Studies in Judaica and the Holocaust
Number Eleven
ISSN 0884-6952

DEFYING THE
Holocaust
A DIPLOMAT'S REPORT

by

Aba Gefen

Edited by Dr. Nathan Kravetz

R. REG
The Borg
San Bernardino, California □ MCMXCIII

D0813261

THE BORGO PRESS

Publishers Since 1975

Post Office Box 2845

San Bernardino, CA 92406

United States of America

* * * * * * *

Library of Congress Cataloging-in-Publication Data

Gefen, Aba.
  Defying the Holocaust : a diplomat's report / by Aba Gefen ; edited by
Nathan Kravetz.
    p. cm. (Studies in Judaica and the Holocaust, ISSN 0884-6952 ; no.
11)
  Includes index.
  ISBN 0-89370-366-4 (cloth). — ISBN 0-89370-466-0 (pbk.)
  1. Gefen, Aba. 2. Jews—Lithuania—Biography. 3. Holocaust, Jewish
(1939-1945)—Lithuania—Personal narratives. 4. Holocaust survivors—
Biography. 5. Diplomats—Israel—Biography. I. Title. II. Series.
DS135.L53G434 1993   93-9283
947'.5004924'0092—dc20   CIP
[B]

FIRST EDITION

CONTENTS

DEDICATION

To my beloved wife,
children and grandchildren.

Aba and Frida Gefen (Peru, 1957)

ABOUT THE AUTHOR

DR. ABA GEFEN, chairman of the Association of the Lithuanian Jews in Israel, was born in 1920 in Simna, Lithuania, and during the Nazi occupation of his country he saw his family methodically slain. However, along with one younger brother, Dr. Gefen managed to survive by hiding in the barns, fields and forests of his native homeland. After Lithuania's occupation by the Red Army, Dr. Gefen remained in Soviet Lithuania for one year, working with Russian police units investigating Nazi collaborators.

Then, under the threat of Soviet persecution and execution, Dr. Gefen escaped to Western Europe and embarked on a career dedicated to the security of the Jewish people. First as a leading member of the Brichah, the clandestine organization that helped thousands of World War II Jewish refugees to immigrate to present-day Israel, then as a member of the diplomatic corps, including ambassadorial posts in Rome, Lima, Buenos Aires and Budapest. Although now semi-retired and surrounded by children and grandchildren, Dr. Aba Gefen today continues to serve his country, often acting as a consultant to the Israeli Foreign Ministry. This is his first book.

PREFACE

The twentieth century has seen some of mankind's worst experiences in all of history: wars, revolutions, the Holocaust. Still, a man may endure them all and find eventual triumph, victory, and renewal. Aba Gefen, from his earliest days, lived through the tragedies of our times. It is his ultimate triumph, tinged with the pain and grief of lost parents, brothers, and fellow Jews, that he saw, also, the rebirth of a state and the renewal of a people.

Dr. Gefen, an obstinate, persistent, and thoughtful man, has come to terms with his century. It was his strength and determination that brought about the survival of his brother, of other imperiled Jews, and of himself. His personal force drew others to his leadership, and his common sense and human sensitivity helped to achieve the difficult crossings of Jews from bloody Europe to the land of Israel.

Writing with vigor, Dr. Gefen bridges those times of war and Holocaust over into the present—uncertain as he knows it is—for the reader. Jews and non-Jews will feel the travails of the victims and know the urgency of their needs to be rescued. He shows how for too many, rescue did not come, or it came too late.

As a diplomat in the service of his country, Aba Gefen observed and dealt with varieties of others, some whose own history included the persecution and murder of Jews. For the Jews at his missions, he represented their hopes and their pride in the achievements of Israel. For the non-Jews to whom he was the representative of a sovereign state, he earned respect, gave valued counsel, and enhanced the opportunities for good will and peace.

In this narrative, a report of one man's life and of the Jewish people, we find the tragedy and the triumph of both. Aba Gefen has defied the Holocaust and so heightened our understanding of its place in history.

—Dr. Nathan Kravetz
Editor
31 January 1993

FOREWORD

Defying the Holocaust: A Diplomat's Report, goes to press several years following the fiftieth anniversary of an inconceivable savagery, begun by the Nazis and their collaborators on June 22, 1941, with the intention—according to Hitler's minister for the occupied territories, Alfred Rosenberg—"to solve the Jewish problem on the European continent through the total biological elimination of the Jews up to the Ural Mountains."

On January 20, 1942, at the Wannsee Conference, the plan to exterminate eleven million Jews of Europe was adopted. Although the Holocaust took place fifty years ago, its relevance to today's issues is beyond doubt.

This book, the story of my life, reflects the principal events in the history of the Jewish people in the last fifty years, including many hitherto unknown episodes.

Part One: "Inconceivable Savagery" describes my years in hiding (1941-1944) during the Nazi occupation in Lithuania, where local collaborators of the Nazis began to murder Jews even before the Germans entered that country. Bloodthirsty Lithuanians travelled to other countries serving as guards in the extermination camps, and notorious for their cruelty.

Part Two: "Hour of Punishment" (1944 and 1945) covers my involvement in the punishment of Nazi collaborators, the activities of reprisal groups, and various individual acts of vengeance.

Part Three: "The Flight" relates the ordeal of 250,000 Jewish Holocaust survivors, smuggled across the frontiers of Europe, who spent the years 1945-1948 in refugee camps in Germany and Austria awaiting an uncertain future. It describes the fate of those survivors; the stratagems used by the organizers of their flight; the expressions of unity and solidarity by Jewish chaplains, officers and men of the United States Army; as well as the help extended by non-Jewish American officers, who protected their "illegal" doings to the point of risking their own careers.

Part Four: "Jewish Statehood Regained" tells of my life in Israel since 1948; of my thirty-five years in the Diplomatic Service in Israel and abroad; and of the main developments in Israel since its founding up to the moment it has been waiting for since the birth of the state: face-to-face bilateral peace negotiations with all its immediate Arab neighbors.

I wish to express my warmest thanks to Dr. Nathan Kravetz and to The Borgo Press for making its publication possible.

—Aba Gefen
Jerusalem
November 1992

PART ONE

INCONCEIVABLE
SAVAGERY

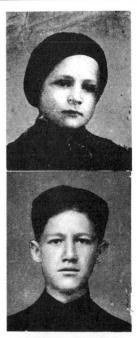

Left: the author's parents, Ruhama and Meir Weinstein; right top: Yehuda, and bottom, Benjamin Weinstein, the author's brothers. All were murdered by the Nazis

Aba Weinstein, left, in hiding from the Nazis, and his brother, Joseph. Both survived.

I.

"LITTLE AMERICA"

I am a Lithuanian Jew, a "Litvak" in Yiddish. The term "Litvak" is to be found in speech, folklore, religious concepts, and literature. I was born in 1920, in the town of Simna in the district of Alitus. I was the oldest of four sons and my name, Aba-Leib, was given to me in memory of my grandfather Rabbi Aba-Leib Weinstein, may he rest in peace.

As was usual for a religious family, my grandfather had ten children: seven boys and three girls. My father, Meir, was the youngest. During World War I, my grandfather was killed by a Cossack.

The Jews of Lithuania were victims of the Cossacks from the days of Bogdan Chmielnicki (1595-1657). Chmielnicki was the leader of the Cossack and peasant uprising against Polish rule in the Ukraine in 1648, which caused the destruction of hundreds of Jewish communities. In the annals of the Jewish people, Chmielnicki is branded as "Chmiel the Wicked," one of the most sinister oppressors of the Jews of all generations, the initiator of the terrible massacres of Polish Jewry from 1648-49.

In the synagogues, before the Holy Ark, Chmielnicki's men slaughtered Jews with butcher knives, after which they destroyed the synagogues. They removed the books of the Torah (the Hebrew Bible) and tore them to bits, and laid them out for men and animals to trample. They made sandals and other garments of them. The Jewish chronicles mention more than one hundred thousand killed, three hundred communities destroyed, and a very severe problem of Jewish refugees created by the pogroms.

The Cossacks renewed their attacks on the Jews during World War I. When the war broke out in 1914, the Russian army was ill-equipped to fight a major war, and neither the political nor the military leadership was competent. The Russian invasion of East Prussia was, therefore, defeated and the campaigns of 1915-16 brought heavy casualties to the Russian forces. Russia lost a quarter of a million men, and its retreating, beaten army vented its anger on the innocent Jews, plundering and killing in the villages and towns.

In one of the pogroms of that time, a marauding Cossack struck my grandfather with an axe and split his head in two. My father, Meir, was then eighteen years old.

Three years later, in Kovno, he met my mother, Ruhama Rubinstein, who was on a visit there. It was love at first sight. They married and settled in Simna where my mother's father, Reb Yossl Rubinstein, was a well-to-do corn merchant.

He helped the young couple to open a textile shop. As time passed, my parents became involved in community voluntary activities, my father on the committee of the local Hebrew elementary school, my mother in charitable organizations, helping poor Jewish families on the holidays, and raising money in secret for the needy.

The Jewish community of Simna was very traditional, as were almost all the towns in Lithuania. On Friday afternoon, Jewish storekeepers were anxious to wind up their business as early as possible to be ready for the Sabbath. Soon Sabbath candles were gleaming from Jewish windows, and Jewish men, dressed in their Sabbath best, hair and beards still damp from a hurried wash, shoes shining, would be heading for the synagogue.

On Saturday mornings, the town looked deserted, stores were closed, no wagons were to be seen anywhere. Parents and children, festively dressed, walked to the synagogue while wives and mothers distributed the Sabbath meal to the poor. Even those who did not observe the 613 *mitzvoth* (religious commandments), would not dare to desecrate the Sabbath in public.

After completing the Heder, the old-fashioned elementary Hebrew school in our town, I was sent to Marijampole to study at the Hebrew gymnasium which was the first Hebrew high school in Lithuania. There I joined the Beitar Youth Movement led by Zeev Jabotinsky. Jabotinsky demanded that the Jews leave Europe where, as he put it, they had no future or purpose for them since the very earth under their feet was burning. But the situation of a quarter-million Jews was good in independent Lithuania. They even called it "Little America," and very few believed the terrible predictions of Jabotinsky, that "if the Jews will not liquidate the Gola (the Diaspora), the Diaspora will liquidate them."

On September 1, 1939, however, Jabotinsky's dreadful warning became reality. Germany invaded Poland, signalling the outbreak of the second World War. German forces converged on Warsaw from all sides, crushing the Polish air force within forty-eight hours and defeating the entire Polish army in one week. With the start of the war, the persecution of the Jews by the Germans and their allies intensified, and eventually turned to slaughter.

Poland was considered the reservoir of Jewish national creativity and, according to the Nazis, the main "biological basis" of the Jewish people. In one year, the Jews of Poland under the Nazi occupation were subjected to a series of debilitating decrees and attacks. Jews were prohibited from earning a living, were beaten, robbed, and forced into labor camps and ghettos. Thousands of Jewish refugees from Poland arrived in Lithuania, but Lithuania also soon lost her independence.

Three weeks after the invasion, Germany and the Soviet Union announced the partition of Poland and, following that partition, the Soviet Union occupied Lithuania.

I was then a student in the Faculty of Engineering at the University of Kovno and, together with many other students, assisted the Jewish refugees from Poland as they tried to find ways to leave Lithuania. Their bodies had already experienced Nazi persecution and atrocities, yet unfortunately, the Lithuanian Jews did not believe the refugees' stories. They continued to live their tranquil lives, blinding themselves with wishful thinking that it would not happen to them, until they themselves experienced the same atrocities.

Among the Polish refugees were two *Yeshiva* (academy) boys who were Dutch citizens. They went to the Dutch consul in Kovno and asked him to help them find refuge in one of the Dutch colonies. There was the possibility of entering Curaçao or Surinam in the Caribbean Sea, and the consul decided to grant fictitious visas to the two boys and to every other refugee. The problem was how to get to Curaçao. The consul checked with the Soviet authorities, who promised that all Dutch visa holders could pass through Soviet territory if they possessed a transit visa for Japan.

In Kovno, the Japanese consulate was headed by a diplomat named Sanfo Sugihara. One day Sugihara saw, through his bedroom window, hundreds of people trying to climb over the consulate fence. He sent his assistant to invite a delegation of five to come and talk with him. The delegation explained that they were Jewish refugees from Poland and that the only way to save their lives was to escape to Japan.

Sugihara sent a cable to his Foreign Ministry in Tokyo asking for authorization to issue visas to the refugees. He received no answer. He then decided on his own to give the visas to anyone who asked for one, even to those who didn't have a passport. It was enough that someone presented a piece of paper with the words, "Country of destination: Curaçao." He gave such visas to 5,000 Jewish refugees in Kovno.

On June 14, 1941, deportations to Siberia began and among those deported were the Jews from Poland who had not succeeded in escaping to Japan.

On that day, Kovno was teeming with Russian soldiers, policemen, and members of the security services who arrested thousands of people, Jews and non-Jews.

I was at the railway station to say goodbye to some friends who were being deported. The screams of those men and women still ring in my ears. It was a hellish scene. I heard a man standing behind me say, "God alone knows whether luck is in store for those who stay behind, or for those who are being exiled to Siberia."

One week later the answer was clear. On June 22, 1941, Germany invaded the Soviet Union, despite their "Treaty of Friendship and Non-Aggression." The German air attack on Kovno began at dawn. Waves of German warplanes descended upon the city, dropping bombs with fearful accuracy, pulling up and swinging around to strafe the people crowding the streets in fear and confusion.

Numerous border violations by German aircraft had taken place months before, and rumor had been rife that war was impending between Germany and the Soviet Union. But up to the very last moment, Stalin did not realize that his country would be smitten, and with a might which would almost destroy his nation. That is why no Red Army planes took to the air to engage the enemy, no anti-aircraft batteries went into action. Taken by surprise, the badly prepared and poorly led Soviet forces retreated rather than risk entrapment in Lithuania.

Panic set in when the Jews of Kovno saw the Russians flee before the Nazi advance. Thousands of Jewish families, surrounded by bedding, suitcases, and household goods, thronged into the train station, praying to God to find them a train to Leningrad or Moscow. Only one train could depart before the bombs destroyed the tracks. Hundreds of bewildered families remained at the station, sitting on their luggage. Thousands of others set off on foot for the Soviet border, clutching small children in their arms, with their possessions on their backs.

German bombers and fighter planes slaughtered many of the fleeing families, forcing the survivors to the ditches, forests, and fields. In the confusion, families were separated and possessions abandoned. Many who reached the Soviet frontier were turned back by suspicious guards for lack of proper permits.

When Moscow finally issued orders to admit the fleeing Jews, it was too late. The German forces had overtaken them and were charging over the border.

Even before the Germans entered Kovno, the Lithuanian Activist Front attacked the Jews of Viliampol, a suburb called "Slabodka" by the Jews. First they forced the Jews to dance, then to recite Hebrew prayers and sing the Communist "Internationale." Finally, when the sadists tired of such games, they ordered the Jews to kneel and shot them in the back. Then they marched down the streets of Slabodka, broke into Jewish houses, and slashed the inhabitants to death.

Slabodka was known for its famous European Yeshiva. The Yeshiva is one of the oldest institutions in the Diaspora, but it reached the climax of its development and achievement in Lithuania. My grandfather studied at the Yeshiva of Slabodka, and I remember my father mentioning with pride that grandfather had been ordained there as a rabbi by Reb Yitzhok Elhonon.

Reb Yitzhok Elhonon Spektor was born in Grodno in 1817 and, after having served as rabbi in various towns, he arrived in Kovno where he officiated until his death in 1896. He established a Yeshiva there for the training of rabbis and attained eminence as a rabbinic authority. He won universal admiration for his broadmindedness, sincerity, and peaceable disposition.

One of the most prominent scholars, who continued in the steps of Reb Yitzhok Elhonon, was cruelly murdered by the Lithuanians when they attacked Slabodka. After a night-long orgy of violence by the Lithuanian assassins, the Rabbi of Slabodka, Reb Zalman Ossovsky, was found bent over his blood-soaked books while his severed head lay in another room.

Even as the Slabodka dead were being gathered up, seventy Jews were seized in the central part of Kovno, dragged into a nearby garage and battered to death with wrenches, hammers, and tire irons. The hose used to wash cars was forced into the throats of some of the men and water poured down their gullets until their stomachs burst. When the massacre was over, the garage floor was covered with human blood and entrails.

In addition to this wanton murder, the Lithuanian pro-Nazi Activist Front, which was preparing to greet the Germans with wild enthusiasm, conducted mass arrests of Jews and assembled them at various places. The commander of the Activist Front announced in a radio broadcast that Jews were shooting at the German troops. He warned that for every German soldier shot, one hundred Jews would be put to death.

Upon hearing this announcement, groups of Lithuanian pro-Nazi activists cast off all restraint. The Lithuanians believed that the more atrociously they behaved toward the Jews, the better they would be treated by the Nazis.

On June 24, I was rounded up along with twenty other Jews and brought to the city square. Standing there with thousands of Jews who had been brought from all parts of Kovno, I watched a group of Jews approaching and noticed that they were headed by Adolf Blumental, the man from whom my younger brother Benjamin and I had rented a room for the 1940-41 school year.

While I was at the university, Benjamin was attending the city's technical school. Blumental had been chief engineer in the Lithuanian air force and held the honorary rank of colonel. When he was arrested along with his wife Zina, a noted photographer, and their son Kolia, Blumental was wearing all his medals.

The Blumentals were separated from the rest of the prisoners by the nationalists' commander, who had served under Blumental in the air force. A discussion ensued among the nationalists as to what was to be done with this much-decorated colonel. He was finally told that he and his family could return to their home. Zina Blumental had noticed me standing there and begged for my release because I was living with them and was part of the family. The commander consented, and I was one of the fortunate few to be saved from the accursed fortress of Kovno. The city of Kovno, between the Nieman River in the north and the Vilia River in the south and the mountains around it, was always an important strategic point where the routes between East and West crossed. Kovno both separated Germany from Russia and at the same time was a bridge between them. Many battles had occurred between their armies around Kovno's gates, and the fortress of Kovno was therefore built: a chain of fortifications which surrounded the city. It was built by the Russians in the 1880s as a barrier against Germany. During World War I the Germans occupied the fortress and the Russians retreated.

When the Germans entered Lithuania in 1941, they began the systematic liquidation of the Jews in Forts IV, VII, and IX of the fortress system.

At Fort VII, in the course of about two weeks, from June 25 to July 7, 1941, eighty to one hundred Jews were slaughtered each day. On the eve of July 8, five thousand Jews were executed. The killings were interrupted the next day when a decree was issued ordering all the Jews of Kovno to move into a ghetto in Slabodka. Every Jew in Lithuania was now to wear a yellow badge shaped like the Star of David.

When we learned about the decree requiring all Jews to wear the yellow badge, I made the Stars of David for the Blumental family and myself. Mrs. Blumental gave one to her husband and said, "Wear it with pride, Adolf." The decree also stated that those having permanent residence outside of Kovno could obtain permits to return to their homes.

On July 12, I received such a permit and two days later I began a three-day hike to my home town of Simna, eighty miles from Kovno, to join my parents and brothers and share their lot.

The German army had entered Simna on June 23, about three weeks before my return, and the pro-German Lithuanians took over the local administration. In stark contrast to the horrors in Kovno, where the local activists instantly seized and murdered Jews, my brethren in Simna still dwelt in comparative peace. They were left in their homes, though the men were sent to labor at all sorts of toilsome tasks for the Germans.

But this was only the calm before the storm. Everything had been contrived and organized so as not to arouse fears or cause the Jews to flee. A state of mind was being prepared in which the Jews could be butchered without hindrance, in accomplishment of the preconceived plan. We began to hear rumors about such a plan in the middle of August.

A Lithuanian farmer friend came to the town's Jewish pharmacist, Boris Ishlondsky, and told him that the Jews from Sirey and other villages were being deported to the district cities. Nobody knew where exactly they would be taken from there, he added, but many believed they were being killed. He advised the pharmacist to run away. Ishlondsky responded he will not run because he had no sins on his conscience. He had never done any harm to anyone, and if they kill him, he will die an innocent man.

At that time, my father visited a Lithuanian friend, Rutkovsky, who had a son-in-law in the town of Shkood. The son-in-law wrote him a letter and added at the end, "Papa, I forgot to tell you that the Jewish men of the town have already been sent to their deaths and now the Jewish women are being deported."

Rutkovsky showed my father the letter. When my father returned home, he couldn't be calm and he walked around in a daze all day, saying that things were going to be very bad for us. My father repeated again and again that he only wanted one thing: that he be sacrificed for the entire family so that we could be spared suffering. That was my beloved father's only wish.

When the rumors spread throughout Simna, people began to collect money to bribe the Lithuanian town leaders. The people fooled themselves into thinking they would thus avoid disaster. But on August 18, toward evening, a drunk broke into our house and started to shout that the Jews should be slaughtered. He was going to hit my father with a bottle. Then he left us and made a terrible uproar in the streets, shouting, "Slaughter all the Jews!"

That night was a terror. At eleven o'clock we heard a siren, and the activists and firemen were running all over with guns. We thought they were getting ready to kill the Jews. My brothers, Joseph and Yehudah'le, hid in the attic, and Papa, brother Benjamin, and I sat in the house. Close to midnight everyone went to sleep. I was on guard. The next day we found out that there was a fire not far from Simna. On August 20, the Simna priest said to my father, "Don't be home tomorrow."

We didn't understand and didn't pay attention to him. Nothing happened on that day, but a day later, on August 22, the German authorities ordered all Jewish males to assemble near the town hall, and all obeyed the summons.

One hundred men were selected and placed in three trucks that left for the town of Alitus. The hundred chosen were all young, healthy, strong men. My father, Meir, forty-one years old, and my brother, Benjamin, seventeen years old and an excellent athlete, were among them. My father, heroically yet with calm logic, saved me from that transport.

When the Lithuanian activists began lining up the Jewish men for selection, he turned to me and said, "Get out of here and go back home. You've only recently come from Kovno and were not in town when the Germans took a census of the Jewish population of Simna. Since you're not listed among the Jews here, they are not likely to search for you. Hide at home, son, until the danger is over!"

I did as he ordered. A few hours later I saw the trucks pass by our home. My father and brother were in the first truck. With the removal of the first hundred, the possibility of any Jewish rebellion disappeared, and all kinds of rumors circulated in town about the fate of the hundred men. There were Lithuanians who told us in confidence, "They have been taken to Alitus and killed, and soon other Jews will be done away with."

At the same time, others reported that on their travels from town to town, they had seen Jews from Simna working on the roads. One Lithuanian came to our house to inform us that he had seen my father and Shalom Rimer working on logs in the Alitus Forest. We prayed to God for that information to be true, and on August 29, my mother went to Alitus to try to find out what had happened to father and Benjamin.

The prison guard told her that the Jews had been transported to an unknown destination. The guard swore that they were taken to work. Sometimes our brother Benjamin would cry, he said, but Papa was merry, making jokes and cheering up the others. I didn't believe the story about their being taken to work and cried bitterly that Papa and Benjamin were dead. Little Yehudah'le would put his head down on the table and cry over Papa and Benjamin. But Mama believed they were still alive.

On September 1st, we were told again to assemble in front of the town hall. Sixty young men and women were selected and sent to Alitus. This time I was saved by my mother's courage. When the assembly order was announced, she forbade me to go and tucked me into bed, as if I were ill. Within an hour, the activist Lithuanians went from house to house to fetch the absentees. My mother stood in the doorway determined not to let me be taken away. God was with me, and the activist who came to our home, turned out to be a long-time employee in the flour mill of my mother's family. Swayed by her entreaty, supplemented by money and clothes, he left without me, satisfied with his booty.

After that second transport, rumors began to circulate about a ghetto to be established on Green Street, and the Jews of our town, my mother included, began to divide up their belongings among their so-called farmer friends in the countryside. On September 10, more than four hundred Simna Jews, all who were left in the village, were told to assemble by three o'clock that afternoon in the barracks just beyond the town limits. Most of them were women and children, the sick and the old. Only seven young men were among them.

Some thought that the intention was to confine us to a barracks-ghetto and keep us as forced laborers. Others believed that we would be taken to some other

ABA GEFEN

city, maybe to Alitus, and used there for all kinds of hard labor. The pessimists insisted that the intention was to kill us, and Ziporah Hasid, my former teacher, was of that company.

At two o'clock that afternoon, I saw her riding on a wagon loaded with her belongings. I went out to ask how she was.

"I am in good health and I feel fine," she said. "I never dreamed that I would be feeling so well only a few minutes before being put to death."

Seeing my consternation, she added, "Aba, do not think that I am crazy. They are going to kill us. All of us! That's what the priest Alexandrovitch told me. He said that they have already murdered all the Jews of Marijampole, even the infants. And I believe it."

At that point I decided to escape. I rushed home to tell my mother what Ziporah Hasid had said. But she would not believe it. She tried to calm me and reassure me that no such thing would happen. They would only take us to do forced labor. Didn't our Lithuanian friend Cherkovsky tell us that he has seen Papa working on the road to Suwalk? She was confident that our lives, too, would be spared. Of course, she added, perhaps because my brother Joseph and I were young and strong, they might give us harder work.

Considering that our youngest brother, Yehudah'le, was only a child, she thought, that they will be more considerate of him, and might even respect her more for his sake.

Turning to me, she continued, "So in the meantime, I suggest that you take Joseph and hide in the home of our good friend, the peasant Slavitsky. In a day or two, when you see what develops, you can decide whether to join the others in the barracks or stay in hiding."

All the while, my little brother Yehudah'le stood at my side, pulling at my coat, and begging me not to go away. Grief-stricken, we took our mother's advice. Joseph and I said goodbye to her and to Yehudah'le, and went to Slavitsky's farm within Simna. They went in the direction of the barracks-ghetto. Slavitsky welcomed us very kindly, telling us to hide under the hay in his barn. Hardly an hour had passed when Yehudah'le came running to inform us that our friends had already arrived in the ghetto and had sent him to tell us that we should join them. Otherwise the authorities would discover our hiding place and kill us on the spot. We tried to persuade our little brother to remain with us, but he stubbornly refused saying, "It will be better for mother if I stay with her."

We kissed him and parted with the farewell blessing, "Go in peace, dear brother, and with God's help we shall meet again." Slavitsky then entered the barn and told us to leave. He explained that the Jews who knew we were hiding there would not be able to withstand the interrogation about our hiding place, in which case his life would be in danger.

I implored him to allow us to stay until the evening. As soon as darkness fell, we would go and search for another place to hide. He consented and gave us the names of a number of peasants, who, to the best of his knowledge, were friends of my father and would be willing to help us. As we prepared to leave the barn, I made up my mind that I would keep a diary in which I would record in Hebrew ev-

18

erything that happened to us from that day on. It was my wish to bequeath it as a testimony to future generations.

In the evening, before we left the barn, Slavitsky returned to us the few gold items Joseph had given to his wife. We made our way through the fields to the house of Bogdanovitch who also lived within the town.

Joseph entered the house and asked permission for us to hide in his barn. Bogdanovitch agreed. Joseph asked Bogdanovitch whether the Jews had been moved from Simna. He said, "Not yet." In complete darkness we managed somehow to climb a haystack and sleep through the cold long night.

The next morning at eleven o'clock, Bogdanovitch brought us a bottle of milk and some bread. I asked him whether the Jews in the barracks will be deported from Simna. He answered, "Figure that out for yourself."

When I persisted, "Will they kill them?" he made a sharp movement with his head that could be understood as "Yes."

No one can imagine our state of mind. It became clear to us that the Jews of Simna would be lost forever, and I thought how right was Haim Dov Flaksman, whom everyone considered crazy when he argued that the path from the barracks leads straight to heaven.

In the afternoon of Friday, September 12, Bogdanovitch came to the barn to tell us that the Jews had been moved out of the barracks. As we were talking, a peasant woman came into the yard and described seeing the Jews being led out of the barracks into the woods nearby. The men were walking with their hands tied behind their backs; the women walked arm in arm, and so did the children. There was weeping and wailing.

At that moment we heard the sound of intermittent gunfire coming from the woods. It went on for over an hour. We were within earshot of the brutal slaughter of the Jews of Simna, innocent, pure souls, murdered only because they were Jews, and among them, our mother and little Yehudah'le.

In the evening, Bogdanovitch came, and his answers to my frantic questions told, in all their horror, the last moments of the lives of the Simna Jews. The Lithuanians tortured them with inconceivable savagery, until their senses and their human image were lost. With no strength to resist any longer, even spiritually, under a hail of blows, from whips and gunstocks, stripped almost to the skin, they were driven to the woods near Kalesnik. Broken and enfeebled, humiliated, they moved in the slow rhythm of the death march.

While still alive, our brethren of Simna were forced into a long, deep pit that had been dug in barbaric readiness and then, in coldest blood, the Lithuanian activists and German soldiers shot them down. After the slaughter the killers came out of the woods singing at the top of their lungs.

We were smothered in gloom. We thought we were going mad, and Joseph asked me, "Do you really believe that our little brother is dead and buried?"

It was hard to believe, but didn't we hear the shots with our own ears? I cursed myself for living, but I didn't want to die, and we had to concentrate on saving ourselves. We prayed to God to have mercy upon us and spare our lives.

7 November 1946

This is to certify that Weinstein, Aba, is the chairman of the Committee for Assistance to Jewish Refugees (CAJR). This committee is engaged in Welfare work with Jewish Refugees in US Zone Austria. Mr. Weinstein, as chairman, is working in coordination with DP Section Zone Command Austria.

Stanley M. Nowinski
Asst DP Officer ZCA

II.

"GOD BE WITH YOU!"

The next morning, Bogdanovitch's son came and brought us a quart of water. Then his father brought us milk and bread, "for the last time." He said that he feared a search at any moment, and his wife, he added, was sick over our hiding in their barn. I showed him our perfected hiding place.

"Just give us enough bread and water to last and then forget about us," I urged.

Bogdanovitch replied, "I will give you food enough for a year, but I can't keep you here."

We pleaded and wept, and he agreed to let us stay for another few days. During the day, some laborers were threshing the wheat, making a great deal of noise. That was not bad, since it gave us a chance to move around.

Three days passed and Bogdanovitch told us that it was dangerous to continue to stay at his place, which was within the village. He ordered us to leave his barn, but said we could come back.

Joseph and I decided to try the barn of our cousin Kapitkovsky, which was also within the town, and then return to Bogdanovitch. We prepared to leave and combed our hair. It evoked memories of how Mama used to wash and comb our hair, and how she continued to do mine even when I was in the last grade of high school. We mourned Mama.

At night we slipped into Kapitkovsky's barn. We struck a match and found an adequate hiding place. Exhausted and thirsty, I consumed a quart of water and soon regretted it. In the morning, we considered whether or not we should make our presence known to Vasilevsky, who had worked for Kapitkovsky and now had "inherited" his barn. If only we could be sure he would not turn us over to the police. We decided that it would be too dangerous.

Vasilevsky and his wife entered the barn and nearly stumbled on us as they approached to examine a plank that appeared out of place. We heard him say, "Maybe some Jews are hiding here. Well, let them." Then they talked about the shooting in the forest. They said that many were buried alive. At most there were fifty assassins, while there were more than four hundred Jews.

"Could one bullet alone kill a man? Could the bullets hit every single Jew?" Vasilevsky said to his wife.

Vasilevsky told his wife to get busy with the hay, and she began pitching hay right over us. It was like a miracle. God was with us. They themselves unwittingly reinforced our hideout.

Vasilevsky and his wife began to talk about the radio announcement warning that if a Jew were found hiding in a barn, both the farmer and the Jew would be executed. They didn't even dream that two Jews were present in the barn they had "inherited." At night, it was torture to huddle in a dark tomb that was about one and a half yards long, one yard wide, and two and a half feet high, covered by a large mound of hay. It was impossible to fall asleep.

I jumped up and began to climb through the hay, shouting at my sleeping brother, "We'll choke to death here!" He woke up and tried to calm me as I hurled myself through the hay. A light breeze made me feel better and I finally dozed off.

In my dream, Papa and Benjamin came to us in the barn. We were overjoyed, but our happiness was dampened by Papa's question, "Where are your mother and little Yehudah'le?"

I responded that they too had, for sure, escaped the shooting, pointing out Yehudah'le's agility. He surely made a quick getaway, I insisted. When we awoke, Joseph told me he had a similar dream. If it would only come true, we said to each other.

One day, I stood up to my full height and peeped through the chinks in the wall out onto the street. People passed from time to time, but certainly none were Jews. "God in heaven," I noted in my diary, "where is your justice? I have lost all my loved ones. All that remains for me now is to say the *Kaddish* (prayer for the dead). I can't bear this! I can't! I just can't!"

Toward evening I felt a little better and Joseph suggested we drink the quart of milk we had, and he would fetch two quarts of water from the nearby stream. I was afraid to have him risk exposing himself, but he insisted that it was not really dangerous. We finished off the milk, and he went and brought back two quarts of water and filled even a broken bottle. I decided to wash myself with my handkerchief.

My face was black with dirt. Since we had gone into hiding, this was the first time I had decided to wash and tidy up, and it made me wonder what the act portended. We looked for some hidden meaning in every act. The idea occurred to me that perhaps we might soon be liberated and would have to leave the barn in a hurry, without time to wash. We fantasized about our liberation, and Joseph said, "What will liberation mean to us? That we will have more or better things to eat, or more leisure? That's not what can be called living. Only then our suffering will begin. Now, we may still refuse to believe that Yehudah'le is no longer alive. Only when we are free, will we be certain whether or not the angel of death has claimed him. If our life is bitter now, it will be far more bitter then. Can you, Aba, really understand what I'm going through?"

Poor Joseph! What he had already endured! Only a while ago I had thought of him as a child, and now I saw the experience of recent days reflected in his face. He no longer looked to me a boy of fifteen but like a boy grown old.

I was about to sit down to eat when the thought struck me that in case liberation does not come that week, we will have to go hungry. We decided to return to Bogdanovitch, comforted by the adage, "A change of place brings a change of luck."

We prayed that God would not abandon us. Since He has chosen us to be among the survivors, we told ourselves, He will surely help us to reach liberation.

We walked safely to Bogdanovitch's barn, quickly located our old hiding place, and slept there through the night. In the morning Bogdanovitch came in. I found him somewhat more welcoming than before. He still warned us of the danger but led us to believe that the war would soon end. He told us that the police knew we had been in the barn. He promised to bring us food after the threshing. I had not expected such a good reception from him.

He did not bring us food until the next morning. When he brought it, he advised us to make our hiding place more comfortable, and told us that Papa and Benjamin were no longer alive. He suggested that we should go to the farmer Smidzun in the village of Glosnik and wait there for the summer. The news about Papa and Benjamin put us in a terrible mood and fueled our fear. During the night we were so cold, our feet nearly froze. We hoped Smidzun might make a place for us to hide in the niche above the oven, or in his attic, where it would be more bearable. We told Bogdanovitch we would go to Smidzun.

One night, Joseph performed a remarkable feat. He went to Slavitsky for food. There, he ate a bowl full of potatoes with sour milk and some sweet milk, and brought from them six pounds of bread, a quart of milk, a big portion of honey, five apples, hard and soft cheese, an egg, and underwear.

We ate our fill, but we couldn't sleep because of the lice. They had discovered that we were wearing fresh underwear and celebrated the event. The crawling creatures continued to be as annoying as ever, our feet ached, and Bogdanovitch informed us of "his firm and final decision" that we must leave. We weren't too upset, but I reminded Bogdanovitch that he had promised to try to get for me the album of pictures from the attic of our house. I said that without the album we would not move.

It took him two days and he brought me my mother's handkerchief containing the album with family photos as well as my matriculation and student certificates.

On October 10, at seven in the evening, we left the barn and, feeling scared, crossed the road near Bogdanovitch's house. We continued straight ahead in the direction of the village of Glosnik.

After a while we came to a village we thought was Glosnik and began looking for Smidzun's place where Joseph had been once. We tried one place and then another. While Joseph went on to look at a third, I sat by the roadside waiting. Suddenly I heard footsteps and saw a woman coming toward me. I jumped up and started walking after Joseph, but the woman began to shout in Lithuanian, "Yushkovsky, thieves are coming! Thieves!"

We started to run and she shouted even louder. I turned toward her and began pleading with her not to shout, saying, "We are not thieves, but Jews from Simna, the sons of Weinstein, the shopkeeper." Providentially, she believed me and calmed down. She knew my father. There was not a single peasant in the Simna area who did not know him, had not bought from him, did not owe him money. The woman, whose surname was Matulevitch, expressed sympathy for us and invited us to her home to rest a while. She gave us bread and milk, while we managed, without revealing our destination, to find out where Smidzun lived. The woman told us of her poverty and that of her children, three sons and a daughter. The boys came down to see us. They were young men, strong and frightening, for they might have been pro-Nazis who would seize us and turn us over to the police. But no! Upon parting she gave us her blessing, "God be with you and watch over you."

Once again we went astray. We wandered until six o'clock in the morning, still unable to find Smidzun's place. Panic overtook us. We must decide quickly. What could we do? I trusted the woman Matulevitch. We dreaded her sons, but what option did we have? We had to take the risk. Her parting benediction still rang in my ears. Was it wishful thinking to believe that a Christian woman who mentions God, who gives you His blessing, must be good, and will not betray you to murderers?

III.

PROUD TO BE A JEW

On the way to the Matulevitches we saw a wagon approaching, so we hid in the field until it passed. When we arrived at the hamlet of Saulinai, where the woman lived, she and her three sons welcomed us very warmly, and the boys gave me some brandy as a remedy for my aching stomach. They told us that searches were being conducted at farmhouses in the nearby village of Glosnik to catch farmers who were making *samagon*, homemade vodka, and it became clear to us that the farmer Smidzun, to whom we wanted to go, would be unable to hide us. He owned a lot of land and employed many farmhands, and that would make him fearful.

I told the Matulevitches I would reward them generously and, then and there, I dressed the younger son, nineteen, in the suit I was carrying. The woman, in turn, said she would wash our dirty underwear.

What at first seemed like a misfortune, encountering this peasant woman, was becoming a blessing. Our meeting her was an act of Providence. The day before she had met us on the road, thieves had stolen her horse's harness and the chain that locked the pigsty. It was because of that theft that she had shouted "Thieves!" when she saw us. God had sent her to rescue us. If we hadn't encountered her, God only knows what misfortune would have befallen us.

In the evening the woman invited us from the barn into her house for supper. After the meal we undressed and she scrubbed both of us from head to toe. It was just marvelous! Who even dreamed of such a reception? We came in wearing dirty, vermin-infested clothing, and they gave us their underwear and shirts to change into while she washed our dirty clothes.

The next day, she again invited us into her house for supper. After the meal we talked for a while and she gave us heartbreaking details about the shooting of the Simna Jews. She told us that four hundred and thirteen Jews were killed in Simna. The trenches had already been dug on September 8, but when peasants told about it to some of the Jews, they were scolded for spreading such rumors. One of them reacted, "Why do the Lithuanians have a habit of scaring people?"

She said that the Jewish women, wearing only their nightshirts and walking barefoot, kept stumbling and falling, and the barbarians accompanying them would whip them. The Pargamuts' infant granddaughter was tossed into the branches of a tree, to fall, still breathing, into the death-pit. Dusia Beinstein hid during the shooting and might have survived, if she hadn't shouted out, "You haven't shot me yet, but you will!"

One of the murderers then shot her in the head, spilling out her brains.

The woman said that the men jumped into the pit even before the order was given. The women tarried, for they held children in their arms, in a last embrace. It was difficult for a child to leave its mother, but a thousand-fold more difficult for a mother to leave her child.

The adults now understood what it was all about. They knew they were being killed because they were Jews, but the poor little children, who walked wailing and sobbing all the way, what did they know? What could they understand? All they knew was to cry out "Mama, Papa!" and cling to them in fear. My little brother Yehudah'le, too, entered the pit holding tightly to my mother's hand. It was their fate that in death as in life they would not be parted, and thus, together, they gave back their lives to the Creator.

Mrs. Matulevitch stressed that there were Lithuanians who did not raise their hands against the Jews, and when she laid eyes on us, she thought that her sons might be drafted someday and find themselves in our situation. She talked to us about her children. Her older son, Sebiastas, who was very gifted, had completed three grades of schooling but had to give up his studies because of his poor eyesight. Her second son, Yozas, did not want to learn but had also completed three grades. Her third son, Vladas, did not want to study at all. The youngest child, her daughter Stase, had already completed two grades and read nicely.

While we were talking, Sebiastas came in and reported that in the town of Alitus they had executed a Jew, Beiral, his wife, and son, along with the Christian in whose house they had hidden. Mrs. Matulevitch began to feel frightened and said she would be able to keep us only for a short while, depending on how her sons felt about it. She reminded us that others in her place would undoubtedly have handed us over to the police, but she could never live with her conscience if we had been executed because of her.

She told us something horrible about the Russian prisoners-of-war. When they arrived by train in Simna, the prisoners were covered with blood. One of them had died, and his starving companions ate the corpse.

Every day, in the morning, I entered a plus sign (+) in my diary to indicate that we had survived one more day. While reading in it, I thought, "If I survive, this diary will stand as a reminder of these times, a testament to what we have endured. To my mind came the days when I dreamt of a Jewish homeland in Zion: to live among our brother Jews in our own country, to speak our own language, to walk the streets of the land of my forefathers, where I could hold my head high, look around me, and say, 'This is mine!'"

I remembered going to the youth movement clubhouse and debating how that country should be built. Recalling my clubhouse, I could hear the national anthem "Hatikvah" (the Hope). Fearing that in my state of mind I might forget it, I decided to write it down in my diary.

On November 3, Yozas came into the barn to inform us that at a meeting called by the local mayor, the farmers were told that the Jews of Kovno were being wiped out, and the people were warned not to hide any Jew. It was in the wake of the Big "Operation" in the Kovno ghetto, which took place on October 28, 1941.

The entire population of the ghetto was ordered to assemble on the main square. The *Aeltestenrat* (the Council of Elders), who were in charge of the administration of the ghetto under the orders of the Germans, were told that those Jews able to work hard would remain with their families in the Large Ghetto, while those considered unable to work would be moved to the Small Ghetto.

"The Germans are not in a position to provide those who cannot work hard the same rations as those who do heavy labor," the Gestapo man, Rauka, explained, adding, "Whoever will not obey, will die."

At the fixed hour all assembled, more than 26,000 persons, and the square was surrounded on all sides by men with machine-guns. Rauka came up to every Jew and according to his view ordered each one to move to the right or to the left. In the ghetto itself searches were carried out in case some were hiding. The selection lasted until the evening. The next morning the transfer to Fort IX of the selected 10,000 persons began under a heavy guard of Germans and Lithuanian collaborators. There they were sadistically murdered.

Yozas said he was told that when the Jews arrived at the fort, they were ordered to strip naked, stack their garments in neat piles, and lie down next to each other, in groups of one hundred, in large open trenches. The more fortunate victims were killed outright; the severely wounded were buried alive.

The Matulevitches became very fearful and decided to prepare a place for us in the barn of their neighbor, the Tartar woman, without her knowledge. They would bring us food every few days. At night, we set out for the Tartar woman's barn, with Yozas leading the way. When he left, we climbed the haystack, where I constructed a proper hiding place.

In the morning we saw the Tartar woman's two children playing happily in the yard, unlike the Jewish children whose bones were lying in the frost covered earth not far from our hiding place.

Joseph commented, "How lucky they are to be Tartars, and what a difference there is between them and us! They are the 'pure' race, and we...."

"Hitler will not succeed in wiping us out completely," I said to myself. "God won't let him destroy us all. The Eternal One shall not fail Israel," I noted in my diary, and added, "Only now am I proud to be a Jew! But only my little notebook and I know it. The day will come when I will be able to tell it to them, too, to those who humiliate us today."

After a week in the Tartar woman's barn, we decided to return to the Matulevitches. It was a dark night, and we could barely see the road, but somehow we found our way back to their house. When Yozas opened the door, they were startled to see us.

I gave a gold ring to the mother, my wallet to Yozas, and promised to bring them various other things left by our parents with friends in Simna: another gold ring and a gold chain for the mother, a silver ring for the daughter, and clothes for the sons.

I begged them to let us stay with them for the rest of the winter. Yozas said that we could spend the night there but would have to leave in the morning, since they expected their place to be searched. I kept pleading until they agreed to

27

let us stay for a week and then decide what to do. Mrs. Matulevitch prepared a place for us to sleep on the kitchen floor.

Early in the morning we went to the barn, and I prepared such a good hiding place that even Yozas doubted anyone could ever find us. But Mrs. Matulevitch said it would be too cold for us there and suggested that we should stay there only in case of an emergency. She invited us to stay on top of their oven, and it was really not bad.

When Sebiastas came from the railroad station in Mergalaukis, he told us that in Alitus they carved the Star of David into the forehead of a woman who had kept some Jews at her place. He also related that he saw at the station seventy Russian prisoners-of-war, guarded by four Lithuanian soldiers and one German. The Lithuanian soldiers saw a prisoner drinking milk and they killed him. Sebiastas said that the Russian prisoners-of-war working in the neighborhood get little to eat, so in the evening, after work, they beg the farmers for food, but get none.

"How cruel people can be!" Mrs. Matulevitch moaned, claiming that she would give them her very last bit of food. One evening, some of them came to the Matulevitches. I didn't see them, but I heard their voices. Mrs. Matulevitch had only potatoes and water to give them. That's what she told them, and they answered, "Never mind, you may still get rich someday!" She gave them also a box of matches, which they were happy to receive.

The next day Yozas asked me if I would teach him how to dance. I was hardly in a mood for dancing, but our situation compelled me to do as he asked. I knew that doing things to please him was a way of buying time. I taught him how to waltz, and he was absolutely delighted. He asked me to forget his one week ultimatum and said he would come every day to practice, giving us one more week to stay with them.

When the two weeks were over and we had to leave, I tried to buy more time by convincing Yozas to go with me to Simna, to bring some clothes from the farmer Cherkovsky. He was considered to be a friend and was the one who had told my mother that he had seen Papa working on the road to Suwalk. My parents had left a lot of things with him. Cherkovsky only gave me my mother's coat and shouted, "Run!" Nevertheless, Yozas agreed that we should continue to stay with them and asked me what would we say if we were caught.

I said that I would say we were in their barn without the knowledge of the household, as was the case in the Tartar woman's barn. He replied, "Even if they should put me in jail, I would evade answering that I knew about it." He surprised me by saying that we could stay with them until the spring. I thanked him, and he said, "When you leave us in spring, I will feel very bad, not afraid for myself, but worried about what may happen to you two. Having lived with us so long, you've become part of the family, and if, God forbid, you should be caught, I will feel terrible."

The next day they told Joseph to stay over the oven and they put me in the attic. This was a safer arrangement, for should anyone come after us, we would be aware of it, whereas in the barn we never knew for sure if we were seen coming or going.

On Christmas Eve the Matulevitches had a festive dinner. It happened also to be our Hanukkah. I gave Vladas and Stase some Hanukkah money, and Mrs. Matulevitch was delighted. After the meal she sat down next to us and said with sadness that it was time for Sebiastas to be married, but he can't find a girl. "You see," she added, "mothers always worry about their children. The children worry much less about their parents. If your mother, for instance, had survived you, she would never stop weeping. And what about you two?"

I replied, "When the orphan weeps, no one sees him; but everyone sees him when he laughs." I had once heard that saying, and at that moment I could fully appreciate its meaning.

IV.

DRUNK WITH FRIGHTENING REGULARITY

On January 1, 1942, I noted in my diary, "We have been sustained in life, thank God, to the year 1942. Only God knows where we, or our bones, will be at this time next year. This year we didn't fast on Yom Kippur or recite: 'Who will be granted life and who death.' Perhaps God will have pity on us, and time will work in our favor."

There was, however, no sign that the war would end. We began worrying that after the winter we might have to hide for another year. It was a horrifying thought, but the most important thing was not to despair, not to lose hope that God would be merciful and we would survive. We started, however, making several plans for the spring. We thought about stealing over the border into Romania, which would require crossing Poland. Or reaching Russia by way of the battle front. Or entering Switzerland by way of Germany. Or perhaps going to the marshes and from there to Iran and then on to Palestine. We were, of course, aware of the fact that those might only remain plans.

Our fantasizing was interrupted by Yozas, who came in completely drunk, followed by Sebiastas, staggering. Yozas could hardly stand on his feet and he said to me, "So what if you're a Jew and I'm a Catholic. We are both human beings. What harm can the Jews do to me?"

I warned him not to say a word about us, and he answered, "I may be drunk, but I know what to do when there's danger."

Just the same, I always worried when they were drunk. In their cups, which was often, they would fight with knives. One day they made a hole in my coat, another time Yozas brandished a knife at my throat.

If they were drunk with frightening regularity, it was chiefly because the family earned its living by distilling and selling samagon. Almost every farmer was making the rural vodka, mainly to sell it in the town. The official brandy had a high tax, while the homemade samagon was sold privately by the farmers without tax. It was therefore much cheaper and, often, much stronger. The samagon brought an important income for the farmers, especially for the poor ones, like the Matulevitches, who had only a few hectares of land.

Joseph and I worked with them by night in this illicit brewing, testing the brandy, finding that sometimes it was one hundred percent alcohol and sometimes like water. We stole firewood from neighboring rich landowners. The impoverished Matulevitches had no wood, and the manufacturing of samagon consumed enormous amounts of fuel. My worries were fully confirmed one morning when a friend of Yozas, Antanas Baranovsky, and a few others arrived. They drank them-selves into a stupor, and Baranovsky, a loud anti-Semite, suddenly said that when the war broke out, Scherbakov, a Jew from Simna, had come to him, but he refused to take him in. "I'm just as happy without the Jews," he said.

Yozas went berserk, breaking the small table and a window. To restrain him, Sebiastas, Vladas and his mother tied him up. The strangers left, and Yozas begged to be untied, but the three of them gave him a good beating. Then Yozas begged me to let him loose, but I didn't answer him. He was livid. More of his friends arrived, but his mother told Vladas not to let them in. Sebiastas kept them in the other room. Yozas continued to plead that he be let loose, but no one paid any attention to him. He shouted to his mother, "Let me go! The Jews ran away, and I'll run away, too!" I whispered to Mrs. Matulevitch that if she didn't untie him, he would tell everyone that she had Jews staying in the house.

I was in a state of terror. Joseph hid behind the stovepipe crying bitterly. I asked Vladas to throw out the friends who had come in. He took my advice, and told them to leave; only one, Navitzky, remained. Yozas was shouting, "Let me go!" But his mother still refused. Then he threatened her. "If you don't let me go, I'll tell", and she replied, "Tell!" Finally he turned to me and shouted, "Get out of here, you frogs, damn you."

Mrs. Matulevitch shrieked at Yozas, "Murderer! You took money and clothes from them and now you're throwing them out!" The day before, Yozas had taken one hundred and seventy rubles from me when the entire family went to a wedding and all were dressed in the fancy clothes we gave them.

Yozas, however, continued threatening to tell all, and then yelled, "Boys—" I jumped off the oven onto the bed and slammed my hand over his mouth, while Vladas ordered Navitzky to leave.

With everyone gone, Yozas quieted down a bit. But suddenly his mother came back in and announced that their neighbor Yushkovsky was coming. I jumped back onto the oven, and, fearing that he would tell Yushkovsky, his mother untied Yozas.

Then he began to beat his mother. It was terrible. Vladas also got his share. And to me he said that he would correct the mistake he had made with the Jews. He would go out and announce that his own family wanted to crucify him, just like the Jews had tortured Jesus.

He went out shouting like that, and suddenly Baranovsky came. Joseph and I hid in the attic, while Yozas went on shouting at Baranovsky about the Jews and Jesus. Then they both left the house.

We came down from the attic. Mrs. Matulevitch was a broken woman. A little while later Yozas came back and begged her to forgive him. We didn't sleep all night. We were afraid that he would either turn us in or turn us out.

The next morning Yozas called himself a stupid fool for beating his mother and promised that he would not drink anymore. His mother wanted to go to Simna and turn him over to the police, but I convinced her not to involve the police.

Like an evil omen, Navitzky meant trouble for us. A few days later, we were sitting at lunch time openly above the oven, talking to Mrs. Matulevitch, and

Vladas was outside threshing wheat. The door to the hallway opened, but we paid no attention, thinking it was Vladas. Suddenly we heard a voice say, "Good morning!" We managed to hide, but Mrs. Matulevitch was so startled and confused that she was almost at a loss to answer Navitzky. He had overheard the last word she had said to us, "Maria," and she started talking about Maria Tzikovsky.

Later the door opened, and immediately I suspected that a stranger had entered. Just as I managed to hide, Yozas and Navitzky came in drunk, and Yozas shouted, "Did we beat up Ignas!" As he was recalling the beating at Ignas' place, the door opened and Sebiastas came in. Not realizing a stranger was present, he said to his mother, "Mama, tell the Jews to go, and hide all the brandy, because Ignas has been to the police."

I was trembling all over. Yozas jumped on Sebiastas and started hitting him. Then Sebiastas saw Navitzky and shouted, "Get out of here!" He turned to his mother and said, "Mama, make them go! I'm telling you, they should leave!"

Sebiastas went out, followed by his mother, and he told her that he had no idea Navitzky was there. Then she returned to the room and tried, with Yozas, to remedy the situation. She asked Yozas what Sebiastas was talking about when he said "Jews," and Yozas said that he meant Navitzky and himself, and Navitzky said, "Obviously us, because there are no Jews here, and he said 'Let the Jews go.'"

Then Yozas turned to Navitzky and said, "Let's go to sleep in my bed," and they went to sleep.

We sat above the oven shaking, not knowing what to do, convinced that Navitzky knew everything. We wondered whether or not to move out to the barn. Mrs. Matulevitch said that, even if there was a search, we could hide under the oven with the chickens. While we were talking, the door opened. We told Mrs. Matulevitch that Sebiastas didn't know Navitzky was sleeping over, and that the same thing would happen again.

I was right! Sebiastas came in and said, "They must go." Mrs. Matulevitch told him, "Sleep over by the stove, they're both in the bed." He understood, lowered his voice, and repeated that we must get out. Ignas had gone to the police. Mrs. Matulevitch told him to be quiet and to go to sleep, and she told us that she would go to Ignas in the morning and find out what had happened. The three of us didn't sleep all night. At dawn we hid, and Mrs. Matulevitch went to see Ignas. When she returned she told us that she didn't believe he had been to the police. That calmed us a little. Vladas reminded everyone that Sebiastas had called them Jews. Mrs. Matulevitch asked, as if she didn't know, "What did he say?" Navitzky answered, "That the Jews should go."

Everyone was confused about those incidents and later Sebiastas asked what could be done to prevent such occurrences. Yozas replied, smiling, "Maybe we should throw these Jews out already." We didn't say a word, and he asked me when we intended to leave. I told him we would leave when they threw us out. He then asked me where we would go, and I told him that I didn't know yet. He turned to his mother and said, "We'll keep them until the summer," and promised that, if they did decide we must go, he would give us two weeks notice.

On March 4, Mrs. Matulevitch went to Simna. On her return, she told us that in the last week the Russians had pushed the Germans back fifty-five miles. She added that she was terrified of a Russian return. I told her she had nothing to fear because, if the Russians came back, there would be no danger to anyone who had been kind to the Jews. I said that I couldn't wait for the day that the Russians returned.

As I said that, I remembered how I had disliked the Soviets when a group of N.K.V.D. (Soviet Security) men searched my room in Kovno and found David Futerman, a Jewish refugee from Poland, in my brother's bed. They immediately made out a warrant for our arrest. When it came to writing down my father's name, the head of the group, a Jew, asked if my father, Max Weinstein, was the owner of a store in Simna who bought his goods from Izraelit in Kovno. When I said yes, he told me that he knew my father well, that he was a good man, that he himself had worked as a porter at Izraelit's, and father had always treated him generously and with kindness. He added that my father didn't concern himself with politics and asked me why I gotten myself involved in this fishy business. When I described to him the suffering of the Jewish refugee from Poland and begged him to have mercy on me, on my father, and on the refugee, the Jewish policeman tore up the arrest warrant and told me he was doing it for my father's sake. He also requested that the boy "disappear" from my room at dawn, because it was known to the police that Polish refugees were staying with me, and he couldn't promise that during the next search I would have the same luck I had this time.

I thought of the biblical adage: "The fathers have eaten sour grapes and the childrens' teeth are set on edge." In my case, it was the exact opposite. My father had done good things, and his children had reaped the fruits. That N.K.V.D. man remembered the generous and kind behavior of my father. The woman, Matulevitch, too, remembered my father with affection and esteem for his unfailing kindness and goodness, and was repaying my father's benevolence by helping his sons.

While in Simna, Mrs. Matulevitch had heard that an inventory would be taken of the animal and agricultural yields, and all the surplus would be confiscated. The family discussed where to hide a little grain, and I thought about where we should hide during the search. Sebiastas suggested that, in case of an emergency, we should hide under the oven. "Surely no one will search under the oven," he said. "At most they will light a match and look."

When a policeman came next morning to the house about the harvest inventory, we scrambled under the oven.

Mrs. Matulevitch also brought me a newspaper and a chill passed through me as I read about a man in Saukiavy who was hanged for hiding Russian prisoners-of-war. The Russians were hanged along with him. Mrs. Matulevitch also told us that in Paulingsot hamlet, hunters found a Jew who had frozen to death. He was young and dressed in rags. Next to him they found a sack containing frozen bread and about half a cup of sugar.

The Catholic Easter was on April 5. It was also our Passover, our first Passover in hiding. The hand of death had taken thousands of our people, but God had led us to the Matulevitches and death had passed over us for the time being. I thought, "If it's God's will that I survive, I will honor the synagogue more than I, and many of our people, did in the past."

Early in the morning, before breakfast, everyone washed and changed his underwear. In the evening, their sitting down at the supper table reminded me of home, and a shudder passed through me when I remembered how we would sit together as a family at our Seder, on the first and second nights of Passover, and Papa would say, "May none of us be missing from our Seder next year."

It was the first time in our life we were to be eating leaven, and I made matzot on the stove from flour and water.

Since it was already spring, and it was very warm outside, we went up to the attic. Only two days passed, and Yozas told us to look for another place to hide. Four armed policemen had gone to the hamlet of Zhuvint to search out Communists and parachutists, and the Matulevitches were frightened. We begged them and they let us stay another few days. The next day, in the middle of the afternoon, Stase came up and asked me to come downstairs. There they told me that the police were coming to search every house for samagon. Everyone knew that the Matulevitches manufactured it and the police were more than likely to visit here.

Sebiastas and Yozas, not unreasonably, told us to quit their place instantly. But where could we go in broad daylight? After months of having been cooped up in the barn and in the house, we were clothed in rags, and our faces were unshaved and as pale as chalk. Any passerby would know that we were fugitives. The longer we lingered in doubt and distress, the more infuriated and nervous the sons became, but the good woman's heart melted in compassion and she decided to hide us in the pigsty. The wrath of her sons broke all bounds and the three of them, together with the little girl, left their home.

Weeping all the while and bitterly lamenting our fate, she dug a pit in the pigsty, pushed us down into it, and covered us with manure. Again we were saved. The police passed by, the sons returned to their mother, and we resettled in the attic. In the evening, when we came to the house, Sebiastas' first words to me were, "Is it good to lie in the shit, Aba? Ah, what a lousy situation!"

In the evening, Yozas saw two people approaching the house. He thought that the women had squealed and he believed the two persons to be policemen, and we suddenly heard loud whistles and Yozas shouting, "Police!"

I ran from the attic to the fields, and Joseph made for the fields with Vladas. But it wasn't the police, just two friends. I lost my socks while running and came back barefoot. At night I went with Yozas to the Tartar woman and stole a sack full of potatoes. There wasn't a single potato or flour in the house. In fact, there wouldn't have been anything at all to cook had we not stolen it.

I went to Bogdanovitch in Simna to bring something for the family. I didn't go to his house, just into the yard and barn. God was with me, because Bogdanovitch had strangers in the house. When they left, I came into the house and he gave me some food and clothes. He told me that three people have already been hanged for hiding Jews. I thought, if only I could bring the Matulevitches more things!

Later, I sent letters to two other Lithuanian friends with whom our parents had left things. I wrote in those letters:

My good friend,

My brother and I have been living in misery for months and only God knows how much longer we shall have to suffer. With difficulties we have managed to get through the hard winter, and all the time we hoped for something better in the spring. But to our great regret, spring has come and our plight is even more difficult. One of the reasons for the worsening situation is that we've already exchanged everything we had for food. We gave it all to the people who are keeping us, and now we have nothing.

For lack of any other choice, and out of our desire to stay alive, I've decided to turn to you as an old friend and ask you to save us. If you remember, we left a package with you, and I need that package desperately now. So I beg you to leave that package with the priest Father Lingis and tell him to give it to whoever comes for it. I'll find a way to pick it up. The main thing is that the package gets to the priest.

I know that this will be a great bother for you, but please understand that for us this is a question of life and death. I believe in your humanity and pity, and I know that you will take care of this for me as soon as you can.

My thanks to you in advance, and if I remain alive, I will be in your debt for the rest of my life.

Aba Weinstein

V.

IN THE WHEAT FIELDS

Navitzky came and said that the police had caught a Jew, Shimon Cohen, the barber. When the Germans began to remove the Jews from Simna, Marta, a Lithuanian woman, deeply attached to Shimon, suggested that he hide with her family in the country. He agreed and lived with her at her brother's house. But his sweetheart's sister-in-law also became enamored of him. The women detested each other and were sick with jealousy and hatred. Shimon did not realize his danger, imagining he would save himself by proving his devotion to both. But Marta was furious and reported Shimon to the hamlet's mayor, who told the police. Shimon and the farmer were arrested.

I asked Sebiastas to go to Simna to find out more about the capture of Shimon. On his return, he said he had seen Shimon through the jail window, and that a woman named Stase Kazlovsky had also been arrested. Stase used to bring Shimon food while he was hiding in the country. After they arrested him, she went and removed a board from the outdoor latrine of the jail. Shimon ran away, but they caught him and he told the police Stase had helped him. They arrested Stase and were interrogating her.

After a week, Yozas was in Simna and told us that the Simna priest asked the German commander not to kill Shimon, because Shimon had saved him during the Russian occupation by warning him that the Russians intended to deport him. Then the priest came to Shimon in jail and suggested that he convert to Catholicism. Shimon replied that if he knew he was going to live he would convert. But as he was going to die anyway, since he was a Jew, he would stay a Jew. They tortured him to force him to ask the priest to come back and convert him. But he didn't.

The Lithuanian activist Piletsky shot him and got fifteen German marks for it. He had already shot seventeen Jews. According to Yozas, when Piletsky took Shimon out to be shot, the two were alone. Shimon begged Piletsky to spare his life, to let him go and say that he had slipped out of his hands. But Piletsky replied, "What makes you think I would have pity on a Jew?"

Shimon could have at least put up a struggle. Either he would have succeeded in escaping, or he would have been shot on the spot. If he did not succeed, what more did he have to lose? Yozas added that they wouldn't have killed Shimon if they hadn't found his lists and his diary, a thick notebook in which he had made notes about taking revenge. When the Jews were being shot, Shimon was up in a tree, and while he was tied to the branch by his belt, he wrote everything he saw in his diary, including descriptions of how the barbarians tortured children.

Yozas told me that he and Sebiastas were unhappy about my keeping a diary and said that they had decided to take it from me before we left their place. If we get out of this alive, they said, they would return it to me. In the meantime, they'll hide it. I told him I would never give him the diary. So he asked me what would happen if we were caught. Would we turn them in? I promised that I wouldn't inform on them. I added that if, for instance, I could save my own life, I couldn't be responsible. But if we were to be shot anyway, why should I turn in the people who had tried to save me?

On the one hand, the Matulevitches were afraid to keep us and wanted to make us go. On the other, the fear that we'd be caught and turn them in forced them to keep us. They got no pleasure at all from the business with us, and Mrs. Matulevitch moaned that she would soon come to a bad end. She said that she trusted me, but if they caught Joseph, he could not resist torture and would turn her in. She said that Yozas already wanted to order us out, but she asked to keep us until the wheat was grown because we hadn't anywhere to go now, and if we are caught, they would all die as well. Even when the wheat is ripe, she said, she will continue being afraid that, if we're caught, we'll turn them in, and they will be killed.

I told her that we'll try to avoid being caught, and I expressed my hope that God will help us and all will end well. But deep inside myself I, too, was scared, and could see myself caught, the game being up. I recalled, however, the Latin saying "There's no cure against the power of death." In other words, no one should fear the worst. If you are meant to live, then you will live. If you're meant to die, then that is the will of the Creator. So we must be brave and not despair.

The next day, near noon, Vladas called us to come down to eat lunch. There were two pounds of bread on the table (Vladas got them in exchange for six eggs) and a quart and a half of milk. Naturally, the portions of bread were meager and Yozas said, "Seriously now, let's try to save on bread somehow from now on."

Then Mrs. Matulevitch gave each of us a glass of milk, neglecting to leave even a drop for herself. I immediately gave her my glass and shared Joseph's portion with him. She didn't want to take it, but I told her that if she didn't I wouldn't eat at all, so she took it.

It wasn't the most pleasant moment for us. I was very uncomfortable when I saw how good they were to us, how willing they were to save us, and that, on top of it, they had to starve. Naturally, we were not to blame for it. After all, we did bring them food and many things in exchange. But the little girl was right when she said, "And what did we get to make up for the fear?" It was true that we would never be able to pay them back for our lives.

The news from the front became more encouraging. The Russians had surrounded seven German divisions, and people began talking about the Germans retreating. In Kovno a railroad car was bombed and there were thirty-six casualties, including eight Germans. The Russians and the British bombed Lithuania and scattered leaflets telling the population to flee from the big cities.

The head priest of Simna announced in church that the Lithuanian young people would be transported to Germany. He called in the mayor and protested to him about registering Lithuanian workers for transport to Germany while there were so many aliens around. So they started transporting the Russian women to Germany. Those who tried to escape were shot. The neighbor Ostrovsky took one of the Russian women working for him, Sura, to Simna. She understood what was awaiting her there and she jumped off the wagon and ran. She was seen running through the Catholic cemetery with the straw from the wagon still sticking to her clothes. People were advised to stay at home at night, because many Russian prisoners-of-war had escaped from the POW camps and were killing villagers.

It was rumored that Hitler and Mussolini had turned to the Pope, asking him to arrange a peace treaty with the Western Allies and that the Allies might be ready to accept. That burned me up. After all the acts of deceit by the Germans, would they still extend a hand to them? I hoped it would not be done. To offer them peace seemed to me an unprecedented sin against humanity, and especially against the Jewish people. Even if it meant that I could walk out as a free man, I didn't want it. I preferred to continue staying in hiding so that Hitler's deeds were not passed over in silence.

All night I dreamed about my family and I couldn't get them out of my mind during the next day. It was hard for me to stop crying—one had to be as strong as steel to bear all that. My strength was drained, and all day my head hurt and I couldn't stand on my feet. It was only toward evening that I pulled myself together a little. Early the next day, Yozas told us that we can stay with them for only one day.

The weather was quite good, so I washed myself all over and got ready to leave in the evening, hoping God would not desert us. Yozas called us to come down from the attic to peel potatoes. While we were working, he said he would keep us for another week. His mother intervened and said she had already promised us we could stay with them for two more weeks. Yozas agreed.

While we were talking, Yushkovsky and two others suddenly came to the Matulevitches, searching for produce. Nobody saw them coming until they had reached the door, and then Sebiastas said to Joseph, "Well, this is the end!" Joseph hid above the oven and I lay down in the attic. God was with us; they didn't search the place, asking only questions. Yushkovsky told the Matulevitches that they would return next week for pigs. When they left, Yozas said we should leave before they returned.

All that night I felt sick. Two fingers on each of my hands hurt very much, and three of my fingers were sore from writing. My shoulders were sore, my neck felt broken, and my head was full of lice and sores.

In the morning, Sebiastas was making samagon, and Yozas got very drunk. He invited me to drink with him and an argument broke out between him and his mother. He beat her and broke a pot and some bottles. She hit him with a stick. The fight pushed us somewhat into the background and the next day Yozas told us we could stay with them longer. He seemed to behave like a real baby, forgetting what he had said a minute before. He asked me to go to a farmer friend and get some food, but there was really nothing to eat here. So I went to Smidzun in Glosnik, the rich farmer to whom we were going the night we met Mrs. Matulevitch. I wasn't in very good spirits, but Smidzun's very warm welcome changed my mood completely. He said that I could hide in his barn and he gave me a pillow and his coat. He added, of course, that if the worst happened and someone picked up my trail, I should say that I had got into the barn without his knowledge. But he hoped that nothing like that would happen to me.

He brought me breakfast the next morning and told me how much he shared our pain, giving me hope that we would get through this after all. He was very nice to me and called me "My dear" and "My boy," and kept on repeating, "What suffering!" I felt much better after such a welcome. His wife was going to Simna and he told her to buy me a newspaper.

Smidzun's child, who was watching for birds, saw me and called out to Zinkevitch, who worked for them. Zinkevitch looked right at me, just laughed, and went away. He went to Smidzun and said to him, "A man is lying up there with a pot and a spoon." Smidzun wasn't very happy about the fact that he saw the utensils and the pillow, but he didn't think that anything would happen before evening. I was again in low spirits, restlessly waiting for dark.

Smidzun gave me a lot of food and I set out to return to the Matulevitches. I lost my way, wandered aimlessly all night, and got lost in the wheat fields. I had no idea where I was. I had lost my sense of direction because when I left Smidzun's I felt that someone was following me, and I went off to the side and got mixed up. I decided to stay in the wheat the whole day and at night to try to find my way. When it was dark, I left the wheat field and took to the road I thought would lead to the farm of the Matulevitches. I reached a forest, wandered around, and got completely confused.

I walked up to a farm, and it looked too big to me. There was a trench by the house, so I crossed it and turned to the farm across the way, which looked more modest.

When I was close to the house, I took off my shoes and put down my sack and started to approach it. The dog barked a little but immediately stopped. When I got close to the garden it looked like that of the Matulevitches. The attic window, too, looked just like the one in their house. The window was open, and I climbed into the house. The family was very happy with the food I had brought.

A week passed and we decided to leave for the wheat fields. The stalks were high and it was easy for us to hide among them without being detected. We fixed a hiding place and it was not bad at all. We were confident that God would protect us. At night, when I went to get water, He provided us with a swamp in the field. I brought a can and two bottles of water. It was of a yellowish color, and we could keep it only for one day. It smelled badly, but we were happy with it. The problem was food. However, during our stay with the Matulevitches, I had gathered enough information about the peasants of the area, and knew which of them were enemies of the Jews and would betray us and which we could trust. So we decided to hide in the fields by day, and to go by night to the peasant homes, tap on the window, explain who we were, and ask for a glass of milk and some bread.

One night I went to get food from a woman who used to visit our store. I asked for some bread. She didn't give me a crumb and wouldn't even open the door. "Where am I supposed to find bread for you?" she shouted. "Go on, get out of here!" So I went to Zinkevitch, a poor farmer who was very nice to me and gave me some bread, butter and milk.

It was already the end of July, the wheat was starting to bend a little, and we knew we wouldn't be able to stay in the field much longer.

A week passed and we decided to try our luck in the barn of the farmer Zhvinak. We went in and were able to arrange a hiding place. We put up a board as a roof. The cow, the horse, and the sheep were a big help, because it was much easier to move around when they were in the barn. After two days Zhvinak's sons found us. Their father came out and laughed. Mrs. Zhvinak also came along, and it turned out to be a very loving reception. Mrs. Zhvinak brought us potato soup, bread, cheese, and milk. The boys gave me a good pencil. In the evening Mrs. Zhvinak again brought us food and we went on our way. Before leaving, Zhvinak told us that we could use his barn whenever we were in trouble.

We heard from Zhvinak that our town's physician, Doctor Angenitsky, was killed in the Kalesnik forest by a young Lithuanian activist, whose name was Zhebrovsky. At first, he only wounded Angenitsky, so the doctor called out to him, "Zhebrovsky, when you were sick, I healed you. Now you heal me and finish me off!" Zhebrovsky turned away and left him to be buried, still alive.

Those who were present during the shooting of the Simna Jews told Zhvinak that while some of the victims were hit by as many as ten bullets, many others were buried alive. They saw how the very earth seemed to rise up in revulsion. I was shivering all over while listening to him, and I thought of my poor mother and little Yehudah'le.

We went again to Zinkevitch and this time we entered his house. He was a poor man, with only two acres of land, but he had a good heart. He also seemed to be a man who knew how to keep a secret. He gave us some food and newspapers. In one of them there was a report that the United States had recognized Palestine as the center for the Jewish people. I was very pleased. It gave me reason to believe that after the war the Jewish question would finally be solved and we would have the Land of Israel.

In the evening we decided to go to the Matulevitches. The reception was lukewarm and I felt uncomfortable for having come to them again. But my mood changed when Mrs. Matulevitch told us that she had heard from a neighbor, that our father was alive somewhere near Alitus. If it were only true! We prayed to God and the difference in our mood was like day and night. They told us to go to the attic to sleep, and I asked Mrs. Matulevitch about Papa again. She swore she had told us the truth, that the man said that our father was still alive.

In the morning we left them, and Mrs. Matulevitch told us to come more often. We continued visiting the various farmers at night. Some of them gave us a warm reception, others a cooler one.

One night, it began to rain and thunder, so we left the field and went to Lazovsky's place. Mrs. Lazovsky was home and we asked her permission to stay in their barn for a day. They brought us breakfast, and when they saw how we were dressed in rags, they brought us Russian army pants and shoes. In the afternoon,

Lazovsky brought us a meal of bread, cake fresh from the oven, butter, and milk. I thanked him and told him that we would leave the next day.

He answered, "No, don't leave. You'll have time enough to lie in the fields. Stay here and you'll be taken care of. If no strangers come over, you can stay on a little longer. Exactly what happened to the Jews could happen to us. These are mad times."

He also told us that we could come back to them in two weeks, after they finished most of their work, and he invited us to come during the winter. He said that all the "colonists" (landowners of Polish origin) would probably take us in for a week or so, and that way we might survive.

The next day the youngsters came in and told us it was safe to go out and walk around the yard. We didn't want to, but they simply forced us. They showed us leaflets distributed by the Russians saying, "Lithuanians! Bury the Jews you have murdered in a place that befits them, and save the trenches you threw them into for yourselves!"

After a few days, Lazovsky's son, who lived in the village of Kavaltchuk, arrived. He reported that someone from Simna had visited him and asked whether it was true that Max Weinstein's sons were hiding out among the "colonists." He answered that he had been to see his family two days before and hadn't heard anything about it. Then he jumped on his bicycle and dashed over to his parents to tell them that, if they saw us, they should tell us to get away from the area. We were in their barn at that very moment, and he came in to see us. When he left we decided to go, parting from them as real friends. I didn't know how to thank them.

We had no idea where to go. But when we reached Lazovsky's potato field, we lay down. After a while we realized that our hiding place was too close to the barley and it was possible to sight us while the barley was being harvested. So we moved to another place in the same field, where no one would be able to see us. We had to find a new arrangement. We would not be able to continue hiding in the fields. The best thing about hiding in the fields was that, thanks to the rain and sun, we got rid of our lice and rash.

VI.

THE GUN

At sunset on August 18, 1942, I left Joseph in our hiding place in the potato field and went to Stephan Pavlovsky, who lived alone in the countryside. I woke him up and asked him to let us build a hideout in his barn, with an entrance beneath the wall and, if possible, a direct exit, so that he would not have to bother about our food. He was in no position to give us any food.

He consented and showed me how to fix up a nice nest where no one could find us. The place seemed to be perfect. He said that he would spread a rumor that he had seen us, and then no one would suspect that we were staying with him. I explained to him that that wasn't such a good idea. While we were talking, the subject of arms came up. He brought out an eight-chambered gun. I told him that if he gave me the gun and fixed up a hiding place for us in his barn, I would do my best to get him a gold ring. He didn't want to take anything from me, neither for the gun nor in exchange for keeping us, and said, "I have no use for a ring. I don't want the last thing you have left. It's not necessary to keep account of it in your diary, and if you want to stay in my good graces, we shouldn't enter into any transactions. If one wants to make an enemy, he should start doing business with someone. If you survive, then we'll worry about our accounts."

He gave me the gun with seven bullets, and I was very happy that I was now able to resist German soldiers or the Lithuanian police if I should encounter them.

We agreed that I would come with Joseph in a few days. I left him and walked to the other side of the railroad track, to a neighbor, a "colonist," to ask for some food. I was given a quart of milk, some cheese, and a pound of bread. I came back to Joseph and we went to get some more food. We became confused, wandered around endlessly, and couldn't find the place. Joseph didn't have any more strength to walk. He would go on a little and stop, and he was sweating. He grew very weak. Having no choice, we stopped in Pavlovsky's wheat field. After a day there, we decided to enter his barn. Pavlovsky received us nicely, and the first night in our new hiding place passed fairly well. We now had food for several days.

We helped Pavlovsky unload a wagon full of peat. While we were working he said that it was pretty dangerous for us to stay with him, because they might come searching. If they came with dogs, all would be over for us. He advised us to dig a ditch and hide further away from the wall, even though that won't be completely safe either. "It never hurts to be careful," he added. I took his advice and started digging a new shelter.

After a few days, Pavlovsky gave me a newspaper and I read about an order to carry identity papers. It said that the order didn't apply to Jews. "That gives me hope that there are still some Jews left in Lithuania," I scribbled down next to the item.

At eight o'clock one evening I left the barn and went for food. I came to Pranas Shupienis in the hamlet of Tcherniukishok. He greeted me warmly, saying he knew my father very well. His wife called me "sir." What a strange feeling I had when I heard that word. I felt that term was somehow improper for me, and I wanted to tell her not to call me that, but I didn't. I ate a little and drank some milk and they gave me some bread, butter and eggs. Pranas suggested that I should go to visit his brother, Antanas Shupienis, in the village of Otesnik. When I got to the edge of Antanas Shupienis' farm, a dog started barking very loudly, and I heard people talking not far away, so I lay down to wait. When the dog stopped barking, I went into the yard.

They received me very nicely. They expressed their sorrow over what had become of the Jews and said, "When someone was in trouble, a Jew would be quicker to help than anyone of our people." They said they were on their way to Simna when the first transport to Alitus was on its way, and they saw my father on the truck.

I left them about two that morning and they invited me to return. It was pitch black on the way back. I couldn't see a thing when I walked out of the house, and it was hard to carry the sack of food on my back. It was so heavy that I was bathed in sweat; my coat and shirt were soaking wet. I drank four cups of water and fell asleep very quickly. At seven Pavlovsky came into the barn and found the door open. Either the wind had blown it open or someone had come into the barn and forgotten to close it. After he left I was still nagged by the thought that someone else was hiding in the barn. We became even more suspicious because there had been a thunderstorm last night. I left our hiding place and looked everywhere but I found nothing.

In the evening, we had almost dozed off when Pavlovsky called us. He told us to get some of our bread because he had brought us fresh milk. I didn't want to leave the barn, but we couldn't just send him back, so we went with him and drank it—a glass for Joseph and one for me. Pavlovsky asked us to drink some more. I thanked him and asked him to give us any potatoes he had left over from dinner, rather than feed them to the dog, and I would give him bread in exchange. He gave us nine potatoes and I gave him half a pound of bread for the dog. We went back to sleep. The next day was horrible. I felt very sick and my head was killing me. I felt like needles were pricking it, and we both had upset stomachs. In the middle of the day, while I was lying quietly in our hiding place, a rat climbed up on my left foot and started strolling around on it. I was startled and brushed it off right away. After a few days, a rat fell from one of the upper rafters right onto my chest and started to scramble all over me. I was scared to death. It almost got as far as my neck. I began to shake and the rat jumped up on one of the side beams.

They had grown so used to us that they were just not afraid of us anymore. In the evening both Joseph and I had swollen cheeks and our teeth hurt. We couldn't think of any connection between that and the rats.

Pavlovsky came to us with news: the Lithuanians were planning a rebellion. They were going over to the American side so that they could have their independence again. Pavlovsky said he was convinced that the Lithuanians would succeed and there would be no revenge on them for what they had done to the Jews; neither America nor Russia was interested in getting back at them for that. "The same activists who slaughtered Jews," Pavlovsky said, "were now going to rebel against the Germans, and everything will turn out fine for them."

I shuddered, thinking that Pavlovsky might be right. It was disgusting to think that those murderers will survive and go on to enjoy their lives. It was their fortune to have it good, while our fate was to suffer.

A week passed and nothing happened in Lithuania to confirm Pavlovsky's news. On the contrary, the Lithuanians started to deport the Poles from Simna to Alitus. While they were doing it, they brought in two truckloads of Jews from Kovno and shot them. People thought they were shooting the Poles, and there was a great uproar. But after they found out it was Jews who were being killed, they quieted down. To kill Jews was permissible!

With the winter approaching, I went to the Matulevitches to ask if we could come back to them. I brought them bread, butter, cheese, sugar, and flour. They were very pleased. They told me they had already prepared the oven for us. I stayed with them for the night, and in the morning, after breakfast, when I was sitting over the oven, a friend of Yozas came into the kitchen and lit a cigarette. We looked straight at one another for a few moments. Then he went into the other room and asked the Matulevitches who was lying there above the oven with such a big head? But he answered his own question by saying it was probably Dzhanuk, and added, that they shouldn't let Dzhanuk sit above the oven. They should throw him out, because he was likely to relieve himself there. Dzhanuk was a retarded boy from the area, and he was credited with every possible abnormal act.

The next day I returned to Joseph in Pavlovsky's barn and brought him a goose egg, half a pound of bread, six biscuits, and a bottle of milk. It was raining and I vomited on the way. Joseph also vomited in the barn. For a few days I was not feeling well and I couldn't go out for food. When I felt a little better and went out, I lost my strength and couldn't take another step. My ears were cold and my head hurt. I lay down in the reeds. After a long rest I got up to return to Pavlovsky's. I was completely exhausted, and Joseph's feet were frozen. So we left our hiding place and lay on the straw the whole day, waiting to say goodbye to Pavlovsky. We had decided to go to the Matulevitches.

The Matulevitches put Joseph on the oven and me in the attic. They told us that Yozas and Vladas had a contagious rash and advised us to watch ourselves. When it became colder, we both were over the oven.

When Yozas saw I had a gun, he asked for it. But I refused to give it to him.

One day, I came down from the oven to relieve myself, but immediately remembered that I had left the weapon there and I told Joseph to keep an eye on it. Just as I was going into the hallway, though, Yozas jumped on the oven to take the gun. Joseph managed to snatch it from him and throw it to Vladas. In the meantime, while they were wrestling over it, I came back and began to tickle Yozas. He jumped off the oven and Vladas threw me the gun.

One evening I went to visit some farmers for food and gathered quite a bit. Among those I visited was Thomas Uter. He told me that he was in the Alitus jail, at the end of August 1941, when the Jews from Simna were killed there, among them my father and brother Benjamin. Uter and his brother were imprisoned there and worked in the kitchen, serving food. Zadok Davidson would give them cigarettes in exchange for food. The Jews were sure they would be freed, he said. They used to say to the Uter brothers, "You're prisoners because you have committed a crime, but we, why are we imprisoned? They will call us in for questioning in a day or two and release us."

He described how the killing was carried out. In the morning, after he had served four hundred Jews breakfast, the police entered and ordered the Jews to strip, because they had to wash. "That's how they fooled them," Uter said. As the Jews left their cells, the Lithuanian activists were already waiting to beat them with guns. Then they chased them to the trenches and murdered them.

A chill ran through my body. It was very difficult for me to listen to what he was saying, and I couldn't escape the fact I no longer had a father or a brother. Until that day, I had still had some hope.

They made samagon at the Matulevitches all night. In the morning, when they were finished, they drank themselves into a stupor, beat one another, broke a large mirror, and did other damage. There were strangers there throughout it all, and we had to stay above the oven until late in the afternoon. Joseph spent the whole night sitting behind the stovepipe and didn't sleep a wink. We also discovered that we had a rash, so I asked Mrs. Matulevitch to bring me a salve.

I went out for some food and was quite successful. But when I was returning to the Matulevitches with more than ten pounds of bread, butter, eggs and five pounds of flour, I was sweating, and my rash was driving me mad. Mrs. Matulevitch had ordered the salve for me in Simna, but it took a few days to get it. When she brought it, I put it on immediately, but since there was nothing to eat in the house, I went out, covered with the salve, to find food. When I returned, I was told by the family that their neighbors knew that Joseph and I were staying with them.

The next morning Mrs. Matulevitch visited a neighbor, and was told that people were saying that the Maxuks (they used to call my father Max, and Maxuk was a nickname for Max's son) were staying with the Matulevitches. Mrs. Matulevitch replied, "How could they possibly stay with us? Where would I keep them?" It became clear that we should leave as soon as possible, and I went out to try to find another hiding place.

So I went to see Bagdon on Dzikautchizna's farm. They greeted me very nicely there, and I ate dinner with them. One of their relatives from the village of

Baksh, Aldona Tarashkevitch, asked me to come to them—they would also help us. She said she may be able to steal the seal of the mayor of Alitus. I gave her a snapshot, and she would see if she could forge Lithuanian identity papers for me. She will either bring the papers herself or send them over with her father.

I stayed for about three hours and got quite a bit of food. When I left, Bagdon accompanied me as far as the river. I crossed it and went home. But I lost my way. I wandered around for about three hours. The snow was up to my knees and I had no more strength to walk. My head hurt, my sides hurt, I was cold, my face was burning, and I was itching like mad. My shoes were torn to pieces, my socks were wet, and I felt broken and trembling, so I went back to Dzikautchizna's farm.

I knew Joseph wouldn't know what to think and would probably be in a panic. But I had no other choice. I knocked on the door and it was a long time before anyone came to open it. They let me in and I went up to the attic. I went to sleep naked under the blanket.

It was a good night, and in the morning, after breakfast, they brought me a pail of boiling hot water and I had a good wash. I really felt like a different man. I dried my socks and put my shoes on the oven.

When I returned, the Matulevitches were delighted with the armload of food I brought, but two days later there was almost nothing left. Joseph and I could have existed in our hiding place for two weeks on that food. Mrs. Matulevitch told us that David Sandler had been staying with a farmer in the hamlet of Krokilovsky for the whole winter. He had lots of money, so the farmer, together with his two sons, took Sandler out and shot him.

We were afraid to continue staying at the Matulevitches, so we went to Yuchnelevitch. They agreed to keep Joseph for two weeks, so I left him there, and went alone to see Pranas Shupienis in Tcherniukishok. He agreed to take Joseph in for a week. His brother Antanas, too, agreed to take Joseph. While I was there, a neighbor, Mrs. Apolsky, arrived. She told me that two Jews from Simna, Gamsky and Bialostotsky, had escaped the shooting and had been with them for two weeks. When they heard that the police were on to them, they took them to relatives, the Bainorovitch family, a woman with four daughters and a son, in the village of Laukintchai, near the town of Sirey.

They were staying there in a warm room, going to sleep clean, and eating like human beings, with forks, knives and spoons, out of shiny bowls.

"They are treated like guests, not like refugees," Mrs. Apolsky said, "and everything is wonderful for them there."

My head hurt very badly and the Shupienises let me sleep in a bed in their hallway, under a blanket. It was wonderful. When I left them the next day, a German and a Russian were suddenly standing right in front of me. I passed the gun into my pants, but I couldn't take off and run right in front of them. They asked me for directions and I showed them the way. I spoke to them both in Russian and German and they went on. Afterward I felt miserable that I had spoken German, because he might have taken me with him as a translator, and that could have been the end of me.

When we started our new phase of hiding, leaving Joseph somewhere for some time, and I wandering daily from one place to another, I was very worried. But very soon I saw that the same peasants, who at first trembled at the very thought of helping Jews, became used to the idea, once they had provided me with some food. They no longer found it so perilous, and they let me sleep overnight indoors or in their barns. As time went by, they were willing to shelter me for one or two days, and Joseph for longer. I found quite a number of farmers ready to give Joseph shelter for a week or two, either by hiding him in the attic or by keeping him openly.

While I was at Shupienis, Apolsky's son came and we played cards. When we finished the game he told me that the police were looking for me. He said that it was dangerous for me to stay in that neighborhood and asked me where I had left Joseph. From the very first I wanted to lie to him, but I sensed that he wouldn't just ask a question like that without reason. I told him that Joseph was with the Berziunases, and he told me that he had been to see a neighbor, to give him a letter from Gamsky. After the neighbor read the letter he muttered, "Thank God he's still alive. You know, they caught one of Weinstein's sons in Simna today."

I jumped out of my seat, put on my shoes, Apolsky brought me my coat, Mrs. Shupienis gave me a cane, and I ran straight to Berziunas. I heard their dog barking next to the house and was afraid that the police were in their yard. I dashed back to Shupienis, and he came with me to the Berziunases. He went into the house, and Yurgis, the oldest son, came out toward me, promising that Joseph wouldn't be caught at their place. I went back to Shupienis with my head splitting from pain. I couldn't sleep a wink all night.

The next day, I decided to visit Gamsky and Bialostotsky. The snow was piled up outside, my feet were freezing, my throat hurt badly, and it was hard to walk in the winter, but I somehow arrived in the village of Laukintchai, and came to the Bainorovitches. It was February 4, 1943, and they told me that Bialostotsky had died on October 15, 1942, and was buried not far from the garden. No one outside the Bainorovitch family knew about it.

They called Gamsky out, and we kissed one another. It was like a reunion of brothers. I showed him a picture I had of him with his son and daughter, and I remained with him for a couple of days. His hosts were very good people. They had not received anything from him and were keeping him out of the goodness of their hearts.

When I took Joseph from the Berziunases, he fell, on the way, into a trench and couldn't get out. With great difficulty I pulled him out of it. Pavlovsky's lawn had turned into one big lake and we ran through the water as if we were bathing in the summer. Joseph had no strength to go on. I took him by the hand and dragged him over to Yuchnelevitch, and we went in and undressed. All three pairs of my pants were wet up to the knees, so they gave me dry pants. Joseph was afraid to stay there for a week, because Mrs. Yuchnelevitch's sister was a terrible blabbermouth. I had no other choice but to leave him there while I went to the Kazakevitches.

Their son Yonas and I chopped down trees, and a branch fell on my left foot. The big toe turned blue and hurt like mad because the nail was out of place. My right thumb hurt because I had hit it with a hammer while fixing my shoes, and the big toe of my right foot throbbed after I took out the pus.

When I left the Kazakevitches, I decided to go to the painter Zigmunt Emart in Simna. I had a stick with a handle and a nail at the other end, so it would be easier to walk on the lake. But my walk was a nightmare, hard, slippery, and against the wind. I also had to walk through the Catholic cemetery. It was very dark, and it was eerie to walk past the graves at night.

Emart gave me a new gun with five bullets. He said it shot accurately and its bullets would penetrate iron. He also gave me three prayer books, one for Rosh Hashanah, one for Yom Kippur, and a third for everyday. They belonged to Bezalel Talkunsky, who left them with Emart so that if he returned he could get them back. He also gave me a leaflet the Russians were distributing to the German population about the fighting at Stalingrad. It said that the Red Army had decimated the German troops who were camped outside Stalingrad since November 23, 1942. On February 2, 1943, the Red Army pushed them back. Of the 333,000 German soldiers there, 240,000 were killed.

When the hard winter was finally over, I came again, on April 1, to Emart. That very day a Communist, Penzin, was being buried. Mrs. Emart described to me how Penzin was caught. Five policemen came. One of them, Karlonis, entered the house with another one while the other three stayed outside. Karlonis turned the searchlight on Penzin and asked, "What's your name?"

Penzin took out a gun and Karlonis grabbed his hand. Then Penzin fired and wounded him in the hand. Karlonis shouted, "Put the weapon down!" while the second policeman shot three times, and Penzin fell wounded. They brought him to Alitus and he died there.

While Emart was talking to me, Karlonis came to their house to drink some brandy. I hid in the attic, and Mrs. Emart went to serve the policeman. They talked about Penzin, and Karlonis said, "We caught one devil. Now we have got to get Maxuk. We know where he is."

I was scared to death.

VII.

ANNOYING PREDICTION

Gamsky asked me to bring him some food. I collected it from a few farmers and went to Antanas Shupienis. He gave me a horse, and I took the food to Laukintchai. On the way back, I rode very slowly and it was fine, but when I tried to speed up, the horse threw me, jumped over me, and ran away. I caught him, got back on, and went to Antanas. My left foot hurt. At night I got sick and I wanted to vomit. Antanas gave me medicines and all kinds of herbs. Somehow the night passed, but I still felt awful. Our Passover was on April 20, 1943, and I went to visit Gamsky again. I trembled, thinking of the Passover we had two years before. When the Bainorovitches saw I was sad, they suggested to me I should convert. "If you die, at least you will go to heaven," they said. "But if you remain a Jew, then it's hell for you."

At the beginning, Gamsky was convinced that the Bainorovitches were hiding him disinterestedly. There were Lithuanians who saved Jews for reward; romance, too, was also a factor in the saving of Jews. The Bainorovitches, Gamsky thought, did so simply out of a solicitude to save a fellow-creature from death. As time passed, Gamsky realized that those good people acted also out of evangelistic motives, seeking to profit from the situation and to persuade him to be baptized. His hosts, a very religious Christian family, did everything that they could for him, in earnest conviction that they would succeed in converting him without coercion. He had been saved physically, they would say, so the time had come to save his soul.

Each of the four daughters was ready to become his wife if he changed his faith, and I am not at all sure that he would not have succumbed if I had not been in the area. I believe that my frequent visits to him, my rejection of all their attempts to convert me, and my encouraging Gamsky to resist the temptation, gave him strength and kept him from taking a step that he would have regretted afterwards.

At Shupienis' I found old Mrs. Zimmerman, who was telling fortunes with cards. She told my fortune, too. All my people have been murdered, she said, except four members of my family who are still alive—two men and two women. The men were dark and blond. In two days something unpleasant will happen to me and for the next ten days I will be very worried. I shall soon meet two other Jews, a man and a woman. I will aid them, but they will be caught. In four months I'll receive good news. In a year or thirteen months I will travel to the east, across the sea, and I will marry a dark woman, who is waiting for me eagerly. I will live eighty-seven years and I will have a two-story brick house.

Even though I did not believe in cards, I was still frightened by what she told me, and I thought I should try to avoid helping other Jews because they might be doomed because of me. If two Jews, a man and a woman, were caught because of me, I would shoot myself, I noted in my diary.

Shupienis was going to the town of Sirey. He gave me a ride and left me at a friend's place in the village of Zhager. When I returned with him, he told me that he had met the police chief of Simna, Vaitkus, who asked him, "Who were you traveling with there, a neighbor?" And he said yes. The police chief said, "He's a good man, the neighbor of yours, isn't he?" Shupienis replied, "Neighbor like all the others." Then the chief said, "So you're not going to tell me who it was? Well then, I'll tell you who it was! It was Maxuk. I knew him personally. But it's not important to me." Shupienis said, "I was driving alone when he met me and asked me to pick him up." Then others broke into the conversation.

When Vaitkus passed us, we saw him. We didn't think he would recognize me, but he did. It was good that he didn't stop. I was scared to death, and I might have used my weapon. Old lady Zimmerman was right. She did tell me that in two days something unpleasant would happen to me.

Even against my better judgment I began to believe in the cards, and I shuddered. The prediction that I will meet two Jews and help them, but they may be doomed as a result, annoyed me and frightened me.

When we arrived at Shupienis' house, we were told that there were Germans in the area and that one German came to a meeting in the village and said, "You're hiding Jews. What do you think they would do to you? They'd send you to Russia!"

There was no doubt that everyone knew that my brother and I were moving around in that area, and it was becoming even more dangerous. Nervous about the news that there were Germans around, I went out to the cold field and lay there sleepless all night. At dawn I went to Shupienis for breakfast, and then took a book and went to lie in the grain again and sun myself while reading.

When it started to rain, I left the grain field and walked through a lot of water. By then, it was pitch black. But I arrived at the Yuchnelevitches and had a good wash. They told me that I was being searched for and warned me to be extremely careful. It was evident that everyone knew which farmers I went to. But I moved from one to the other and tried not to spend too much time in any one place, hoping that would help me not to be caught. The main problem was to protect Joseph, who was staying at each place a longer period, and often worked there as a farmhand. He was delighted about it, for it was infinitely preferable to spend the day out of doors, in the sun, than to lurk in a granary or behind an oven. The arrangement was equally convenient for the peasants, who gained materially from his work and my contributions.

Yuchnelevitch told me that people were saying there won't be any Jews left in the world, so it was pointless to protect them. He said that a few days before there were a lot of people at his place and they were drinking. Among them was the policeman Kvadrulis, who said that there were Jews hiding in Otesnik, and sooner or later they would have to be caught. Everyone else remained silent.

Then I went to Berziunas' uncle. The uncle himself was like the other Berziunases, a good man. But his wife was a shrew. She insulted me deeply. It was obvious that she was afraid to leave me alone in the room. She was afraid that I might steal something. She didn't say it, but I could tell from the way she was acting. I wanted to stay in the room where I was sitting, but she pushed me into another room and shut the door to the first room. I asked her why she was closing the door, and she said, "We don't let anyone in through this door."

I thought about sleeping there, but considering the way she was treating me, I left and slept in a field. In my dream, I saw Papa and my dear little brother, Yehudah'le. I hugged and kissed them, and I was deliriously happy. But suddenly I woke up and found myself in the field, and I felt miserable.

The following day I worked in the field all day, and I wounded Shupienis' right foot. It hurt him badly. Mrs. Shupienis also hurt herself because of me. I had left the pitchfork pointing up, and she stepped on it and hurt the big toe of her right foot. Early in the morning I sat at their table thinking what to do. We were running out of places to hide. A bee had stung me on the nose, my head was killing me, and I was so tired that I fell asleep right there.

In the evening, I went to find places for Joseph to hide. I walked by way of the swamps and I was soaked up to my knees. On my way, two people passed me and one of them shouted, "Hello!"

I stopped, and when I got a little closer I was scared, but suddenly I recognized him: it was Pranas Dainovsky, a shoemaker from Simna and a member of the clandestine Lithuanian Communist Party. He was arrested when the Germans entered our town and was released after a short time. A year passed, and he was arrested again. When we met that night it was for the first time since I had gone into hiding. He was on leave from the prison for a few days. He told me that he decided not to go back to prison but to join the anti-German partisans in the forest.

I then went to Yermelevitch's in Kalesnik. There, we heard two encouraging broadcasts, one from London in Polish and the other from Moscow, in German. Italy had surrendered. There were uprisings in Yugoslavia, France, Greece and Albania, and demonstrations in Bulgaria. The Russians were advancing, and Germany had been given an ultimatum to evacuate all the conquered territories.

While I was there, the policeman Mishkinis visited them. They talked about the killing of the Jews, and Mishkinis said that when the Jews of Simna were in the barracks, he saw the wife of Tuynila, from Kalesnik, bring some cheese to the Mirkus family.

"So I arrested her," he boasted, "and made her wear the yellow Star of David because she had brought food to a Jew. Everyone made fun of her for wearing that badge of shame on her back."

When the policeman left, Yermelevitch told me to be very careful. He said that some of the farmers, among them a certain Petrovsky, were saying that because the Russians were drawing near, if I remained alive they would be the first ones to be killed. They claimed that I was very dangerous and that no good will come of me because I was keeping a diary and writing down everything, and when the time came, I would get my revenge. I must, therefore, be turned over to the police.

Petrovsky was among those farmers who buried the Jews of Simna after they had been killed. The Lithuanian activists ordered the farmers to cover the trenches where the Jews had been shot, even though some were still alive. One of the farmers, Zhuk, protested, "People are still alive! How can you fill in the trenches?" Petrovsky answered, "I don't care!" Zhuk said to him, "Hundreds of people have been slaughtered and you don't care. When your pig died, you wailed for three days. But you don't give a damn about people, you don't feel any pity on them at all."

At night Yermelevitch's daughters, Zosia and Anela, and I decided to go to the railroad station. While we were walking along the track, not far from the station, someone called out to us, "Halt! Halt!" I thought that some boys were playing a trick on us, and we kept going toward whoever was calling out to stop. They called out, "Halt!" again, but we still kept going. Suddenly we heard a bullet being loaded into the chamber of a gun, and again someone called out "Halt!" We froze in our tracks.

A policeman from Simna and a Lithuanian soldier approached us. The girls were very frightened and so was I, but I couldn't escape. I told them we were students on our way to the high school in Alitus. When they asked why we didn't stop, I said that we thought some boys were playing a joke on us. "You would have had a big laugh if you were stretched out on the tracks right now," said the policeman. I stood shaking for fear that they might search my pockets, because they would have found the gun. But they left us. My salvation came from my being with the girls. That way I wasn't suspicious. If they had met me alone on the railroad track, they would have searched me, and that would have been the end. God was with me.

I learned later that when the girls arrived at the station, they found the soldier and the policeman there and taunted them that less than an hour before they had stood in front of a Jew and didn't know it. The two men rushed out to search for me, but didn't do anything to the girls and let them travel to Alitus, because they claimed they had just met me by chance.

On November 7, at night, we heard an important radio broadcast from Moscow. Stalin himself announced that the Russians had liberated the city of Pastov and were about to liberate Kiev. The population of Pastov celebrated and sang the praises of the Red Army. Many of those who had collaborated with the Germans were shot. It was also announced that a meeting was held in Moscow of the foreign ministers of the Soviet Union, the United States and Great Britain (Molotov, Hull and Eden) and, according to what people said, they had decided to open a second front.

VIII.

INTENSIFIED CHASE

I went to see the Miknevitches and sat all day talking with their daughter. She was married to a Russian colonel, who had fled with the Russians. Unlike most of the farm women, she was an intelligent woman. Being with her was very different from being with the farmers and, naturally, the food, the way of eating, everything was different. When I was there, she wouldn't take food with her fingers. This was the only place where they acted like city people.

I had grown so used to country life, I simply didn't know how to behave when I was in company like that. Even breakfast was different. They had coffee, bread, honey, butter, and cheese. I ate until I was full. In the countryside they left you alone in the room. She never left me by myself. She called her father to come in and talk to me.

In the evening, Yonas, an anti-German partisan, came to visit them and we talked for a few hours. The Russians had parachuted him into the area. The anti-German partisan movement started, in effect, immediately after the German attack on the Soviet Union. People who had held official positions during Soviet rule, members of the Lithuanian Communist Party, Russian soldiers who were isolated from their units and who did not want to become prisoners-of-war, all went into hiding in the forests. Later, those partisan groups were joined by Jews and by Russian soldiers who had been taken prisoner but escaped.

From the Miknevitches I went to Emart. He said the police were offering a reward for my capture, dead or alive. A six-year-old child came in. Mrs. Emart asked him something and the boy told her, "You talk like a Jew." A little one like that and he was already picking on the Jews.

Emart told me that a Jewish woman was in the village of Shostakova with the farmer Vinzas Slavenas, so I left for Slavenas' place. I found a Jewish girl, Regina Kaufman, from the city of Lazdey. She had survived with her sister, Guta, whom I knew before the war. Regina was living there almost openly as a weaver. Guta was staying with a priest, completely free. Both sisters converted, and that was very painful for me. I tried very hard to explain to Regina why they mustn't adopt the religion of those who slaughtered her parents and entire family. I went to see Guta and spoke to her, too, for a while. But I did not succeed in changing their minds.

On December 23, 1943, I took Joseph to Kazakevitch. They agreed that he should stay with them over Christmas, and I went on to Pranas Shupienis. He informed me that there were three Jews staying with Smadziun in the village of Kavaltchuk.

I immediately went there and found Zvi (Hershel) Levit and his wife and Gita Zeliviansky. The three of them had come to the outskirts of Simna on foot, following the road at night, hiding in the woods by day. They were born in Simna and then had moved to Kovno. They told me that the situation in the ghetto of Kovno was becoming more and more difficult, and rumors were circulating that the ghetto was to be wiped out. So they decided to escape to Simna in the hope of finding friendly peasants willing to help them and give them cover until the storm passed. The three of them knew Smadziun well, and Smadziun let Levit's wife stay with him. I took the other two with me. We left at night, and we three stayed one day at Pranas Shupienis, who agreed to give Gita shelter for a month.

Zvi and I went to see Burbon and I left Zvi there for a few days. At three in the morning Zvi arrived at Shupienis' place, terribly frightened. He had heard the Burbons talking about a reward and thought they were going to turn him over to the police. I explained to him that they were talking about the reward the police were offering to whoever caught me, and he had nothing to fear. Since he was still afraid, I took him back to Smadziun in Kavaltchuk, to his wife.

With the help of Shupienis I found in the village of Susnik a farmer, Gurevitch, who agreed to take in Zvi Levit's wife as a maid, and promised to try and convince his brother-in-law to hide Zvi. I went back to Smadziun, who gave me a horse and a wagon, and I took Levit and his wife to Gurevitch in Susnik. I returned the horse and wagon to Smadziun and went to see my brother Joseph with the Balkevitches, where I left him for another week.

After a week, I took Joseph from the Balkevitches. We visited five farmers and they were all afraid to take us in. When we arrived at Yermelevitch's place, he took us in for a day. He said that the police knew we were moving around in the area and the searches for us had been intensified lately. I told him that I needed his help and that of my other farmer friends more than ever. More Jews had escaped from the Kovno ghetto. I assured him that they needn't be afraid because the war was about to end anyway.

For some time I had to move around with Joseph. On January 10, 1944, we went to Strolis in Otesnik, and there we heard about Gita Zeliviansky's tragedy.

Pranas Shupienis, with whom she was staying, was still making samagon and one day the police arrived to search for it. When Gita saw the police coming, she thought that they were searching for her, and she fearlessly jumped from the window and ran. She tried to escape, but a policeman ran after her and caught her. When it became clear who she was, both she and Shupienis were arrested. Gita was taken off to Alitus, where she was shot by a firing squad.

Poor Gita! It drove me mad that another one of old lady Zimmerman's prophecies had come true. She said that two Jews, a man and a woman, may be doomed after they meet up with me. When she told me that, I wanted to avoid meeting Jews. I even wanted to stop helping Gamsky, and I thought that if anything like that happened to me I would kill myself. Now I didn't know what to do. What if they caught another one of the Jews I had met? Joseph tried to calm me by saying that it was only fate.

Pranas Shupienis was tortured savagely and imprisoned in jail for a month. But through the mediation of influential friends he was set free. Much worse was the fate of another friend who had helped us enormously, Stephan Pavlovsky.

Three days after Gita was caught, Joseph and I were at Berziunas' and there we were told that the day before, at six o'clock in the evening, eight policemen came to Stephan Pavlovsky's place. He opened the door for them and they snapped, "Hands up!"

Pavlovsky was a brave man, and he made up his mind not to surrender. He took out his gun and shot two of them. One died on the spot and the second was going fast. Then Pavlovsky went down to the cellar below his granary. Germans came from the railway station and threw grenades into the granary, but it didn't blow up. Then they set fire to the building and Stephan was burned alive.

Poor Stephan, who had helped so many others, died in the hiding place he had prepared and was so proud of. He was sure that no one would catch him there.

God was with us. A week earlier Joseph and I had passed Pavlovsky's. Two days later we were there again. We sat with him for a long time, until midnight. On the very Wednesday the tragedy happened, I was at his place toward evening, when I could only stay for a few minutes. I wanted to stay with him longer, but he advised me not to because he was expecting a search. Soon after I left, the police came and it happened.

Poor Pavlovsky. A kind fellow, we were not his only wards. He also assisted young Poles who were wanted by the police, and Russians who had escaped from the German prison camps and sought hiding until the Red Army arrived. So were nobility of soul and steadfast friendship shamefully rewarded.

I left Joseph at Berziunas' and went to the village of Kavaltchuk. While walking, I met a man on a wagon who offered to take me on his wagon. I introduced myself and asked him who he was. He said he was Gradetzky from Kavaltchuk and invited me to his home. Once there, he told me that two Jews were staying with Ivanovsky in the village of Skovagol. Gradetzky took me to Ivanovsky, and I met the two Jews who had come from Kovno, Leah Port and Samuel Ingel. I stayed overnight with them at Ivanovsky's.

Leah and Samuel had escaped from the ghetto of Kovno and were heading for the woods to join the anti-German partisan groups. Halting near our town, they found shelter for a few days at the farm of the woman Ivanovsky, who was a deaf-mute.

After I had spent the night and promised to try to find hiding places for them, they decided not to continue to the woods, but to stay with me. I left them at Ivanovsky's and continued my daily trips in search of new hideouts. Leah Port was a good seamstress and could sew for the farmers, so the Berziunases, as well as the Bainorovitches, agreed to take her in for a month or more.

In the meantime, strangers visited Gurevitch in Susnik, saw the Levits and understood that they were Jews. So I took them to Bantzevitch, who also lived alone in the field and was not in a position to give the Levits food. He gave me a large wagon hooked up to one weak horse, and I went out to gather food, taking Samuel Ingel with me.

At one point, near a bridge, the horse stopped and wouldn't go on. It almost threw us into the river. With great effort we made him move. We gathered a quantity of food and on our way back we entered a swamp and we had a hard time getting the wagon out. We arrived at Bantzevitch's soaked. We climbed up onto the hay in the barn and fell asleep.

Bantzevitch came to the barn the next morning and said, "Get out of here, men. Things are very bad!" He didn't explain himself and we didn't understand what had happened. We were happy he did let the Levits stay on and we wanted to leave immediately, but we couldn't get our boots on. It was the middle of February. Our boots and our clothes were soaked. We waited for about an hour, got our boots on with great difficulty, dressed in our wet clothes, and went out in the freezing cold, our bodies literally shaking.

On the way we came across a wagon carrying seven people. We were frightened and turned off the road, lost our way, and wandered around. It was impossible to keep going in the boots, so we ran the last mile barefoot in the cold and wet. Samuel was having great difficulty walking at all. After we had covered thirteen miles, we got to Balkevitch's place convinced that we would be sick from the journey. We took off our clothes and placed them out to dry. I slept by the oven and Samuel stretched out on the bench. In the morning we went to Yermelevitch in Kalesnik.

While we were there, the mayor of the village came. He asked us who we were, when did we arrive in his village, and were we hiding out in the forests. He demanded that we tell him whether we were from Berlin or Moscow, and asked to see our papers. I told him that not only were we not from either, but we had never even been near Berlin or Moscow, and introduced myself as the son of Max Weinstein, who was the owner of the clothing store in Simna.

He said, "It can't be! Why just a while ago you were a little boy like that!" and he held his hand down toward the floor while telling me of his friendship with my father and that he used to lead my little brother around by the hand. He didn't believe it was me. Then I showed him my student card. He copied down everything in his notebook and assured me that I had nothing to fear. I asked him if we could come to his house and he said yes. I took Samuel back to Ivanovsky's and I went to see Mrs. Zubrowa, the mistress of the farm in Metel. She was a very good friend of my father and let me stay at her farm for a couple of days. She considered herself a friend of the Jews and told me she was related to the Count Valentine Potocki, the righteous proselyte.

Potocki was a celebrated Polish aristocratic family, known in southern Poland since the thirteenth century. A scion of that family, Count Valentine Potocki, while studying in Paris, was visiting a tavern whose owner was a Jew. Once, while in the tavern, he noticed the owner immersed in the study of the Talmud, and he expressed a desire to be instructed in the principles of Judaism. Potocki vowed that he would become a Jew if convinced of the error of Christianity. From Paris, Potocki went to the Papal Academy in Rome.

After some time at the academy, he went to Amsterdam and became a Jew. Then he went to Lithuania and settled as a Jew in the village of Ilya, near Vilno. Once Potocki scolded a boy for disturbing the prayers in synagogue. The boy's father, a coarse tailor, reported the existence of the proselyte to the authorities, thus leading to his arrest. Potocki was put on trial and, despite the pleas of fellow aristocrats, refused to recant. On the second day of Shavuot, in 1749, he was burned at the stake at the foot of the fortress of Vilna, on his lips the prayer of "Shmah Israel, Hear, O Israel."

A local Jew, pretending to be a Christian, succeeded in collecting some of the ashes and a finger from the corpse, and these were eventually buried in the Jewish cemetery. From the soil over the grave of Potocki, there grew a big tree which drew vast pilgrimages of Jews. The grave was demolished by Polish vandals. The Jews of Vilna commemorated the anniversary of Potocki's death by reciting the Kaddish and by making pilgrimages to his purported grave on the Ninth day of the month of Av, and on the High Holidays.

A week later I returned to Zubrowa, this time with food for the Levits and for Gamsky. I had so much of it that it was hard to manage, and I tore my pants on the way. So I went to Zubrowa, who mended the pants, and I left the food with her and went to get a horse from Smadziun in Kavaltchuk.

Smadziun gave me the horse, and told me I should be very careful. He said he had been in Simna and heard that my movements were being followed closely and the police hunt for me had intensified. He added that some of the farmers were inciting the people against the Jews and against me in particular, saying I should be killed, because otherwise I would make trouble for everyone.

When I returned to Zubrowa with Smadziun's horse, I took the food and distributed it. I then returned the horse to Smadziun and went to see Joseph at Navinsky's. While Navinsky's son, Vinzas, and I were standing and talking, a car pulled up. We jumped behind the barn, and it became clear that it was a truck full of policemen. The police drew up to the house, and Vinzas and I ran to the nearby forest. Joseph and Vladas Navinsky, who had been in the attic when they saw the truck approaching, ran after us. We four stayed in the forest until dark.

In the evening we saw someone running down the mountain. We thought it was a policeman and started to run, but the person called out to us. It was Navinsky's daughter, Anna. She reported that a lot of policemen had been there, more than ten, but they didn't find anything in the house and went on. Vinzas and Vladas Navinsky went home and Joseph and I stayed in the forest. About two hours later the police passed again. Then Joseph and I went back to the house, ate dinner, and I left for Shupienis in Otesnik.

I stayed there overnight and left for Berziunas. When I arrived there, the police arrived at Shupienis' place, and I was told that two searches had also taken place at the Yuchnelevitches, where they looked for us. The facts that the chase after us had been intensified and a number of searches had been carried out in places we used for hiding were not encouraging. Even the farmers who wanted to help us and were generous in providing food were beginning to be fearful. The Berziunases themselves, who were making much fun of the police and were saying that neither

Joseph nor I would ever be arrested in their house, got scared that time and told me to be very careful. "The police have really decided to get you," they said. And this was happening when we needed even more hiding places, both for the Jews who were already hiding out and for those I still hoped to bring from Kovno.

IX.

THE CONTINUING SEARCH FOR SHELTER

On April 8, 1944, I went to Simna to see Stase Kazlovsky. She told me she had been in Kovno and had seen Leib Frank, a Jew from Simna. He told her he was planning to escape from the ghetto and come to Simna. During her stay in Kovno, she said, the "Children's Operation" took place in the ghetto. On March 27 and 28 the Gestapo and their auxiliary Lithuanian police arrived in a fleet of canvas-covered trucks and surrounded the ghetto. While loudspeakers blared military music they moved from house to house, seizing every old person and little child they could find. Stase said she saw how they threw all the children up to the age of twelve or thirteen and all the old people onto trucks and took them off to Fort IX to be slaughtered.

Since it was forbidden to bear children in the ghetto, many of the infants were hidden in closets, bureau drawers, attics, and basements while their parents were at work. "If their cries didn't betray them," Stase added, "trained dogs smelled out their hiding places."

From Stase, I went into the Kalesnik forest and flung myself on the common grave of my brother Jews of Simna. After reciting the Kaddish, I went to visit Joseph at Navinsky's. A tailor sewed him a pair of pants and asked where he was from. Joseph became flustered, and afterward the tailor told the family that Joseph surely wasn't a Russian, but a Jew. So Navinsky decided to move Joseph to Yonin's place, and for the same reason I decided not to bring Leah there. I visited Joseph at Yonin's where he was feeling all right.

From Joseph I went to the farmer Yanushon and found Olga Levin and her son, Abrasha. Olga was the sister of Max Goldberg, who had a farm in Mergalaukis. She and her son had papers that identified them as Lithuanians. Her husband, Moshe Levin, was the chief of the Jewish police in the Kovno ghetto, murdered by the Germans in the "Policemen Operation."

"The Gestapo feared the Jewish policemen," Olga said, "and decided to dispose of them in advance of the March 1944 'Children's Operation'." The Gestapo ordered the Jewish police to assemble for inspection. More than one hundred and fifty of the men on the force turned out, their boots carefully polished, their jackets brushed, and their faces closely shaven. For an hour the men stood about joking and laughing, waiting for the German officials to arrive. Suddenly a line of trucks approached. Police auxiliaries and Gestapo agents jumped down and surrounded the waiting men. At gunpoint they ordered the Jewish policemen onto the trucks, and drove them to Fort IX where they were questioned about the ghetto underground. Most told the Gestapo nothing. Some gave away the location of a few bunkers. Whether they broke or held out, all were shot. Yanushon gave me a wagon, and I went to collect food for the Levits. On my way I visited Adela Baravik, who agreed to take in Olga Levin and her son. At Smadziun's in Kavaltchuk, I found Leib Frank and his wife, Rachel. They had arrived from Kovno by car. Rachel, who was also a seamstress, was going to stay with Smadziun, and for Leib I found a temporary hiding place with another farmer. When I came the next day to Yanushon's to return the wagon, I found there a Jewish child from Kovno, who was sent by a certain Margolis. The Yanushons agreed to keep the child.

I arrived at the Berziunases' soaked in sweat, lay down, and fell asleep immediately. I arranged to bring Rachel, Leib Frank's wife, to their place, and she would sew for them. Stase Kazlovsky came and told me that Stephan Pavlovsky's sisters had found my diary in the barn and buried it so that no one else would find it. At night Samuel and I went to Pavlovsky's barn to get the diary. We searched all over, but we couldn't find it. I went on to Mrs. Emart in Simna and sent her to the Pavlovsky sisters to ask where they had buried my diary. They explained that it was hidden in the corner next to the big stone. I left the Emarts and ran out of the town in the middle of the day because the police were on the street next to Emart's.

In the evening I returned to Pavlovsky's barn. I dug with my fingers, but I still couldn't find anything. Then I went to Yuchnelevitch and got Samuel and a spade. We went to Pavlovsky's barn, used the spade to dig, and we found the diary. I went to Yonin's and it hurt me to see Joseph, exhausted and thin. He had lost ten pounds and had been working very hard. Although it broke my heart, the place was very safe and I left him there for a little while longer. The Yonins were very happy with him and were glad that I would leave him with them for another few weeks.

But I had difficulties in finding new places for the other Jews. Some of the shelters we were using were quite dangerous, and some of our farmer friends had begun to fear that it was common knowledge they were hiding Jews. The police had intensified their searches. I didn't know what to do. My head was spinning and it was really maddening. I took Samuel and we went to Smadziun to take Rachel Frank to Berziunas in Otesnik. She told us that Smadziun was getting very nervous and was waiting for me anxiously. He had already asked a number of times, "Where is Aba? Why doesn't he come?"

I had a talk with Smadziun. He wanted me to take Mrs. Frank away, but didn't object to bringing the Levits to stay in his barn. As we were walking by the river, two people walked out of a house toward us, and we ran. We sat in the wheat for a while and then we went on to the Berziunases. Rachel and Samuel remained there, and I went to see the Krashnitzkys in Skovagol to arrange a place for the Levits. The Krashnitzkys were two brothers, devout and meek people who wished to help Jews. But they were a bit odd. They did not get on well together and there was a lot of fighting between them.

When I asked the elder, Yonas, to give the Levits shelter in his barn, he said that he would, provided the younger brother, Alphonse, knew nothing of it, a condition I readily accepted. He made it clear that he could not feed the fugitives and was only offering them a place to sleep. This, too, I could accept. I quickly contacted other peasants of the area, to obtain the needful provisions, and one of them was the younger brother. He said he would willingly furnish me food for the Jews hiding out in the area, but with the condition that his elder brother must not find out. He did not dream that we were talking about the Jews who would be hiding in his own barn with his brother's consent.

I took the Levits from Smadziun and brought them to the Krashnitzky farm and told Yonas they were settled in. He was in a very good mood. He only repeated his request that his brother mustn't find out. We agreed I would come from time to time to the barn and bring food to the Levits, without bothering him at all. I brought them food every week.

After a few weeks, Alphonse, who gave me food for the Levits without knowing they were in his own barn, went out one night and heard talking there. The Levits were having an audible conversation. Never imagining that it was the Jewish couple whom he was himself helping, he began to shout, "Thieves! Thieves!" Yonas, his elder brother, was in the house and heard the shouting, but he didn't want to tell his brother that the Jews were staying in the barn with his consent. And in the midst of the uproar, I arrived with a package of food. When Alphonse saw me he understood what was going on. I calmed him and explained that the Jews in the barn were those he was aiding by giving me food. He cooled down.

In the meantime, it was dawn already, and I was afraid to leave the Levits there, because the neighbors had heard the shouts and someone might even have seen what took place in the yard. It was too risky to stay on. I decided to move the Levits elsewhere, and we left the Krashnitzky barn in broad daylight.

On our way, two German soldiers suddenly appeared in front of us. We were stricken with fear. The Levits' faces would have betrayed them at once. They had not seen the sun for months and were as pale as ghosts. Flight was out of the question. The Germans would have pursued us or shot us. I told the Levits to jump into the haystack in an adjoining field, and I went on alone. The Germans apparently had not noticed the episode and only asked if I spoke German, in which case would I accompany them as interpreter to the nearest farmstead. They had come to requisition pigs for their regiment, stationed nearby.

It was evident that it was the farmstead of Ivanovsky's, the very one where I had intended to lodge the Levits. The deaf-mute woman of the house would be frightened out of her wits at the sight of me, escorted by the Germans, and would think that they had come to search her place for hiding Jews. I could not gainsay the soldiers. When we neared her home and she came out towards us, I signalled to her that all was well.

I explained to the Germans that she was a poor peasant woman. If they had to requisition pigs, why not take them from the rich? They thought this a good idea and asked her who the wealthy peasants were. She knew the neighborhood thoroughly and named a few, especially the ones who had been mean to the Jews.

Soon after the Germans had disappeared, I returned to the haystack, took the Levits to the woman's home, and I went to the Yanushons. I found there another child, sent from Kovno by Margolis (it was his daughter) and two letters from Kovno. One was for Leah Port from her father. The second was for me from Miriam Idels, who had studied with me at the university. The situation in the ghetto, they wrote, was very bad.

From the Yanushons I went to visit Joseph at Yonin's. It was clean and pleasant there, and he was very happy. They agreed to keep him for as long as necessary, and they told me not to worry about him. If it should become necessary, they said, they would take him to one of their acquaintances. I was very pleased because that made the search for places for the other Jews easier for me.

X.

GOD WAS WITH US!

I decided that the time had come for my people to join the partisan movement and play their modest part in the combat against the Nazis. It was no longer the poorly organized Lithuanian partisan movement, with low morale and negligible exploits, largely ignored by the Germans because of its lack of aggressiveness. The movement had been brought under close Moscow control and now became part of the general Soviet partisan movement which was, no doubt, the largest and the most elaborately organized guerrilla movement in the history of warfare. At its peak, it might well have mustered more than 150,000 members, men and women, and it combined all the classic features of such movements of the past with modern weapons and modern means of communication and transport.

Trained commanders were sent to the woods in Lithuania; arms and equipment were supplied in abundance; and a system of controls had been set up to coordinate operations with the tactics of the Soviet Army. In the spring of 1944, the reorganization of the movement was complete and the partisans were perfectly prepared to exert an important influence on the coming battles.

On May 31, 1944, I went to see Alphonse Rushkovsky, who was one of the leaders of the Lithuanian anti-German partisans, and told him my decision. He said that he was pleased with my decision, but they would only accept young people and those who were armed into the movement, none that were old, and none of the women who were in my group. "Let them stay here and look out for themselves," he said.

Only Samuel and I carried arms. Joseph and Abrasha would, of course, also be accepted. But all the others who made up my group were for them just "extra mouths," unwanted competitors in the procurement of provisions from the peasantry. I also had heard that the partisan leadership was disturbingly overpoliticized and that it had had clashes with Jewish partisans who tried to assert their Jewish identity. The Soviets were against the existence of nationally oriented Jewish combat units, and among the Gentile anti-Nazi partisans there were Jew-haters. Many a Jew died at their hands.

While I was important for them as a partisan, I saw things in a different way. Every Jew was important to me, and I told Rushkovsky that I'll join up with the partisans only when I'll be no longer needed by the Jews. I meant when the Levits, Franks, Levins, Gamsky, Leah, and the two children are taken in and cared for. He said that was impossible. So I decided not to join them and to carry on independently.

I noted in my diary: "As long as I am needed to help even one Jew, I'll stay here. They are willing to fight side by side with us but not assume responsibility for us."

In the first week of July 1944, planes were flying over and dropping countless bombs. People said the Germans were in retreat and that that the Red Army had already reached Vilna. I went to Amshey's in Verniger to visit Joseph and to start preparing ourselves for the return of the Russians. Joseph was feeling fine and the Amsheys told me not to worry about him. They even agreed that in case of emergency I could bring five or six Jews to their barn. They promised to set up a proper hiding place.

Amshey told me that there was a great uproar in Simna. The cooperative was robbed and documents were destroyed. The Germans had taken the arms away from the Lithuanian police. Everyone was running from Simna, even the police, and everything pointed to the fact that the Soviet army would be coming soon. It was like the beginning of the end—anarchy, in the full sense of the word. Everyone was terrified.

On July 11, I was at Adela Baravik's place. The Germans were on the run since morning, and they were taking POWs with them. Three Lithuanian soldiers, making their escape, told me that the Russians were approaching. Some wagons stopped at Adela's place. One of them was carrying two Germans and a policeman with a sidearm. Mrs. Levin was terrified. She left the house with her son, and they went to a nearby hamlet. I remained there with Margolis' daughter and we decided to pose as Lithuanians. For a whole day we shared our roof with the Germans, helped them with their cooking, waiting anxiously for the night. Daylight could betray us, darkness gave us hope. In the nocturnal shadows we felt safe. The night was our friend and savior.

The Russians were advancing toward our town and the front approached about a mile and a half from where Gamsky was staying. Five shells fell in the Bainorovitches' field. Gamsky was right under the shrapnel! I went to the partisan Rushkovsky, who gave me some white cloth for Leah to dye red so we would have a red flag when the Russians arrived.

On July 20, I slept with Joseph at Amshey's. That place was also near the front, where there was a lot of fighting during the night, and I was really sick. My head was killing me, my legs were tired and sore, I felt awful, completely limp from weakness, and I couldn't eat anything. So I remained with Joseph for a couple of days, waiting for the Russians to come. Some people said that the Russians had been pushed back thirty miles; others claimed that they had already reached the town of Balbirishok, about eight miles from Simna.

Four days later a number of Germans came into the village of Verniger, so Joseph and I went into the forest. But toward evening we returned to Amshey. I left Joseph there and went to Pranas Shupienis. Making my way by the Metelitze River, some Germans shot at me without knowing who I was. They could have killed me, but God was with me.

On July 27, I came to see Joseph at Amshey's and we decided to go closer to the front, to welcome the Red Army. Before meeting Joseph, I had arranged a place for everybody from my group to stay and wait for the final battle between the Russians and the Germans. Zvi Levit and his wife were at the Krashnitzkys. The two brothers had finally agreed on something: to keep the Levits hidden until the war was over. Leib Frank and his wife were at the Berziunases. Gamsky was at the Bainorovitches, Olga Levin, her son, Margolis' daughter, and the other girl, were at Adela Baravik's.

Samuel Ingel and Leah Port asked to join Joseph and me on our way to the front. We met in the village of Kumatch and we decided to stay there, hiding in a bunker. There was a lot of shooting and for two days the bombs were raining down over our hidden heads. We were almost in the midst of the battle. The moment that we had dreamt of so long, the end of the Nazi presence, was at hand. After all the suffering and horror that we had endured for the last three years, we had no wish to die at that eleventh hour. In all the years of hiding, flight, and constant peril, when I knew that the police were hunting me, and that a price had been set on my head, I had never feared death as much as in those moments, being trapped on a bloody battlefield.

Faith, trust, confidence in God were as a sun lighting up my life throughout the war, and under the rain of shells we prayed silently and hoped that God would save us. One must hope, I said to myself, for the man who has no hope in his heart is doomed. As long as a man is alive he can hope.

On the afternoon of July 29 the shelling stopped, and the battle ended. The Germans retreated, and the Russians entered the village of Kumatch. We came out of our hideout, which was near the woods, and the first thing we saw were Russian soldiers, marching out of the forest, in small groups, each group in single file and all the groups in line abreast, each about a hundred meters from the next. We stood still, waiting for the first group to reach us.

There were ten men in it, and what a wonderful feeling it was! The captain in charge was a Jew, named Polak. One can imagine his excitement to find himself liberating four Jewish survivors of the Nazi oppression. Ours was not less: our liberator, the man whom we embraced and kissed, was a brother Jew.

Captain Polak asked us for our guns, because if Russian soldiers found us armed, they might take us for anti-Russian partisans. We gave him the guns. He also whispered to us that some soldiers took watches, so it would be wise for Leah to hide hers.

We left the Russian officer as free men, starting a new life. We believed it, and yet we couldn't quite take it all in. It seemed like a dream. In the morning everything around us was in flames, but we came through it untouched—except that some Russian soldier stole my boots.

PART TWO

HOUR OF PUNISHMENT

XI.

O LORD GOD OF VENGEANCE!

Free of the murderous Nazi menace, my brother Joseph and I went first to the Kalesniki woods and flung ourselves on the common grave of our brother Jews of Simna, where our beloved mother and little brother Yehudah'le were buried, and we recited the Kaddish.

It was summer, the sun was blazing, but we were shivering, weeping, numb. The martyrs cried out from the ground to the Lord God, to whom vengeance belongs, to avenge their innocent blood, and to our minds came all our vows, during the three years of hiding, to wreak vengeance on the twentieth-century monsters for their unspeakable crimes.

A few days after the murder of the Jews of Simna, while we were hiding in the barn of Bogdanovitch, we had heard laborers talking about the killing of the Jews. One said that one of the victims was hit by ten bullets, and dozens of people were buried alive, and Mikulsky the woodcutter shouted at him, "Why should you pity the Jews! Why should the priest defend those dogs?"

I trembled listening to Mikulsky and noted in my diary, "If I survive, that man is dead! I must remain alive to avenge the death of my little brother Yehudah'le."

While I thought of revenge for the little children who were thrown alive into their common grave in the forest, I felt a murderous rage rising within me, and I imagined what I would do if faced with one of the killers. I felt like a beast sure of its prey, and I remembered the words of the Jewish poet Haim Nahman Bialik in one of his poems, "Vengeance for the blood of a child, the devil has not yet created."

When rumors reached me about the negotiations of peace between the cursed führer, Adolf Hitler, and the Western Allies, I trembled at the thought of making peace with Hitler before exacting revenge for the innocent blood that had been shed. I quoted in my diary that Hitler had declared, "Not one Jew will remain wherever a German has set foot," and I noted, "Some Jews will remain, here and there, and they will reveal to the world what has been done to us, and, if they only have the chance, they will surely avenge our people."

When revealing to the world what had happened, one must recognize that there were Christians who did not raise their hands against Jews. But many of the Christians who committed sadistic murder on Friday, were absolved in the confessional on Sunday, and resumed the slaughter on Monday.

While we were hiding with the woman Matulevitch, she told us that in one village the men were assembled in the synagogue and murdered; the women and children were given a day's grace. They were brought the next day to the death-pit in wagons. The girls were raped, then killed. The women were forced to undress, were thrust into the pit, and shot. Only the little children were left. Even the most hardened killers shirked the task of the murder of infants.

But there was one volunteer—the Lithuanian chief of police. He donned a white smock, so as not to spoil his uniform, and with methodical bestiality that guardian of law and order dashed out the brains of Jewish babies against the stone wall of the Christian cemetery, adjacent to the killing site. Then he calmly returned to his wife and four little children, and on Sunday he attended chapel in the friendly company of the parish priest.

Yozas asked me what I would do if I could leave as a free man. I told him that I would take my revenge on the Jew haters.

I noted in my diary, "The blood of the slaughtered must be avenged/God will avenge the blood of His people." I also wrote a poem:

"Forests of Fate"

O little woodland, hapless as thou art,
Within my soul is graven deep thy name,
And for thy torment mourns my aching heart.
Was not my agony thy impious shame?

Thy shadows veil all that I held most dear.
The old, the young, the babes, beloved kin
Drew a last lingering breath in prayer.
They were but Jews, that was their only sin.

Murder unmasked, its bestial features glare
Upon cadavers of my martyred folk,
Answer, O woodland—is it near or far
The time to pay for what the crime bespoke?

No, hapless woodland!
Say not that "they" will never pay
The righteous penalty of godless guilt!
No!
With Heaven's favor, on a destined day,
I shall avenge my people's lifeblood spilt!

After all the consolatory illusions we fabricated for ourselves and offered to each other, the hour of liberation was not joyful; it occurred against a tragic background of destruction, slaughter, and suffering. Just as we felt we were again becoming free people, the sorrows returned.

Joseph and I met an officer of the Russian counterespionage and discussed how to proceed. He advised Joseph to join his unit as an interpreter and suggested that I join the local militia, the police under the Soviet regime, and help track down the Nazi collaborator. Joseph joined the counterespionage, while I approached the Simna militia.

But a difficulty arose. Pranas Dainovsky was the secretary general of the Communist Party in Simna and he remembered that, while he was active in the clandestine Lithuanian Communist Party, I belonged to Beitar. Beitar was a right-wing Zionist Youth movement, and Zionism had been outlawed in the Soviet Union since the late twenties. In Communist Russia, Zionists were the scapegoat for any protest by intellectuals, and anti-Zionism was a pretext to harass Jews and to limit their religious and cultural lives.

At the outset of the Russian Revolution, in spite of hostility to Zionism, anti-Semitism was considered a crime. But in the 1930s, during the years of mass purges, it gradually changed from a breach of the law into the virtually official policy of the Soviet Union. During the Moscow Trials of 1936-38, nearly all the institutions of Yiddish culture were closed down. During the Soviet rule in Lithuania many Zionists were deported to Siberia.

Pranas Dainovsky ignored the fact that, though a Zionist, I was a Holocaust survivor who had lost his entire family. He considered me a person who could not be trusted by the Communist authorities. He advised me to go to Kovno, enter civilian life, give up the idea of joining the militia, and leave the problems of security in the hands of him and his friends, the Communists.

I was very upset and warned him that if he would not let me join the militia, I would fight back by bringing to the attention of the Soviet authorities the fact that he had turned his coat when the Germans entered Lithuania.

As a member of the clandestine Lithuanian Communist Party, Dainovsky was one of those Lithuanian Communists who had become government officials during the period of Soviet rule in Lithuania from June 1940 to June 1941, professing to be ardent Communists. When the Germans came, they claimed that they had never been Communists, but that the Jews had forced them to collaborate with the Russians. Many were believed and set free, to become collaborators of the Nazis against the Jews and any Communists who remained loyal to Moscow. There were rumors that Dainovsky, too, had blamed the Jews for his joining the Communist Party, and I told him I had such information.

I said to him, "When you were arrested by the Germans, you asked forgiveness from your interrogators for having been a Communist and claimed the Jews had forced you to collaborate with the Russians. You were set free. True, you were later arrested again, escaped from jail, and joined the partisans, but your behavior during the first days of your arrest is unforgivable."

Such an accusation against Dainovsky would not only have caused his removal from the post as the local Communist Party's secretary general, but might have brought about his arrest. Immediately after the return of the Red Army to Lithuania, there was very close collaboration between the Jews and the Soviets, considered by the Holocaust survivors as their savior. Moscow trusted the Jewish survivors more than those who had been anti-Communists before the war; more than the Lithuanians who were Communists in the past but behaved in a doubtful way under the Nazis.

Dainovsky denied any misbehavior on his part and was very angry when I mentioned it. But when he realized I wouldn't give in, he said he would let me join the militia, if I promised to forget the story I had heard about his interrogation. We shook hands, and I prepared myself to bring to account those Lithuanians who had been assassins of the Jews.

To begin our searches, I had a list of roughly one hundred Lithuanians of Simna, who had been Nazi collaborators. I gathered all the necessary information about these people and the first day of my militia service, the Russians, using the addresses I had supplied and myself accompanying them, rounded up forty men who were taken to Alitus prison. I did not intend, of course, to confine myself to punishment activities, and I did everything in my power to reward the peasants who had helped us in the dark days.

When, years later, the State of Israel was proclaimed, Gentiles who saved Jews during the Nazi oppression at the risk of their own lives, were recognized as Righteous, and awarded a medallion which, in artistry and symbolism, bespeaks the Talmudic saying, "He who saves a single being saves a whole world." They stood out as a beacon of light in the blackness of Hitler's occupation of Europe.

The good Lithuanian woman, Ona Matulevitch, who helped my brother and myself to save our lives, at the risk of her own, was recognized as a "Righteous." The most renowned "Righteous" was the Swedish protector of thousands of Jews, Raoul Wallenberg, about whom much has been written.

As they did everywhere, the Russians imprisoned or deported to Siberia many Gentiles who had saved Jews during the Nazi period. Some of the Lithuanians who had helped me survive were nationalists, and/or men of affluence, and thus not favored by the Soviet regime. I had to make great efforts to have the Soviets modify their adverse attitude toward them.

More than once my intervention might have boomeranged against me. One example, among many: the Berziunas family from the village of Otesnik. They were fanatical Lithuanian nationalists and, when the Soviets entered Lithuania in 1940, the Berziunases had been among their most open enemies. Two members of the family were arrested by the Russians and spent months in jail. When the Germans took over, the pair became leaders of the pro-German people who had collaborated actively in rounding-up Lithuanian Communists. But they were also known to be friendly with many Jews in Simna, including my father.

When the Germans began their anti-Jewish activities, the Berziunases spoke out against it and advised many of their Jewish acquaintances to flee before the massacres began. When I started my wanderings through the hamlets and villages, they were among those to whom I went for aid, and they lavished it generously on my brother and me. They gave us supplies and sheltered my brother for weeks, as well as any Jew whom I brought along.

Times changed. The Germans retreated, the Russians returned to Simna. Power reverted to the town Communists, and the Berziunases were now at the top of the list of candidates for arrest. However, the local branch of the Communist Party, headed by Pranas Dainovsky, knew about the help given to the Jews by the Berziunases and did not take extreme measures against them.

But the Red Army warred pitilessly against the nationalist guerrillas. I fought alongside the Soviets against the guerrillas whom we called bandits. They were mainly men who had collaborated with the Nazis, even in the slaughter of Jews. One night, more than twenty bandits fell in a clash between Soviet troops and the anti-Communist guerrillas. The dead were displayed the next morning in the public square as a warning. Two of the Berziunas brothers were among them.

Pranas Dainovsky, as secretary general of the Communist Party, took me to the square, showed me their bodies, and asked me whether I still thought that the Berziunases should be treated as friends because they had helped Jews. I, a survivor of extermination, wished, as far as I could, to help those who had aided the Jews and saved them from certain death. The Soviet authorities were prepared to take this into account, being sometimes inclined even to forgive their former enemies, if only they would accept the new regime. The Lithuanians who did so were pardoned. Those who persisted in their opposition were punished severely, despite all my efforts to save them.

After what happened to the Berziunas brothers, I left for Alitus and was admitted there by the N.K.V.D. as an interrogator of the Nazi collaborators. I was to visit the towns of the Alitus district and to supervise the interrogations there, as well as to interrogate personally those who were brought to the Alitus prison.

I rented a room from a Jewish doctor who had survived the Holocaust. Belkin, his wife and child, had managed to escape death. The parents had gone into hiding; a friendly girl looked after their baby and, after the war, not unnaturally went to live with the family. At the beginning, it was normal for the child to call the girl "mommy" and call her real mother "aunt," but, as time went on, she showed more and more affection for the girl. No protestations of the real mother availed, and the girl declared that she would never be parted from the child. Money was no inducement and, after all that she had done for the child, the parents were unwilling to evict her. But, in the end, they had no alternative.

That any Jewish child at all lived through the terrible massacres was often thanks to adoption by well-meaning Christians. The guns silent at last, there were Gentile families who were reluctant to give the children back to their families or to a Jewish institution. Many insisted that they would yield the children to their parents and to no one else. Some demanded large sums for the succor they had given, and there was bitter bargaining at times. Others refused to give the children back, either because they had come to cherish them and could not bear to let them go, or because they wanted to convert them to Christianity. Herculean efforts had often to be made to rescue the orphaned children speedily, lest Christianity took too strong a hold or the anti-Semitism instilled in so many of them become irreversible.

During a visit to the town of Butrimonis to interrogate a peasant suspected of having participated in the killing of Jews, I found a nine-year-old boy. He denied it and claimed, in his defense, that he knew a peasant neighbor who was hiding a Jewish child and he had not betrayed that child to the Germans. I went to see the peasant and found that a Jewish child was in fact living with him. It took all my insistence to persuade the man to surrender the boy for placement in the Jewish orphanage of Kovno.

While still in Butrimonis, I was invited for supper one day by the local Lithuanian pharmacist. I was very much surprised, because according to the information we had about him at the militia, the man was an anti-Soviet nationalist whose activities we were following closely. It didn't take me long to realize the reason for that unexpected invitation. A side door opened, and in front of me stood Feliks, one of the sons of Mrs. Zubrowa, the Polish woman, owner of the farm in Metel, who was related to the righteous proselyte Potocki. She was among the Gentiles who had helped me during my years of hiding. She had given me food and let me stay at her home for a couple of days.

Feliks explained the purpose of the meeting. He reminded me that in June, 1940, the Russians were going to deport his family to Siberia for being wealthy Polish nationalists. It was because of the German attack on the Soviet Union that they had not been deported. However, in spite of being sympathizers of the Germans, they condemned the persecution of the Jews and helped me when I came to them. Now, they needed my help.

He told me that when the Russians returned to Simna, he and his brother, Vacious, had gone into the woods and joined the anti-Soviet guerrillas. He said he knew I wasn't a Communist. I was only pursuing those Nazi collaborators who had taken part in killing Jews. He, therefore, hoped I would be ready to disregard their being Polish nationalists and help him and his brother at a very critical hour in their lives.

There would be a repatriation of Poles from Lithuania to Poland, he told me. The head of the Polish Repatriation Commission in Vilna was a relative who had offered the brothers jobs there. But in order to go to Vilna, they needed certificates attesting that they were respectable Lithuanian citizens. They could not get such certificates in Simna, so they decided to come to me and beg my help. They needed an official statement, with the seal of the militia, saying that, before they departed for Vilna, they were living as peaceful citizens in Butrimonis. It wasn't easy for me to give them this help. It meant the risk of my own life. I knew the Soviet Criminal Code: if I were caught, I would be accused of treason, and I would have been punished by imprisonment for up to a life-term and deportation to Siberia, or by execution. Still, how could I refuse to help somebody who had helped me in my critical times, one who had taken great risks for me?

I knew I could trust the boys and their mother, but I feared the pharmacist. What if he decided to betray me in revenge for my fight against his fellow-nationalists? I issued them the certificates, and prayed to God the N.K.V.D. would not find out.

When I visited the town of Varena, I found a group of Jewish Holocaust survivors, Leon Kaganowicz, Benjamin Rogovsky, Lippa Skolsky and Abraham Widlanski, roaming the nearby villages and hamlets and exacting revenge on the Nazi sympathizers responsible for the murder of Jews, on farmers who had betrayed Jews to the Nazis, and on the civilian officials who had collaborated with the Germans.

The group was executing prisoners found guilty and was sending to Alitus only those in whose cases there was no hard evidence of their participation in the murder of Jews. In many cases, they told me, they had evidence for a conviction, but lacked the ability to write it up in Russian, as required by the Russians. Thus, criminals whom they had spent weeks tracking down were set free once they got to Alitus for lack of proper documentation. They told me about talking with a Russian officer of the N.K.V.D. who visited Varena and invited them for dinner. When dinner was over, the officer told them he had heard about their exploits in the partisan movement and complimented them on their bravery. Suddenly, changing the subject, he asked them, "Do you like herring?" and they answered, "Of course!"

The officer, "How much do you pay for it?"

"Ten kopeks," they said.

"And where do you get it?"

"At the fish store!"

"How is it sold to you?"

"The owner takes it out of the barrel, puts it in some newspaper, and hands it to us."

The officer leaned back in his chair and asked, "Were you ever in Moscow?"

They shook their heads, and he continued, "Well, in Moscow they sell herring in the Metro Café. It costs there a ruble and a half. Do you know why it costs that much? Because in Moscow, they take the same herring, arrange it artistically with onions and capers, and serve it with style. That's why herring costs you ten kopeks in Varena and fifteen times as much in Moscow."

"That's what wrong with you here!" he added. "You keep sending herrings, but you don't serve them up with style! You need someone to write your reports so that your herrings arrive the proper way."

They got the message. We agreed that in the future they would send the prisoners to Alitus, to me personally, and I would interrogate them and document the cases before processing them.

They told me how difficult, time-consuming, and dangerous their work was because most of the wanted men, desperate to escape from justice, had gone into hiding and were armed. They questioned their families, but most of them claimed to have no information. They had to rely largely on ambushes and stakeouts to capture the men on their list. They made bargains with some of the farmers who were guilty of lesser crimes in order to catch the big criminals, and many were willing to cooperate. But often, after receiving a tip that led to one of the men on their list, they would arrive too late to make an arrest. Naturally, this didn't deter them. They returned again and again until they caught him.

Abraham Widlanski caught the farmer Danielewicz who had betrayed him. After he had escaped from the town jail, Widlanski came to Danielewicz, who was considered a close friend of the family, and the Widlanskis had left a lot of their things with him. Danielewicz welcomed him warmly and told him to hide in the attic. After three days, a German soldier and a Lithuanian gendarme arrived straight to the attic and ordered Widlanski, "Hands up!"

When the Lithuanian gendarme shouted at Widlanski, "Tell us immediately where other Jews were hiding," he decided that if he was going to be killed, then at least let it be on the spot, and he said, "I will tell you everything, even where their gold and jewelry were, but not in the presence of the German."

The Lithuanian agreed and went with Widlanski into another room. The German remained with Danielewicz to drink samagon. In the other room, Widlanski went near to the window and the gendarme followed him, anxious to get the information. Then, Widlanski grasped his rifle, and bit the gendarme's nose with all his strength. The gendarme managed to fire a shot. But before Danielewicz and the German came in, Widlanski jumped through the window and escaped into the nearby woods.

Danielewicz was executed and, just a few days before my visit, one of their biggest fish walked into the net himself. About two o'clock, they were just finishing dinner, when something made them look up. The dining room window overlooked the street and there walking calmly down the sidewalk was Baderas, the killer of the Eisiskes Jews. They dashed out of the house, but they were too late. Their quarry had vanished. They ran into all the shops down the streets searching. Then there he was again, standing confidently in the wide foyer of the city hall, talking to the Lithuanian who was secretary of the Communist Party.

They rushed in and began pounding Baderas with their fists, smashing him into the wall, while the tiny Lithuanian secretary danced around them, screaming, "Stop it! Stop it! Why are you doing this? Why are you hitting my friend?"

Leon Kaganowicz told him all the crimes that Baderas was accused of, but the little secretary just kept shaking his head.

No," he said, "you are wrong! This is not Baderas. His name is Markovicz. He is my old and dear friend. He's not the man you're looking for!"

Kaganowicz demanded Baderas' identification, and he naturally produced papers to show he was Markovicz. Kaganowicz, born in Eisiskes, knew Baderas well. He pushed his face into Baderas' and asked, "Don't you recognize me?"

"No! I've never seen you before in my life!" His eyes were filled with fear.

The jail was only two doors away and they hustled Baderas along and locked him in a cell. In the evening, they took him for a walk. He understood what was going to happen. He fell on his knees on the cobblestones, weeping desperately. "No, please, don't! I've got gold and money! I'll give you anything you want! I'll give you anything, anything!"

They forced him to get up and walk again, prodding him along the street. Each of them carried an automatic rifle containing seventy-two bullets, and at a signal, they emptied them into his body.

Those were days of "partial" retribution, when not only Jewish survivors were anxious to track down the Nazi collaborators, but also Soviet officers were ready to carry out irregular activities to punish some of those who had lent their support to the Germans. The Soviets were very willing to exact revenge on the Lithuanians, who went so far in their hunger for Jewish blood as to volunteer to finish off the Jews of Latvia and other areas under the Nazis.

One non-Jewish Russian officer had known very little about the Jews before the war. Now he came to grasp the bitter reality of the Holocaust. Belonging to the N.K.V.D. as he did, he had to question arrested Lithuanians who had helped in mass killings of Jews. One night, in the presence of a Russian major and myself as a witness who identified the murderer, the officer went on tirelessly with his interrogation. At a certain point, the major and I went out to breathe the fresh air. Suddenly, we heard two shots. We ran back into the station, and found the Lithuanian lying dead.

What had happened? The officer asked him to recount in detail how he had killed the children, with what weapon, with what finger he pressed the trigger. The Lithuanian left out nothing. The Russian could not master his revulsion, he drew his revolver and shot him.

Among those involved in tracking down the Nazi beasts and their collaborators, were also Russian officers who had liberated the extermination camps of Treblinka and Maidanek, where Jewish prisoners would immolate themselves on the electrified wire fences. It was better to die that way than in the gas chambers. The dead were deemed luckier than the doomed living.

With the aid of my brother, myself, and other Jewish survivors, the Russians caught many Lithuanian collaborators, interrogated them, and judged them. Hundreds were either sent to prison for many years or faced a firing squad.

Captain Stanley M. Nowinski, Displaced Persons Control Officer, at his post in Salzburg, Austria, 1945

XII.

WHY DID THE JEWS NOT REBEL?

Lithuanian Jews, who had either fled or been deported to Russia or managed to survive the Nazi horrors, began to return to Lithuania, where they found their country soaked with the blood of their families and friends. The repatriates, who during the war had heard rumors about the Nazi atrocities, now learned about the crimes committed by Lithuanian neighbors, once close friends. Young Lithuanian schoolboys had sadistically riddled with bullets the bodies of yesterday's classmates.

When the repatriates heard of the savagery, many of them refused to believe it. Most people were inclined to reject the atrocities because of their very enormity and, therefore, there was disbelief in what had taken place. On many occasions, the survivors were not only not believed, they were not even listened to.

Among the repatriates, there also were those who ignored the Talmudic saying, "Judge not thy neighbor until thou art come into his place," and did not resist asking, "Why did the Jews not rebel?" They were ready to judge without asking themselves in absolute honesty whether in a similar situation they might not have done the same.

Years later, I heard people offer, from the comfort of their peaceful surroundings, ready-made prescriptions for what the Jews should have done in the countries occupied by the Nazis.

While we were hiding, I heard the same question from Stephan Pavlovsky. He said to my brother and me, "If you're going to be shot, then at least let it be on the spot, not by marching down to the trenches," and he himself acted in this way when the police came after him. He resisted and died on the spot. Abraham Widlanski resisted and survived, and if a policeman had tried to arrest me, I, too, would have used my gun.

But I could not rebel when I was arrested unarmed in Kovno, and taken with twenty other Jews to the city square. Our Lithuanian escort insulted, taunted and menaced us. "Accursed Jews, we shall send you all to the next world!"

I had no doubt as to what awaited us. My classmate Moshe Strasdansky of Marijampole marched at my side. I suggested that we try to escape, but he rejected the idea as utterly hopeless. Nevertheless, I decided to make the attempt when I reached the gate of a familiar courtyard. As I contemplated the move, another of the group forestalled me in the attempt, only to be shot dead at once. So I resigned myself to my fate and went on to the city square, to what seemed certain death. Yet a spark of hope still flickered: Maybe? Perhaps, in spite of all?

And my brethren from Simna, the old and the ailing, the women and children, who, after being starved and tortured, were marched barefoot and half-naked for two endless miles, lashed and clubbed, to the Kalesniki woods and the waiting weapons of destruction in the hands of bestial Nazi and Lithuanian murderers. Could they rebel?

Or the Jews of Eisiskes, Leon Kaganowicz's home town, who were herded together into three synagogues and, after three days of threat and torment, were taken, first the men and, the next day, the women and children, to freshly dug trenches and pitilessly shot by Lithuanian neighbors. Could they rise up?

Or could the Jews from the ghetto of Radun, chosen to provide a day's "hunting sport," rise in revolt? One day after lunch, the regional German commander decided to go hunting. Forty Jews from the Radun ghetto were rounded up and put in a truck, The Germans, Lithuanians, and Poles followed in a second truck. About a mile from the ghetto, the Jews were ordered to get out and run for their lives. The hunters remained in their truck and used the terrified Jews as their quarry.

How could the thousands of Jews rebel who were lulled into false confidence by the Nazi tactics of deception and treachery, and were then pushed into pits that the victims, with their last breath, had been made to dig?

Or the thousands who were lined up facing the open pits and shot down by bursts of machine-gun fire! Or those Jews who were hung upside down to determine how long it took for death to come. Could they rebel?

German officers and their Lithuanian allies lusted for naked Jewish women before thrusting them into their graves. They pulled gold teeth out of Jewish mouths, sometimes before, sometimes after, these cold murders. Iron nails were plunged into women's eyes, fingernails were torn off, tresses shorn to fill Nazi pillows.

Could they rise in revolt?

Among the six million Jews assassinated were one and a half million children. "I did not deem myself justified in exterminating the men," declared Heinrich Himmler, "while allowing their children to grow up to avenge themselves on our sons and grandchildren."

Infants were torn from their mothers' arms and hacked to pieces before the eyes of their families. Babies were thrown into the air like clay pigeons, to see how many bullets would pierce the pitiful target in flight. Children were burned alive and massacred in ghettos, asylums, hospitals, prisons, and Gestapo torture chambers. They were injected with tuberculosis bacillus and poisoned. Thousands died in the concentration camps, victims of hunger and disease.

Could those children, those babies, rise up?

When the Germans began to deport the Jews from the ghettos to the death camps, they told them they were being sent to work camps where they would enjoy better food and accommodations. Postcards arrived in the ghettos from those camps where the inmates were forced to write to their friends, "We are well here. We have work and the behavior toward us is nice. We are waiting for you!" Many went, therefore, to the camps voluntarily, expecting better conditions and, on arrival, found a lovely spot: an orchestra playing at the entrance, flowers blooming, as though in a rest-camp for German soldiers, and on the camp's gate was proclaimed, "Work makes you free."

Once past the gates, they realized the awful truth—bolted and barred behind an electrified fence and a perimeter of armed guards, with kicks and punches right away, often in the face, and a torrent of orders screamed with rage. Complete nakedness after being stripped, the shaving off of all one's hair, and the dressing in rags.

Then, led to a barrack and, again, selection: to the right and to the left, to hard labor for as long as they could stand it, or to the crematorium. Who shall live and who shall die, in the fatal words of a penitent prayer of the New Year and the Day of Atonement. Now, not in synagogical liturgy, but in a confrontation with a frightening reality, Jews spoke the grim catalogue, "Who shall perish by fire and who by water, who by sword and who by beast, who by hunger and who by thirst, who by strangling and who by stoning."

Could they rebel?

Those who thought they could rebel, resist, or flee, did try to do it, even if only to die with honor. Altke Bialotzky, a woman from our town of Simna, when brought to the pit in the woods, fervently resisted and struck a young Lithuanian, Vite Yatkovsky, who had been brought up in her home but now pointed his murderous rifle at her breast, crying, "You too, Vite?"

That was real heroism!

Take the case of Shael Kaganowicz, Leon's father, who was in the ghetto of Radun. The ghetto was surrounded one day by Nazi troopers and Polish policemen and the Jews were told to stay indoors. Whoever opened a window would be shot. On the pretence of a count of heads, the ghetto was beleaguered for three days and nights, awaiting the arrival of the arch-murderers, the special commando made up of Ukrainians and Lithuanians. Many Jews tried to flee. Most lost their lives in the attempt. Those who tried to buy their way out handed over their valuables and then were killed by the Poles and Lithuanians, who had promised them salvation.

On the third day, the police rounded up a hundred sturdy Jews, gave them shovels and marched them to the Jewish cemetery, to dig burial trenches for their five thousand fellow-Jews. Polish policemen and five German troopers escorted them.

Shael Kaganowicz, one of the hundred, passed down the word that, on reaching the outskirts of the town, they should attack their escort party with their shovels, kill as many as they could and make for the forest. It was done. They killed all the policemen and four of the troopers, and lost twenty-eight of their own number. The seventy-two survivors reached the woods and that was the beginning of the local partisan movement, which carried out a number of attacks on German military and civilian installations.

When the mass graves of the assassinated Jews at Fort IX in Kovno were full, the Nazi authorities decided to cremate the corpses in order to eliminate the traces of their crimes. A special group of Jews from the Kovno ghetto was set up to pull the corpses out of the mass graves and burn them. The group was kept at the fort under a heavy guard. They knew that the Nazis would take great care to ensure that no witness survived, and that, as bearers of the secret, they must be disposed of and would be shot and burned the moment their task was finished. A plan for escape was born.

Sixty-four tried to escape. Thirty-seven were caught and shot. Twenty-five reached the gates of the ghetto, but six were arrested by the guards. Only nineteen succeeded in joining the underground that existed in the ghetto, whose main activity was to send young boys and girls to the forests. All nineteen escapees reached the partisans.

At Treblinka one of the most courageous expressions of resistance took place when a group of Jews from Grodno refused to undress. They had thrown themselves in unison at the guard, but only achieved being shot by automatic fire instead of being gassed in the chambers.

In the Sobibor camp, too, there was rebellion. After having learned what was in store for them, some three hundred Jewish laborers decided to kill the camp commandant and escape. Poorly armed, they revolted on October 14, 1943, and killed several German supervisors and Ukrainian volunteers. The Germans and Ukrainians opened fire on the fleeing Jews and prevented them from reaching the camp exit. The Jews then came to the area of barbed wire fences and mine fields. There some one hundred and thirty Jews found their deaths while about thirty fled to freedom. The remaining one hundred and forty Jews were captured and returned to the camp where they were all shot.

Even in the most terrible of extermination camps, in Auschwitz itself, there was, in spite of the hopelessness of the situation, an attempt to rebel by the Jewish "Special Squad."

"Special Squads" were auxiliary troops, forced to assist in the exterminations. It was their task to maintain order among the new arrivals who were to be sent to the gas chambers, to remove the corpses from the chambers, to pull gold teeth from jaws, to cut women's hair, to sort and classify clothes, shoes, and the contents of the luggage, to transport the bodies to the crematoria, and oversee the operation of the ovens, to extract and eliminate the ashes.

Conceiving and organizing these squads was one of the Nazis' most demonic crimes. Their operation represented an attempt to shift onto the victims, the burden of guilt, so that they were deprived of even the solace of innocence. The idea of the Nazis was to destroy not only the bodies but the souls as well.

A group of four hundred Jews from Corfu, who, in July 1944 had been included in the "Special Squads," refused without exception to do the work and were immediately gassed to death. A survivor who had belonged to the squads declared, "Certainly, I could have killed myself, but I wanted to survive to avenge myself and bear witness."

The "Special Squads," bearers of a horrendous secret, were kept rigorously apart from the other prisoners and the outside world, but would not escape everyone else's fate. They knew the Germans would prevent any man who had been part of their group from surviving to tell. The squads succeeded each other, each working for a few months, whereupon it was suppressed, each time with a different trick to head off possible resistance. At its initiation, the next squad burned the corpses of its predecessors. In Auschwitz, twelve squads succeeded each other. On October 7, 1944, the last squad rebelled, set fire to a crematorium, killed several S.S. men, cut the barbed wire, and escaped. Yet few of them survived.

The finest expression of Jewish resistance was the Warsaw ghetto uprising, the only open European insurrection against the Nazi military power, a heroic hopeless revolt, when there was no possibility of getting assistance from the outside. It was launched in the clear-eyed conviction that death, if it came in battle against the Nazis, would give meaning to the lives of others and their own.

The fighters of the Warsaw ghetto were few in number, but they made history, redeeming the honor of their people. Mordechai Anilevitch, commander of the uprising, wrote in his last letter from the ghetto, on April 23, 1943, "The last aspiration of my life has been fulfilled. Jewish self-defense has become a fact."

Not less heroic was the spiritual resistance. In the face of prohibitions, backed by immediate death penalties in case of discovery, Jews in the ghettos and extermination camps clandestinely celebrated the Sabbath, lighting candles on Hanukkah, gathering for prayers on holidays, and organizing schools.

At the risk of their lives, many smuggled their prayer shawls and phylacteries into the camps. They hid them in their barracks under the rafters of the ceiling, and every morning heroically put them on very quickly, saying only, out of fear not to be caught by the camp commander or one of his assistants, "Shmah Israel. Hear, O Israel, the Lord our God, the Lord is One!"

Jews marched to the mass graves in prayer shawls, chanting psalms, while others proudly sang the "Hatikvah," the Jewish national anthem. A specific form of Jewish civil resistance was the resolve to bequeath testimony of all that had transpired in the Jewish communities under the Nazis. Young and old recorded events, intellectuals accustomed to writing, simple folk penned painfully. Just recently, a testament of forty-seven inmates of the most horrible Chelmno extermination camp, thirty-seven miles from Lodz, where about three hundred thousand Jews were killed, was discovered.

The Germans had carefully camouflaged that camp. An innocent-looking ancient palace, surrounded by a high fence, bore inscriptions "To the showers" and "To the doctor." After passing through a dark corridor the victims were driven into a large truck, which was in fact a gas chamber. The engine gassed the victims within a few minutes. The truck then continued on its way to a mass grave in the nearby forest. The Germans constructed two crematoria following a typhoid epidemic in the district caused by the decaying corpses. The ashes and bones were put into ditches, and later into sacks and disposed of in the river. A few Jews were kept alive temporarily to strip the corpses of their valuables, burn, and bury them. The belongings taken from the victims were sent to Germany.

From August 1944 till January 1945 the only function of the German crew was obliterating the traces of the extermination installations. In January 1945 when the Soviet troops were approaching, the S.S. men started executing the remaining Jewish workers, some of whom attacked the Germans, killing two of them. The

S.S. then burned the building in which the Jewish workers were housed. Only two Jews survived the Chelmno camp.

The forty-seven wrote their testament on January 9, 1945, just nine days before the arrival of the Red Army, and they expressed their "deep pain for the fact that the American and British governments did not stop the Nazi arch-butcher, which they could have done if they had only wanted."

They concluded their testament with the words: "We beg you, the lucky ones who will find this testament, to avenge us, our families, and the other tens of thousands of Jews assassinated in such a horrible manner."

What some transcribed, the photographer pictured. In the ghetto of Lodz, one day, a whole family was seen dragging a cart full of dung through the street, father and mother in front pulling, son and daughter pushing behind. The ghetto photographer came toward them. He stopped but did not take out his camera, unwilling to film such degradation. But the father bade him proceed, "Let the snapshot be preserved, let others that come after us know how downtrodden we were!"

The photographer hesitated no longer.

All that was to be a link between the generation fated to die and the generation that arose after the Holocaust. It displayed that consciousness of history which Jewry developed when its very existence was at stake: the compulsion to record each daily torment, to maintain a secret archive, to scratch a name on the wall of a prison cell, and next to the name of one condemned to add the word "Vengeance!"

XIII.

BIG CATCH

I continued to interrogate the Lithuanian Nazi collaborators in the Alitus prison and to visit the towns of the district. There were some cases where collaborators were shot while trying to escape. The interrogations took place, in general, during the night. When an interrogation ended, the prisoner was escorted, by a Russian soldier or a Lithuanian militia man, to his cell. If he tried to escape in the darkness of the night, he was shot on the spot. The escort filed a formal report about the case, and the interrogator added his signature.

One day, while I was questioning a prisoner at the militia station in the town of Yeznas, a gendarme burst in to report that a picture of Joseph Stalin had been found in an outdoor toilet at the local school. In those days, there could be no bigger crime than that.

Our prisoner was immediately taken to his cell and I left for the school, accompanied by two Lithuanian gendarmes and a Russian soldier. I asked to see the principal, and I couldn't believe my eyes: in front of me was sitting Gedraitis, who had been a teacher in my own town of Simna. As soon as the Nazis came, Gedraitis was appointed prosecutor-general and, by his direct actions, Jews were murdered in the first days of the Nazi occupation. He had them arrested as Communists although not one of them was a member. When the Red Army arrived, he fled to Yeznas.

I was no longer interested in Stalin's picture lying in the outhouse. Here was a really big fish! I placed him under immediate arrest and took him to the militia station. I telephoned the headquarters of the N.K.V.D. in Vilna and informed Colonel Sabitov about my catch.

We interrogated him all through the night, and he told us everything, leaving out nothing. When he was finally taken to his cell, he tried to escape to the nearby woods, but a gendarme's bullet brought him down; I then signed the formal report.

When I informed Vilna about what had occurred, Colonel Sabitov gave me real hell, shouting at me, "There was no reason to kill him. You will pay for it!"

It was July of 1945, the war had ended, and political factors began to play a major role in regard to the Nazi collaborators. The Russians started to set many assassins of Jews free, on the pretext of "lack of sufficient evidence." After the Gedraitis case, they started an investigation about my activities. They discovered that I had signed quite a number of reports on escape attempts, and they decided to arrest me. By sheer chance, a Jewish doctor, employed at N.K.V.D. headquarters, heard someone say that a militia major was leaving for Yeznas to arrest a Jewish interrogator for "complicity in illegal acts of revenge against Lithuanians."

The doctor immediately forwarded the information to a friend and, within twenty-four hours, my brother came from Vilna to Yeznas. We decided to flee, very conscious of the possible consequences. We went to Vilna and straight to Feliks Zubrov, at the Polish Repatriation Commission. He provided us with forged papers certifying that we had been born in Poland and, on August 25, 1945, we were put on the 46th Polish repatriation transport. We crossed the border smoothly and arrived in Lodz, where, at the outbreak of World War II, 230,000 Jews had lived.

After a few days in Lodz we moved on to Cracow, arriving during the High Holidays, shortly after a pogrom had taken place there. It was the first pogrom after the end of the war, and it occurred thirty-two miles from the Auschwitz-Birkenau concentration camp. Fear and worry stalked the house at Miodova Street when we arrived there. About sixty Jews had gathered, anxiously waiting for a chance to negotiate the Polish-Czech border, which had been closed some weeks earlier.

Tension reigned; the services of the New Year and of the Day of Atonement were held in inexpressible dread lest fresh violence break out. The Poles had been happy with the idea that the Nazis would free them of the Jews once and for all. But the war came to an end and trains with Jews began streaming in, bringing back to Poland thousands of Jews who had survived.

As repatriates soon began to reclaim their stolen property from Polish pilferers, it was not unusual for an engine-driver to stop his train far out in the countryside and let peasants from the neighboring villages fall upon the hapless passengers. There were Poles who tried to finish the work started by the Nazis, and many a Polish Jew who had lived through the hell of the Holocaust was found murdered with a scrap of paper in a pocket: "This will be the fate of all Jews who survived Hitler!"

Anti-Semitism, far from having been extirpated, was deeply planted in the minds of many Poles, intellectuals and clergy not excepted. Hatred of the Jew was their heritage. It had been so even in the underground.

Jeanette Nestel, who had fled from the ghetto and lived in Lublin on false papers, posing successfully as a Catholic, told me that at a meeting of the anti-Nazi Polish nationalist underground, one leader had said: "We Polish intelligentsia should not dip our hands directly in Jewish blood, but if any of us knows where a Jew is hiding, be it man, woman, or child, it is our duty to go to the German authorities and report the knowledge. By so doing, by the end of the war we shall be able to rid ourselves of every Jew, along with the Nazis."

Jeanette told me also that a Catholic friend, shamefaced, had confessed to her that he was himself an anti-Semite and wondered why, for he had never really mixed with Jews.

"The only reason I can think of," he cried, "is that I must have sucked in the hatred at my mother's breast."

No wonder that a Jew's life was in jeopardy in the street, on trains or busses, everywhere, and he had to take up the wanderer's staff once again.

After having been in Cracow for two weeks, we were informed that the headquarters of the *Brichah*, the clandestine Jewish organization whose mission it was to smuggle Jewish survivors westward across the frontiers of European states, had decided to send on several groups in an attempt to make the crossing. Instructions were that only "adequate" people might join these groups, in other words, only those devoid of even the most essential personal belongings. Otherwise they could not plausibly pass as recently freed inmates of concentration camps with no more than the shirts on their backs.

As Joseph and I fulfilled the condition, we were included in the party, and I was put in charge of a group of twenty people. I organized my travel companions and, pass in hand, we set forth for Katowice. The pass was a slip of paper covered with signs, unintelligible at first sight to any layman, but fully understandable by the Brichah's headquarters in Katowice. My instructions were to contact a Polish physician in Katowice with whom a Jewish boy named Avner lived and ask whether Avner "wished to bargain with me." If he did, I should offer him a sack of sugar, and only show him the credentials if he put the question, "From which factory is the sugar?"

We reached Katowice without incident and Avner lodged us temporarily in the doctor's home. A friend of Avner's provided us with International Red Cross documentation and a permit for me and my group to cross the Polish-Czech border in transit for Greece, "our mother country." The permit certified that we were Greek Jews whom the Nazis had transported to concentration camps in Poland and, now that the war was over, we were returning to our homeland.

My brother and I were given the names of Joseph Bohiah and Aba Bohiah respectively; the other members of the group also assumed Greek names. We were ordered to speak Hebrew throughout the journey and over and over again to proclaim: "*Ani ivri Greco*," a strange polyglot rendering of "I am a Greek Hebrew."

In those days, unsettled and nomadic refugees were wandering across Europe from country to country. The wholesale disorganization, the lack of proper frontier controls, made it easy for them to cross borders with the weirdest of documents. Best of all were Greek papers, apparently approved by the Soviet commander of the city, because very few in Central Europe knew Greek. Our groups could either pretend not to speak the local language and give no reply, or answer in Hebrew, which passed as Greek. Besides converting us into nominal Greeks, the members of the Brichah taught us some Greek expressions, such as *kali mera*, good morning, and *kali spera*, good evening. We went off to the station, fearful of any encounter with genuine Greeks or with anyone fluent in the language who might thwart our exit.

On the train, we met several other groups of "Greeks," but avoided all contact with them. Five such groups arrived at the station of Dzerzice, where we stopped for two hours. The Gentiles simply stared at us and, while some really believed that we were genuine Greeks, others undoubtedly knew the truth and thought,

"What does it matter to us if the Jews leave Poland?" That Jews were again quitting Poland did not disturb the Poles. The very thought made many rejoice.

We arrived at Zebzidovice, a frontier stop on the Polish side. Neither the Poles nor the Czechs controlled it very strictly, and we entered Bohumin, the first border town in Czechoslovakia, without harassment. We were supposed to stay there overnight and take the train to Bratislava at daybreak, but rumors were circulating that, only a few weeks before, a group of "Greeks" had been sent back from Bohumin to Poland. So we decided to board the first train out. It was bound for Prague and, on the way, we changed to one going to Bratislava.

In its twenty-five rooms, the Yelen Hotel camp in Bratislava could house two hundred refugees under relatively humane conditions; the Brichah had no choice but to squeeze in up to a thousand people. Consequently, the situation was wretched, the filth and slovenliness were indescribable. Not surprisingly, we could not snatch a moment's sleep that night.

Within two days, my brother and I left with a group of eighty "Greeks" for Vienna. We left in a passenger train and then traveled in a freight train that crossed the Czech-Austrian border at a point where there were no frontier guards. Our Brichah guides left us at the Vienna railway station from eight in the morning until five in the afternoon while they went into the city to arrange our accommodations.

The atmosphere was tense. The refugees were nervous; some wanted to go to the city on their own, others to return to Czechoslovakia. The Austrians at the station kept asking us who we were, what we were doing in Vienna, where we had come from, where we were going?

The reply was "I am a Greek Hebrew." But not all the refugees were disciplined, not all obeyed the instructions given in Poland and Czechoslovakia. Many of them spoke to each other in German or Polish, in Czech or Russian, in any language except Hebrew. The Austrian police guards, it seemed, understood the situation well. We were not Greeks at all, one of them said, but Polish Jews fleeing from the Russians to the American zone of Austria.

Our Brichah guides finally returned and took us to the refugee camp at the Rothschild Hospital. For the first time I could breathe freely. We had come to sanctuary at last.

XIV.

SIX MILLION WOULD-BE ACCUSERS

Conditions were not ideal in the refugee camp at the Rothschild Hospital in Vienna, but they were superior to those at the Yelen Hotel of Bratislava. After the war Austria had been, like Germany, divided into four occupation zones: Russian, American, British, and French. Vienna lay within the Russian zone, but that was in turn subdivided into four sections. The Rothschild Hospital was in the American section. The moment we arrived there, we ceased to be "Greeks," and became Jewish refugees from Poland, protected by the "International Committee for the Assistance of the Displaced Jews from Poland," which looked after the affairs of the Brichah in Vienna.

In a week, we were converted into Austrian-born Jewish refugees. Each of us was given papers attesting to his birthplace in a town or village in the British zone of Austria; the bearer had been taken to a concentration camp during the war and was now returning home. Armed with these documents, we were supposed to cross the frontier between the Russian and British zones, get to a camp at Gratz, and thence to Italy to be shipped to the Land of Israel. One hundred and fifty of us left the Rothschild Hospital and reached the town of Semmering where we would slip across the frontier. But there was a snag.

Two days earlier, a group of two hundred and fifty refugees had left Semmering. The Russians had let them cross into the British zone, but the British suspected the authenticity of their papers and ordered them back to Vienna. The refugees declined to obey. When our group got to Semmering, we met the guides of the rejected contingent and heard the tale. We took all our bread to feed our hungry and forlorn predecessors and, at their bidding, we retraced our footsteps to Vienna.

Brichah headquarters in Vienna decided to stop sending groups to the British zone for a while and to try to slip them into the American. Therefore, we were given new identity papers, establishing birth in this or that town or village in the American zone. For example, my "home town" was now Gmunden. There was nothing new about sending transports to the American zone, but it was exceedingly complex and difficult—and exhausting.

The refugees had to go by train to Saint Valentin and from there, through Mauthausen, to Linz in the American zone. From Saint Valentin, they traveled by cart or on foot to the Danube, crossing the river by boat under cover of darkness. The Brichah, naturally, preferred the British zone, but the hitch at Semmering warranted a second try at the American. My group was the first to make it, after a long interval.

On our way, we were astonished to find out that our train, whose last stop, until then, was to be Saint Valentin, would this time cross the border between the Russian and American zones, and continue to Linz. Our guides were now faced with a choice between getting us off the train at Saint Valentin as originally planned, or only when forced to. We were still wondering and all discussing when the train pulled in to Saint Valentin, then on to Linz.

For our guides, it was a miracle, a new, easy route for getting refugees from Vienna to Linz had been opened up. They were overjoyed. One guide hurried back to Vienna on the same train in high spirits to report; the other stayed with us. He took us to Wels, about fifteen miles from Linz. All the members of my group were resolved to go on as soon as possible to Salzburg, from there to Innsbruck and thence to Italy. But there were priorities. First come, first go was a law of the Brichah, and we had to stay a while in Wels.

All the refugees wanted to go to Italy because there were many possibilities of getting to Eretz Israel, the Land of Israel, from there. But, as British regulations severely narrowed all entrance into Palestine, and the numbers of the mass migration from Europe were vast, it was necessary to find temporary asylum until a way could be found of getting those Jews there. The American occupation zones in Germany and Austria served that indispensable purpose.

We intended to cross the border between Wels and Salzburg carrying papers as persons freed from concentration camps. The two cities lay within the American zone of Austria but there was a frontier between them, guarded by a different Army division on either side. In general, the American army was very considerate toward the bearers of ex-concentration camp papers, whom they saw as hapless, uprooted people who had suffered agonizingly during the war and were searching in despair for lost kin.

But we were unlucky. The Americans stopped us and sent us back to Wels. Undismayed by this rebuff, we set forth again. Now the guards were less rigorous and we got to Salzburg, lodging at the "Ridenburg" camp.

We arrived in Salzburg in mid-October 1945, at a time when the principal prosecutors of the four main occupation powers in Berlin were presenting an indictment against twenty-four former heads of the Nazi regime. Political, military, and economic leaders, captured by the Allies, were charged with numerous crimes against peace, conventional war crimes, crimes against humanity, and conspiracy. The proceedings of the International Military Tribunal were to take place in the city of Nuremberg, where the two anti-Jewish "Nuremberg Laws" were adopted on September 15, 1935.

The two anti-Jewish statutes had been placed before the National Socialist National Convention following orders given by Hitler, and they had marked a new phase. The first, the Reich Citizenship Law, created the "legal" definition of the Jew, by origin, religion, and family ties, and the clear distinction between German and Jew, depriving the Jews of their status as citizens of the Reich and reducing them to "subjects of the state."

The second, the Law for the Protection of German Blood and Honor, forbade intermarriage (while special provisions were made to deal with existing mixed marriages) and prohibited sexual intercourse between Jews and non-Jews, which was branded as *Rassenschande*, "defiling of the race," subject to severe punishment. In order to stigmatize the Jews further and brand them as licentious people, the employment of "Aryan" maids in their households was also prohibited.

Thirteen regulations were published following the Nuremberg Laws, by which Jews were barred from all positions and professions, were forbidden to hoist the national flag and to display the colors of the Third Reich, their movements were limited, the letter "J" was to be printed on their identity cards, along with other anti-Jewish restrictions. The Nuremberg Laws were a prelude to the "final solution" of the Jews. Addenda were made to the Nuremberg Laws until July 1, 1943, when the thirteenth order was promulgated, declaring Germany *Judenrein*, "clean of Jews."

The proceedings of the tribunal at Nuremberg began on November 20, 1945, and continued for more than ten months. They concluded on October 1, 1946, with a judgment in which twelve of the war criminals were sentenced to death, three to life imprisonment, four to various prison terms, and three acquitted.

The death verdicts were carried out by hanging on October 16 and 17, 1946, except for Hermann Goering, who took poison and killed himself before he could be executed, and Martin Borman, who was tried in absentia and may still be hiding in one of the Latin American countries.

One week before Germany was forced to surrender, on April 30, 1945, Hitler committed suicide. When the Americans recovered his will, written a day before he chose to die, they declared it "Hitler's final anti-Semitic tirade." It showed vividly Hitler's recognition that he had lost his war against the Jews. He had fought for the "final solution" of the Jewish "problem," for not a single Jew to be left on the European continent and, having lost this war, he feared facing trial and being confronted by six million accusers, the six million innocent Jews he had murdered. In his last moments of life, Hitler felt defeated by them, and it was their symbolic revenge on him that he killed himself while the Jewish people were to continue to live.

The displaced persons camps in Austria were crowded with survivors of the ghettos and the Nazi labor and death camps, with Jewish partisans and families of non-combatants who had hidden in the forests, with Jews who had been kept alive in the villages by denying their Jewish identity, and with adults and orphans saved by gentiles, virtually each the only survivor of a once numerous family.

On settling temporarily in the DP camps, many of them asked themselves, why were only twenty-two Nazi war criminals judged at Nuremberg? Why have so many others, who had to answer charges, escaped judgment and lived now in prisoner-of-war camps, in comfort as if in rest camps? Others circulated freely among their families, relatives, and friends. They all watched with disdain the Allies' slow and slack, easygoing judicial actions. They hoped to escape punishment for their crimes, since the potential witnesses of their savagery had all been murdered.

In the hearts of those Jewish survivors, who left behind them lands which had become the graveyards of thousands of their brethren, the longing for revenge burned like fire, and some of them organized the Nekamah, "revenge" group. They were mostly young people who had belonged to the partisan movement during the war. They did not wish to leave Europe, soaked with the blood of thousands of their relatives and friends, before dealing a deadly blow to the Nazi criminals.

The "revenge" group planted members in the camps of the Nazi criminals and executed some of the assassins. They decided to carry out a massive liquidation and, since they agreed to accept the discipline of the emissaries of the *Haganah*, the Jewish underground self-defense organization in Palestine, they presented the liquidation plan to them for approval.

The Haganah as an organization refused to approve. But among the emissaries were some who not only encouraged the survivors to avenge, but who also participated themselves in such actions. They would come in a team of three to a certain address, find the wanted criminal, bring him out of the house, specify the list of his murderous deeds, and inform him of his death sentence. They would shoot him on the spot.

In some cases, they caught Nazi criminals hiding among the Jewish refugees, after they stripped off their clothes and discovered they had not been circumcised.

One of the Haganah emissaries, committed to apprehending Nazis still at large, was Asher Ben-Nathan, known as "Arthur," who had arrived in Vienna to direct the activities of the Brichah in Austria. In 1944, Arthur had been on the staff of the Investigation Division of the Political Department of the Jewish Agency in Haifa, collecting intelligence, especially for Jewish volunteers from Eretz Israel who parachuted behind the enemy lines. In that capacity, he and his colleagues assembled vast amounts of oral evidence from survivors concerning what had happened in the camps and about Nazis known to have been involved in the plans to murder the Jews.

The material was carefully compiled and checked and, on the strength of it, a list made of the principal planners and executors of the massacre. The list was delivered by the Jewish Agency to the Allies, and all the documentation was in evidence at the Nuremberg Trials. In the classification of the vilest murderers, appeared the name of Adolf Eichmann, the fanatical executor of the plan for the "final solution of the Jewish problem." This was the devil who undertook to accomplish the largest and bloodiest crime in history, who had said that he would "gratefully go to the tomb with the death of five million Jews on his conscience, for that would be a source of special pleasure."

It was Eichmann who prepared and organized on January 20, 1942, the conference at Wannsee, a suburb of Berlin, where the heads of the Nazi regime adopted the plan to exterminate eleven million Jews and discussed different killing methods. After the conference, Eichmann was given extensive powers to direct the deportations of European Jews to the death camps. He determined the pace and the timing of the deportations, and was responsible not only for ensuring the extermination of the Jews, but for the plundering of their property, planning the sterilization of part-Jews, and deceiving the outside world about the true facts of the mass murders. The relatively less deadly ghetto at Theresienstadt, in Czechoslovakia, was, among others, used to hide German methods and actions, and was subject to Eichmann's personal direction.

Arthur believed that his chances were good of finding Eichmann, for everything pointed to his being still alive, in hiding. He was an Austrian and his family lived there. Persistently, Arthur set out to hunt him down. Rumors were rife that Eichmann was hiding in a prisoner-of-war camp in the American zone. Arthur asked the Office for Special Services (O.S.S.), the American agency that tracked down fugitive war criminals and handed them over to justice, to check on Eichmann. This was done, but nothing emerged. Neither Arthur nor the O.S.S. had a photograph of him, and that means of detection and identification was vital. Arthur organized a group of young men to follow up any Nazi of Austrian origin who might be connected with Eichmann; the Austrian police provided a list of the Nazis in Austrian jails; Arthur visited each one in his cell. But it was still all in vain.

Arthur learned that Dieter Wisliceny, murderer of Slovakian Jewry, was in a Bratislava prison. He reasoned that this would be the man to help him in picking up Eichmann's trail. By devious ways, Arthur got to see Wisliceny, who was sure that Eichmann was alive. Thus informed, Arthur tracked down one of Eichmann's mistresses in Austria. One of his agents won her confidence with cigarettes, chocolates and cash, and she gave him a photograph of her lover. From then on, now with better prospects of success, the quest was unrelenting, but it was not until 1960 that Eichmann was found hiding in Argentina.

At the end of the war he had been taken prisoner, but his true identity was not discovered and he succeeded in escaping, under a false name, with papers prepared by friends in the Vatican. Eichmann was brought to justice in Jerusalem in 1961. He was indicted of crimes against the Jewish people, crimes against humanity, and crimes of war, under the Nazi collaborators (Punishment) Law of 1950, in the sovereign State of Israel.

In his opening remarks, the attorney general of Israel, Gideon Hausner, said, "When I stand before you here, Judges of Israel, to lead the prosecution of Adolf Eichmann, I am not standing alone. With me are six million accusers. But they cannot rise to their feet and point an accusing finger toward him who sits in the dock and cry, 'I accuse.' For their ashes are piled up on the hills of Auschwitz and the fields of Treblinka, and are strewn in the forests of Poland. Their graves are scattered throughout the length and breadth of Europe. Their blood cries out, but their voice is not heard. Therefore I will be their spokesman and in their name I will unfold the awesome indictment."

Eichmann was tried and found guilty. A sentence of death was passed and upheld in the Court of Appeal, and he was hanged. "The Eichmann trial," wrote Abba Eban, who was in the aircraft that brought the captured Eichmann to Israel, "had risen above the level of retribution, vengeance and even formal justice."

PART THREE

THE FLIGHT

XV.

TANGIBLE GOAL

On arrival in Salzburg, there were three possibilities for us refugees: to settle down in a camp in the American zone of Austria; to go on to Italy, where economic conditions were bad, but with good prospects of clandestine immigration to Eretz Israel; or to go on to Munich in the American zone of Germany, and settle down in a camp there, with poor prospects of getting to Palestine, but with good camp conditions.

In Germany, at the beginning, American authorities were against separate displaced persons camps for the Jewish refugees. They had favored the idea of common camps for all refugees, without distinction of nationality or creed. They felt that such divisions meant perpetuating the racist policy of the Nazis. But the refugees demanded that they be left each with their own, and, in the end, it was agreed to separate them by nationality and to recognize the Jews as a national group. The camps, however, were still under military surveillance, guarded by barbed wire, and had the semblance and air of concentration camps rather than brief sanctuaries for survivors of the Nazi horrors.

Soon, military surveillance was abolished and the barbed wire torn down. This was the result of a report which President Harry Truman was given by Earl G. Harrison, his special envoy of inquiry into the living conditions in the DP camps. The inquiry was prompted by General Eisenhower's visit to the camps and by an appeal of David Ben-Gurion, as chairman of the Jewish Agency for Palestine.

I quote from Harrison's report: "The present situation is as though we were giving the Jews the same treatment as the Nazis [did], with the difference that we do not exterminate them. A large number of them live in the concentration camps under our military instead of under S.S. surveillance, and I would not be surprised if, on seeing this, the Germans will not be convinced that we are continuing the Nazi policy, or that at least we condone it."

Ben-Gurion and Eisenhower agreed that the American zones in Germany and Austria would be used as temporary asylum for the homeless remnants of European Jewry. A delegation of the Jewish Agency, which acted within the UNRRA (United Nations Relief and Rehabilitation Agency), came to Germany to see that the Ben-Gurion/Eisenhower agreement was faithfully carried out.

The living conditions in the Ridenburg camp in Austria were none too pleasant, with a dozen families and more crowded into each large room. The Jewish chaplain of the American garrison, Captain Bonen, an enchanting man with a warm Jewish heart, obtained approval from the military commander of the region for the

Jewish refugees to move to a group of buildings on the outskirts of Salzburg, a former American army billet. The rooms were small, but each family could have its own. The refugees called the billet "New Palestine."

Officially, Chaplain Bonen was liaison officer between the military commander of the American zone of Austria and the Jewish refugees. Like so many American Jewish officers and soldiers, he lent his utmost aid to the refugees, even if it meant endangering his position. Co-religionists from the New World were resolved to redeem and rescue the survivors of the Holocaust and to inspire them with hope for peace and safety. Their help was doubly precious because it came before any organization of protection and rescue had begun to function. Bonen helped the Brichah people a great deal, being careful always to remind them, "I know nothing of your illegal activities."

My group's plan was to make our way to the camp for displaced persons in Innsbruck, in the French zone of Austria, and then to Italy. We had to stay in Salzburg a while, anyhow, so I offered my services to Pinhas Koppelberg, local leader of the Brichah, who was in charge of sending the refugees to Innsbruck. Pinhas was a Holocaust survivor himself and he, too, wanted to go to Italy, so my offer was to his liking. He suggested that I remain for a time in Salzburg to replace him.

I was attracted by Pinhas' proposal that I stay in Salzburg, but I had little authentic knowledge of the fate of those who reached Italy. When I thought of everything that these fellow Jews had already gone through, I was reluctant to be responsible for sending them anywhere, without knowing what exactly was in store for them. I told Pinhas that I would accept his proposal if I were first allowed to go to Italy and find out, on the spot, what transpired there. He agreed.

I prepared to cross the border into Innsbruck and proceed to Italy. Just then, by sheer chance, the president of the Salzburg Jewish Community, Doctor Boris Roisin, asked the Brichah for a young man to escort three Jewish girls to Villach, in the British zone of Austria, where a Jewish unit from Palestine was stationed. Roisin procured the necessary papers.

I volunteered as escort, but only on Roisin's promise that he would get me into Italy from Villach. So he gave me two letters: one for Major Sacharov, commander of the Jewish unit in Villach, and one for Private Mordechai Surkis, of the Jewish Brigade in Milan. In a few days, we were off. We crossed the border without any trouble. At the Villach railway station, we met a soldier in British uniform, wearing a Star of David on his sleeve—the first Jewish soldier from Palestine that I had ever seen. We explained our assignment there and he took us to his camp.

Major Sacharov undertook to get me to Milan with all speed, but warned me that the transit to Italy had become very hazardous. The British Military Police stopped and checked all vehicles marked with the Star of David. Just the other day, they had arrested two girls in army uniform at the frontier.

On October 20, 1945, I left Villach in the guise of a soldier of a Jewish transport unit. Private Alexander, in charge of the transit to Italy, furnished me with a name and army number and familiarized me with such cardinal facts as where I came from, how I had been mobilized, where I had served, so that I could stand up to questioning at the border. The journey was uneventful and, still in the truck,

I changed from my uniform into civilian dress. That same afternoon I was in Milan, at 5 Via Unione, a house that resembled Yelen Hotel in Bratislava in filth and disorder.

The next day I met Surkis, a Pole by birth, who had settled in Palestine in 1933, and was a leader of the Histadrut, the Labor Federation, in the village of Kfar Saba. As one of the leaders of the Haganah, he enlisted in 1941 in an artillery unit of the British army, then transferred to its Jewish Brigade.

The Haganah, rigidly subordinate to the civil authority of the Jewish Agency for Palestine, was formed in 1920, when the problem of protection of the Yishuv, the Jewish community in Palestine, became an integral part of its development. It grew out of Hashomer, the Watchman, a small self-defense militia formed of fighters and farmers, pioneers in Jewish villages, standing guard over remote outposts lying isolated amid hostile Arab populations. They looked upon their work as a personal mission undertaken for the good of an entire nation. Their example was to inspire the Yishuv with an audacity and self-defense that proved decisive later against massive Arab assaults.

The Arab attack on Tel Hai in 1920, on Jewish Jerusalem in the same year, and the riots in Jaffa in 1921, all demonstrated the need to organize Jewish self-defense in a new way. Provision had to be made for procuring arms and training people to meet the growing threat of now systematic Arab terrorism. It was clear that the British would not sacrifice their soldiers to save Jewish lives. And it was no longer enough to furnish watchmen for the farm villages. The towns, too, had to be defended. The entire Yishuv must look to its security. The handful of "watchmen" who went out at night to guard the crops, would become a central instrument in the shaping of Palestine's political destiny. Without it, settlement, Aliyah, and communal defense would have been impossible.

The military strength of the Yishuv was mainly marshalled in the Haganah. But there were two dissident Jewish underground groups: the Irgun Zva'i Leumi, National Military Organization, and the Lohamey Herut Israel, Fighters for the Freedom of Israel. Both were militantly anti-British and were responsible for numerous attacks on British targets. The two organizations were at loggerheads with the Haganah as to the best ways to thwart British policy.

When Britain declared war on Germany after the Nazi invasion of Poland, the Jewish authorities in Palestine issued a statement supporting that declaration. The war that had been forced upon Great Britain was also the war of the Jews. The Yishuv had a threefold concern in those days: the protection of the Homeland, the welfare of its people, and the victory of the British Empire. Thousands of young Jewish men and women were eager to join the British forces. Yet, far from welcoming these Jewish volunteers to fight in the British ranks, the Foreign Office put many obstacles in the way. The Palestine Mandatory administration brought to trial Jews who clamored for the privilege of fighting the Nazis, accusing them of illegal possession of arms. Forty-three members of the *Palmach*, the Haganah's spearhead, who belonged to Colonel Orde Wingate's "night squads" and had been trained by the British army for special duties against Arab terrorism, were prosecuted for committing that "crime!"

But in October 1940, after Italy joined the Axis powers, the British granted the Jewish appeal and approved a limited plan for the enlistment of Jews in distinct units of the British army. So Jewish contingents, led by Jewish officers, came into being in Palestine and were soon on active service. The attitude of the Arab world towards the Allies was, to say the least, unfriendly, ranging from open hostility to grudging neutrality.

In the end, the advance of Rommel's columns in North Africa and the need for more manpower made the recruitment of Palestinian volunteers an urgent necessity for Britain. After lengthy discussions, a Jewish Brigade was formed in September 1944, and the number of Palestinian Jewish soldiers on the Allied side rose to 30,000. They were part of more than one million Jews who fought Hitler in the ranks of the Allied armies.

The flag and the insignia of the Jewish Brigade featured horizontal blue stripes on a white background, with a blue Star of David in the center. Every Jewish officer and man in the brigade was also a member of one of the three underground groups. After having played their full part in the war against the Nazis, the officers and men of the Jewish Brigade now devoted themselves to the rescue of their brethren, the survivors of the Holocaust. These fighters from Eretz Israel were the soul of the Brichah.

In its beginning, the Brichah was a spontaneous effort. The flight (or escape), for that is what Brichah means, was disorganized and chaotic at first, lacking explicit direction and clear purpose. It took on form, system, and planning when the first fugitives made contact with the soldiers of the Jewish units and the Jewish Brigade. The contacts with the soldiers from Eretz Israel gave the meaningless wandering a purpose, a tangible goal, an ultimate direction, in the classic Hebrew term, *Aliyah*.

In their encounter with the displaced Jews, the soldiers from Eretz Israel took on the task of instilling the pioneering spirit of Eretz Israel into the inmates of the DP camps. The Star of David rekindled the wish to live and gave hope for the future, and the Brichah became the biggest illegal emigrating movement in our century. Approximately 250,000 refugees passed through its routes, half of them through Salzburg.

Surkis was the first commander of the Brichah in Europe and, in fact, all the underground work in Italy was in the hands of members of the Haganah, whose people served in the units of the Jewish Brigade and in the separate Jewish units of the British Army. My conversations with Surkis and with the other Brichah people in Milan brought me to the conclusion that I should accept Pinhas' proposal. The chances of getting to Palestine from Italy were good, and that was paramount. Any other considerations must take second place.

The main part of the Brichah work was the hard and unending labor of the *Brichah'nikim,* the barrier-breakers, who moved the refugees using all possible stratagems: with false papers, along "black" (illicit) trails, through forests, over mountains and rivers, through snow and rainstorms, in the shadows of the night.

In the words of the prophet, "And I will bring the blind by a way that they knew not, in paths that they knew not will I lead them; I will make darkness light before them, and rugged places plain."

However, when we could make it easier for the refugees with the help of our American friends, we were happy to do so, and American officers and men, Jews and non-Jews, helped. They often provided us with transport to move the refugees across the borders officially from Salzburg to Munich and from Salzburg to Innsbruck. We especially appreciated the help of the "Joint," the American Joint Distribution Committee. Most of these American Jews were unreservedly sympathetic and helpful. They were, in truth, brothers who shared our feelings, believed in our common destiny. They did not look on their job as a narrow philanthropy of giving out rations, in their mercy, to the survivors of the Holocaust. They meant to be active partners in a mission to realize the longing for safe havens.

One of the Joint directors in Europe defined it thus, "It was the collaboration of an institution of the wealthy North American Jews for the recovery of the survivors, with the valiant leaders who fought in the vanguard, and who took on the duty of saving the survivors and making the dream of generations come true: to reestablish the State of Israel."

They not only did everything possible to improve the conditions of life of the Jewish refugees by supplying them with provisions, but helped them cross European borders by issuing passes which, for some time, had been honored at the various frontiers. But when the Brenner Pass between Austria and Italy was closed by detachments of French, Italian, and British guards, the documents of the Joint became useless, and our transit camp at Innsbruck was flooded with refugees impatiently awaiting entry to Italy. I went to Innsbruck to see what could be done.

One of the refugees, Frenkel, had made his way from Munich on his own and tried to go on independently. A French captain, in the DP Bureau of the French zone authorities, gave him a permit to Italy and, at the Brenner Pass, the French and Italians let him through, but the British turned him back, for they had the strictest orders not to let a single Jew into Italy. Back in the camp, Frenkel was planning to cross the border at the village of Nauders, about eighty miles from Innsbruck. His information was that there were no British there, but French and Italian guards who had no compunction about admitting any bearer of a paper with a French stamp. Beyond the border, in Merano, was a convalescent home of the Joint for tubercular patients. Frenkel urged that I prepare a certificate stating that the bearers had tuberculosis and were going to Merano to convalesce.

Frenkel then set out for Nauders with two other men and got safely through. I went to Salzburg to discuss it with the Americans who were providing us with official papers for some of our transports. The American official papers to transport refugees from Salzburg bore two stamps, one from the 42nd Division, the other from the Allied Military Control. We promptly printed replicas but, instead of specifying Munich or Innsbruck as the destination, we inserted Merano, Italy. With these documents, I went to see the officer in charge of the Bureau of Displaced Persons to get the corresponding stamp.

This officer was only too glad when DP's left his area and he signed the papers, as he had done more than once before, without so much as a glance. Once we had his signature, it was easy to get the second one.

I now had a document signed in quadruplicate, for passage through the DP camp, for the members of the transport, and for the sentry post at the border. But our plan was different; we intended to use the four copies to get four separate contingents across. Off we went to see an Austrian Jew, a manager of an automobile company, and told him that we needed a vehicle to drive from Salzburg to Merano. He knew a few things about our business and understood perfectly well what we planned. He was aware of the possible risks that vehicle would run, but was confident that, in case of accident, we would pay for the damage. I returned to Innsbruck with his truck.

We squeezed thirty-five people into the truck and set out for Nauders. All we had was the American certificate. For that journey I became Moritz Aizikovich, and the pass in that name permitted me to move freely anywhere in Austria. It actually belonged to one of the Brichah drivers. At the frontier post, the French soldiers ordered the refugees to alight. But they did not budge. I descended, informed the soldiers that I was in charge and asked to see the commanding officer.

The commanding officer received me most courteously. I explained that I was transporting thirty-five DPs, all of them Jews who had survived the Nazi concentration camps and had been liberated by the American army, to the Joint's convalescent home in Merano. All the expenses were taken care of by the American army, and I hoped that the commanding officer, as a son of magnanimous France, would understand and cooperate. He did, communicating with the guards in Landek, explaining the situation and adding, to impress his superiors, that the DPs were escorted by a British and an American soldier. The guards allowed our truck to pass.

The officer wanted to know why the passengers lacked individual identification papers, and I told him I had not known that they were necessary. I promised to be armed with the required papers in the future. He then treated me to a cup of quality French wine, to go with my sweets and American canned fruit. We were very comradely.

The Italian inspection was superficial, limited to noting the number of the vehicle, the drivers' names, and my own, in other words, only of the persons who would be driving back. On the way back, I had a second friendly talk with the French officer and this time was quite frank. He was most understanding. His people, too, had suffered terribly at Nazi hands; he could understand our feelings, and was ready to help us as needed. We agreed that I should be back that same night with fifty more people, and I reappeared at ten o'clock.

Again the French guards asked no questions. But this time, the Italians were less accommodating. They had strict orders not to let Jews cross. We needed an Italian stamp and must use the Brenner Pass and not this short-cut. In vain I told the Merano convalescent home story. My Italian was nil and so I asked the guards to accompany me to the French officer, in the hope that he might convince them, and, indeed, he did his best.

The Italian was stiff-necked and insisted that "the Italian stamp was essential." Finally, the French officer succeeded in convincing him to let us through, and I promised that in the future we would get the Italian stamp.

We were determined to use the new route to Italy. But the Americans told us it would be difficult for them to furnish crossing passes to Merano. So we decided to travel on forged ones.

It would have been immoral not to use every possible advantage for the achievement of the lofty purpose: to move the survivors of Nazi extermination to their homeland or, at any rate, out of the lands of their oppression. We did not consider military regulations by foreign armies binding upon us. After what had happened to the Jews during the years of the Holocaust, we believed that the moral right of the non-Jew to tell Jews what to do and where to go or stay had ended. It was in this light that all problems of legality were approached.

The American officers, however, could not, at the outset, comprehend it and were not altogether happy about our infractions, for all their shared interest in getting as many refugees as possible out of their zone. They were very formal at first, probing every issue for its strict legality. But soon they began to judge differently, recognizing that certain things were beyond the written law, and that not to do all they could to ease the way home of the survivors of the Holocaust to Eretz Israel would be a moral wrong.

They showed humane understanding for our position, and our irregularities were viewed not as an objective but as a means to a praiseworthy end. As time went on, our American friends helped the Brichah to the point of covering up for its "illegal" doings.

When one of them was asked why they were doing it, he replied, "I was with the 42nd Division which liberated Dachau extermination camp. I was among the first to enter it. I was shocked and I trembled when I saw what had happened there, and I decided to help the survivors of those cruelties in whatever way possible."

To carry out its activities, the Brichah found a refugee in the DP camp of Bad-Gastein, Eliezer Alpert, who specialized in manufacturing rubber stamps. I ordered from Eliezer the Italian, French, and American stamps, as well as the one of the British liaison officer in Salzburg. Thus equipped, and after preparing the necessary papers for the passengers, we issued corresponding ones for the vehicles and got under way to Italy, each refugee carrying an identification card. Our convoy of forty-five crossed the frontier smoothly.

A few days later, we sent another group to Italy, escorted by one of the Brichah guides, Moshe Vaisand. He left with two trucks, a convoy of one hundred and five, among them forty-five children traveling in the first truck. The first truck set out alone for the frontier, the other remained behind in Innsbruck. When the truck with the children reached Landeck, Moshe telephoned Innsbruck that all was well, and that the second truck could proceed. But, in the meantime, the French soldiers had surrounded the truck and, as the children did not stop talking and chatting in Polish, the soldiers suspected that there were Poles inside trying to cross the border illegally.

Moshe and the children went on to the frontier, but the French soldiers had alerted all neighboring posts that a truck was on its way with Poles trying to get into Italy illegally. So, when the truck came to the frontier, the soldiers, with rifles pointed, called on it to halt. But the drivers did not understand and accelerated instead. The soldiers opened fire from different angles, injuring one of the two drivers in the right eye. He stopped at once, and the guards from the nearby border posts came hurrying to see how the "Polish transgressors" had been captured.

Imagine their astonishment at finding in the truck forty-five children, saved from hell; lonely children who "graduated" from ghettos and concentration camps and whose wide-opened eyes implored. The French trembled. Their officer told Moshe, "Even though we should not let you pass, get out of here as quickly as possible."

It was deep winter. The road to the Italian village of Schluderno was covered with snow and, for all the drivers' efforts, the truck stalled. So the children crossed on foot, and were taken on to Schluderno in hired sleighs. By now, the second truck, with sixty passengers, arrived at the frontier. Moshe was ready and waiting, and got them safely and swiftly across. He stayed with the refugees in Italy to help them onward to Milan.

At the end of March 1946, I went to Munich to discuss the transport of one thousand pioneers, who were originally to have gone from Germany to Belgium and from there to Palestine. The plan was changed and it was decided to transfer them to Italy, via Nauders. In Munich, I learned that a transport of five hundred children was about to depart for Palestine, on immigration certificates issued by Great Britain. I was told that some children from Salzburg would join that group. The transport had been arranged by Youth Aliyah, the Jewish Agency's Department for Children and Youth Immigration, established in 1934, after Hitler came to power.

Many Jewish parents in Germany then, and subsequently in other parts of Europe overrun by the Nazis, were so concerned to save their children that they entrusted them to the agency's care, to be brought to a safe haven in Palestine.

To meet this greatest of human needs, the Jewish Agency invited Henrietta Szold, founder of Hadassah, the American Women's Zionist Organization, to take charge. Thus thousands of Jewish children were rescued. Most of the parents perished in the Holocaust, but some survived and were later able to come to Israel and to settle with their own sons and daughters, now fully grown and integrated.

When the war ended, Youth Aliyah turned heaven and earth to get visas from the British government for the children who had survived the Holocaust. Very few were granted, and the transport from Munich was the first authorized contingent for Palestine. The Salzburg children, my brother Joseph among them, left for Munich on April 8, 1946. It was a day of jubilation for the Brichah in Salzburg.

The next day, Peter Moore and Jimmy Cafin arrived from Milan to Salzburg on a mission to Poland. They had a letter from the Vatican declaring that the Pontifical secretary of state supported the rescue of Jewish children, and asking the Polish, Czech, and Romanian authorities to aid the humanitarian task as much as possible. Peter and Jimmy meant to organize the transfer of three thousand Jewish children from Poland to Italy, but the Vatican's letter did not contain a firm commitment that it would take care of the children on their arrival in Italy.

It was our job in Salzburg to "repair" the text of the letter, and we did it with the help of Marek, a specialist in manufacturing metal stamps.

Redemption of the children who had survived the Holocaust, and transporting them to the shores of Eretz Israel, were among the paramount missions of the Brichah. Most of those children were transported as "illegal entrants," whom the members of the Brichah literally carried on their backs for mile upon mile, along lonely tracks, across rivers, over mountains, through forests. The Brichah boys were, after all, themselves survivors of extermination. Most of them mourned their own murdered kin, and they felt it their profound obligation and duty, their privilege, to save the children with their actions, their love and their devotion.

XVI.

GLORIOUS WEEK

In the first week of April I received a very pleasing telephone call from Innsbruck. The Joint there had been authorized by the French to send as many people as it wished to Italy over a period of three days. After that, however, the frontier would be sealed. Would I, therefore, start sending contingents without an instant's delay?

We began to work at a feverish pace, contacting our people in Munich. They, however, informed us that their refugees could not possibly arrive before three days. But transports started coming in from Linz. The Brichah guides, Yona'le Aizenberg and Haim Max, drove uninterruptedly to and fro along the Salzburg-Innsbruck line. When the three days of agreement expired, we were asked to stop. In three days we had moved seven hundred refugees into Italy.

We asked our people in Germany to hold up their transports. Ernst, the head of the Brichah there, notified all the exit points forthwith, but warned me that a convoy was already on its way, and it was physically impossible to halt it. So nothing could be done and, difficulties or no difficulties, four hundred more Jews entered Italy. A few days later, I was informed that a transport of about six hundred refugees was waiting in Landeck railway station. It had been sent despite instructions to the contrary.

I arrived in Innsbruck in the uniform of a soldier of the Jewish Brigade, Nadaf Ben-Zion, number 32091, and met there with Moshe Vaisand. I set off for the frontier with three hundred and seventy refugees and we reached Merano unscathed. Close behind, Moshe came with two hundred and twenty people.

The congestion at the camp in Merano was indescribable. People were literally "housed" on the sidewalks, and a few hundred more were waiting in Innsbruck to cross over. Nor were we lacking in refugees who made our task even harder, unappreciative of its true value. One refugee, who had been in a Nazi concentration camp, crossed the frontier smoothly in one of our lorries, came to Merano, and lay down to sleep. He was aroused the next day for lunch and, finding the soup not to his liking, cursed the people of the Brichah for daring to wake him for a miserable meal. He concluded insolently, "If you don't know how to work, then shut down the center."

People like this didn't understand what we were doing. Our work seemed simple and easy to them. We got thousands of Jews across the frontiers in convoys of trucks escorted by soldiers. We took advantage of the transports of Italians and Germans, of prisoners and repatriates of all nationalities, when they themselves were totally incapable of organizing their own repatriation. All this was beyond the understanding of many of the refugees.

When I returned to Innsbruck, I learned that another transport of three hundred refugees had come from Lindau to Landeck. We had no other choice but to try and get them, too, across the frontier. I set out with seven trucks filled to overflowing and, thankfully, things went well. One Italian soldier even remembered seeing me in the British soldiers' club in Naples. I had never been there in my life!

It was a glorious week—two thousand entrants to Italy. But our raptures were short-lived. Bad news came. The ship *Fedah* was at anchor, ready to take twelve hundred *ma'apilim*, "illegal" immigrants, to Palestine under the aegis of Aliyah Beth, but they were detained at the port of La Spezia in a convoy of lorries of the Jewish Brigade. Things became more troublesome, too, on the border between the American and Russian zones of Austria, and on the Austrian-German frontier. Abruptly, the Czech-Austrian border was closed and refugees were denied entry into Austria.

The American army no longer gave us certificates for legal transports from Vienna to Linz, and forbade transit from Austria into Germany. We had no choice but to move them to Germany clandestinely.

Yona'le Aizenberg and our other guides were quick to find "black" routes, and along those illicit channels we started moving people en masse. More than once, in attempts to traverse a forest or ford a rivulet, refugees were caught and sent back to Camp Mulln as their likely origin. But we did not give up. If a group was trapped the first night, it tried again the next, and so on until it finally got across. The frontier guards came to know Yona'le well, and every time they sent him back to Salzburg with a transport, he would proclaim defiantly, "It doesn't matter. Today you reject us, but we'll meet again tomorrow, and so on, night after night, until you get tired and stop persecuting us, for we have reached the point of no return."

One night, a transport of one hundred and fifty refugees was caught on the border trying to cross illegally. They couldn't put one hundred and fifty refugees in jail, so an American sergeant and an Austrian guard escorted the group back to Camp Mulln. The American sergeant left and the Austrian guard remained to finish up the formalities. I entered into a conversation with the guard and convinced him to help the Brichah, assuring him that he would not be the loser: he would benefit doubly, as the doer of a good deed and the recipient of a material reward. He was to telephone us, where and when he was on frontier duty, so that we could move our transports accordingly. His code name would be Moishele. His remuneration was chocolate, American cigarettes, and liquor. Incredible miracles could be performed then with a bottle of whisky and a few packs of American cigarettes. Moishele helped many Jewish refugees cross the frontier safely.

The stream of refugees continued flowing into Vienna, large convoys kept arriving there, and we had to move them onward. So we added to our collection the seal of the Supreme Command of the American army in Austria. The Russians, who collaborated with us since it suited their policy of making life more miserable for the British in Mandatory Palestine, knew nothing about the change in the American attitude, and permitted our convoys to cross into the American zone. We were well aware, however, that the situation could not last much longer, for the Americans in Linz were equally aware that these permits were not being issued any more.

One day, inevitably, a transport of ours, with "our" documentation, would be held up at an American frontier post. Our people were, therefore, given precise instructions that, if there should be a border control, they were to get off the train, sit on the ground and in no circumstances return to the Russian zone. To give in was out of the question.

Our worst fears did materialize. The Americans stopped a group of two hundred and fifty young refugees who had passed the Russian control uneventfully and were waiting for the Linz train, with some of our best guides in charge. Ordered by the Americans to go back to Vienna, the answer was a "sit-down" strike. They were there, they would not turn back. In vain the Americans used force; there was no budging the refugees, and their persistence and unflinching will-power won the day. They were sent to Salzburg. They were young and strong, and we decided to send them all to Italy for Aliyah Beth. But the contingent failed to cross into Italy.

Although the transport was approved by the French and Italian controls, it had been rejected by a British sergeant. This was the first time that we had run into the British at Nauders. The sergeant did not question the authenticity of our papers, but claimed to be under orders "not to let the Jews pass." They would have to wait until the next morning when he would get in touch with his superiors. Our guides, not wishing their papers to fall into the wrong hands, took them back from the sergeant and returned to Innsbruck with the convoy.

Captain Stanley Nowinski of the Displaced Persons Bureau of the Supreme Command in the American zone of Austria, informed me that General Collins, the commanding officer of the zone, insisted that not a single refugee re-enter the territory under his jurisdiction. I promised Nowinski that this wish would be granted. I asked the director of the Innsbruck office of the Joint to go posthaste to the Brichah camp and inform Moshe Vaisand of my agreement with Nowinski. He must lodge all the refugees in the French zone. I sent Yona'le Aizenberg to Innsbruck to make sure that the refugees did not return to our zone.

We were on very good terms with the Americans in Salzburg and were anxious to keep our promise to General Collins. I gave Yona'le provisions and three certificates to move from one zone in Austria to another; such certificates were meant for certain of our guides in Innsbruck. Yona'le left by express train in uniform.

One day after Yona'le left for Innsbruck, the transport was back in Salzburg, in violation of my pledge to Nowinski. The director of the Innsbruck Joint had not transmitted my instructions to our men in time, and Yona'le had never arrived. I soon learned that a young Jew in uniform had been arrested that morning at the railway station by American Military Police. I explained the situation to Captain Nowinski at once. I had sent Yona'le to fulfill my promise, and the group had come back as a result of his arrest. He had worn a uniform to get to Innsbruck with the least possible delay, and not have to wait his turn in endless lines.

Nowinski and his superior, Major Schutz, said that they would help to liberate Yona'le. This was not the end. His real name was Aizenberg, of Polish origin, but he had also a birth certificate in the name of Wilhelm Rechnitz, Viennese-born, and an interzone pass in this name so that he could move freely in Austria. His German was far from sounding Viennese.

His trial was to take place within a few days. Captain Nowinski and I agreed that I would accept full responsibility for the charges against Yona'le, declaring that I had sent him to Innsbruck, had provided him with everything found on his person, and that everything had been done on the instructions of Captain Nowinski, who would corroborate my statement.

The charges against Yona'le were many: wearing a British uniform; attempting to pass illegally from one zone to another; trying to carry dollars illegally across the frontier; trying to transfer mail illegally across the frontier; trying to transfer provisions from one zone to another; and being in possession of four interzone passes with different names.

I spent half a day preparing my speech for the defense. I wrote it in Yiddish, had it put into English, and handed a written copy to the court. The president of the court was an American captain. Nowinski asked for a private word with him on a secret matter. On their return to the courtroom, the president gave Yona'le a conditional sentence of one month in jail, and he was free once more.

When Sergeant Harvey, the American commander of our refugee camp, saw me come back with Yona'le, he could not believe what had happened. The charges should have meant drastic punishment. "It's too much for me!" he exclaimed. "If I'm condemned to six months in jail, will you be able to get me out as easily?"

From the Brichah point in Einring, Germany, I received a message that the American border police there wanted to know with what papers our transports were crossing the border to Germany. They had gone to the Einring refugee camp and asked to see the documents of arrivals. Our people there, of course, showed them nothing and hurried to warn me. We knew that showing our legal papers might get our American friends in Salzburg into hot water.

The American army command in Austria was not in the least interested in looking after refugees and was only too glad to be rid of them, which is why it helped us to get the largest possible number into Germany. However, its counterpart there hardly welcomed the influx. It was aware of the limitations on Jewish entry and could not fathom why, nevertheless, so many were entering legally. The frontier guards had reported that the refugees had American papers, and the American border police in Germany wanted to see those documents. The border control was so managed by us that our transports could pass without their documents falling into the hands of the American authorities in Germany.

The Austrian frontier post was in the railway station at Salzburg; the comparable German post, in the railway station of Freilassing, the first border town in Germany. The Austrian guards at Salzburg allowed anyone with a pass to board a train. The German guards at Freilassing allowed the refugees, who had arrived legally, to alight there. It never entered their minds that the Austrian guards were conniving at illegality. As for the Americans, apparently on the strength of an agreement between headquarters in Austria and Germany, only the Austrian sentries at Salzburg checked passengers. There was no American control in Freilassing, for surely the Salzburg sentries would not play a dirty trick on them!

Now we learned that the Americans in Germany would no longer allow passengers to leave the train in Freilassing without showing documentation. Naturally, we did not want to show the papers provided by our American friends in Salzburg, so we altered our procedure. Besides the American army papers, we prepared a certificate from the Mulln refugee camp for the entire transport, describing it as a group of refugees on its way to Germany, and had it stamped at Salzburg railway station. After the document check, we kept the American papers, giving the guide the camp's stamped certificate as proof that the refugees had entrained legally.

Yona'le left with a transport. In Freilassing, he showed the certificate to the Americans. They did not reject the transport, but informed him that the certificate was not enough and demanded the replica with the stamp of the 42nd Division. I asked the staff of the 42nd Division to stamp the camp certificate and they obligingly did. The American control in Freilassing was content. So we carried on that way, adding a 42nd Division seal of our own making, for our American friends just could not handle the volume of documents that the amount and speed of our work required. Yona'le would thus safely navigate two convoys each day. But this happy situation only lasted until June 18. He set out that morning with one hundred and thirty people and crossed the frontier with no bother, returning at midday. An hour later he left again with one hundred and six more. At Freilassing, Yona'le saw that the station was full of American military police. Rightly guessing that they were there to "welcome" him, he ordered his "wards" to get off the train and scatter. The Americans gave chase, but only caught eighteen, Yona'le among them. His Camp Mulln papers were taken away and he was charged with illegal crossing.

As civil director of Camp Mulln, I had signed the papers, and I left for Germany that very afternoon to free him. The border police in Freilassing told me that he was in the jail at Bad-Reichenhall. Back I went to Salzburg and saw Captain Nowinski. He agreed that I should go to Bad-Reichenhall on my rescue mission, and I did. Not that we did not try to send a transport of one hundred and seventy five refugees that same day to Germany, but it was returned without being permitted to leave the train. Control was manifestly stringent now.

I asked Lieutenant Evans, in military command at Bad-Reichenhall, to release Wilhelm Rechnitz, that is, Yona'le, who, on this occasion, too, carried the papers of an Austrian citizen. After telephoning his superior, Colonel Kent, Lieutenant Evans ordered me into the corridor in the custody of an armed soldier. I was under arrest. I was given permission to send my driver home to tell Nowinski what had happened.

After more than three hours in the corridor, I was taken to the headquarters of the border police, thoroughly cross-examined about Camp Mulln, the papers, and our links with the army. And what were the names of the officers who stamped our papers with the 42nd Division seal? I said that I simply could not remember the names of all the officers with whom I was officially in contact as camp director, and, furthermore, the staff frequently changed. My duty was to prepare documents, lists, and letters, get them stamped by the military command, and send on the people.

Did I know Captain Nowinski? Yes, as officer in charge of the DP Bureau of the 42nd Division and that he frequently visited Camp Mulln on official duty. I guessed that my interrogators had already found out what was going on.

My answers did not satisfy them and I was sent to a German jail. There I met Yona'le. "Aba, what are you doing here?", he asked.

"The same as you," I could truthfully say.

We tried, unsuccessfully, to be put into the same cell, and I had to share one with eight other prisoners, including a Pole on a "black market" charge, a Russian suspected of anti-American espionage, a Yugoslav with a shady past, and run-of-the-mill Germans who had attempted to "hop" the frontier. I was hungry and asked for food. A German jailer brought me a crust of bread, but Yona'le got nothing. The warden showed me an order from the American officer to the effect that Wilhelm Rechnitz was to be given food only once a day. The other criminals had three meals.

I lay down to sleep, much depressed at being stuck in jail. The next morning, I persuaded the warden to allow Yona'le to come to my cell, and we started a game of chess. At lunchtime a parcel of food arrived from Salzburg, with a message that Captain Nowinski was intervening vigorously. The American commanding general in Salzburg, even the Supreme Command in Vienna, had been notified. Our informers were highly optimistic.

Within a few minutes, we had a most welcome visitor, Leon Fisher, director of the Joint in Salzburg. He telephoned Lieutenant Evans and asked why I had been arrested, but all that Evans could say was that it was on orders from Colonel Kent. Fisher called Kent, identified himself, and explained that he came on behalf of General Collins, commander of the 42nd Division, to find out why Aba Weinstein and Wilhelm Rechnitz were in custody. Kent answered that Rechnitz had attempted to get Jews across the border with false papers and Weinstein had come to intercede for him.

"If that is so," said Fisher, "I have come to intercede for Weinstein; will you arrest me also?"

Colonel Kent, of course, disclaimed any such intention.

"In the name of the commander of the 42nd Division," Fisher went on, "I demand that you set both men free here and now. They crossed the frontier legally in broad daylight, under orders from the American army in Austria. If you want them for questioning, they will come whenever you say. You can always find Aba Weinstein through Captain Nowinski of the DP Bureau of the 42nd Division. He is the civilian director of Camp Mulln and you may contact him directly by phone 1478."

Kent, vastly impressed, ordered our instant release. The German jailers were amazed. As the warden turned around, I took away from his desk the order putting Yona'le on "short rations" as a souvenir. At the frontier, the American guards stopped Yona'le, who had no official papers, but a quick call to Captain

Nowinski, at Fisher's instance, overcame their doubts. In Salzburg, Nowinski was delighted to see us. In the midst of his greetings, the telephone rang: it was Colonel Kent wanting assurance, and getting it, that Fisher had been in Bad-Reichenhall on army business.

In jubilant Camp Mulln, we held our horses for two days. On the third, Nowinski told me that he had a chance of sending five hundred people legally from Austria to Germany. We made up our minds to seize the opportunity and add a few hundred to the legitimate documentation. In fact, we got seven hundred and twenty survivors into the coaches. Afterward, Nowinski could predict the possibility of sending a legal transport of one thousand people to Germany. Again, we "overspent our budget" and sent off sixteen hundred, the "surplus" being methodically dispersed en route by the escorts.

Lieutenant Colonel Stanley M. Nowinski, Retired, 1961

The U.S. Holocaust Memorial Council
hereby expresses appreciation to
Stanley Nowinski
for valiant service during the 1944-45
liberation by Allied forces of Nazi concentration camps.
International Liberators Conference
Oct. 26 through 28, 1981
The United States Department of State
Washington, DC

XVII.

A POGROM AND A RABBI

On July 4, 1946, a "ritual murder" story caused a massacre of Jews in a Polish town. Few had believed it was still possible in postwar Poland, assumed to be a civilized country.

That morning, a nine-year-old boy, the son of a shoemaker, appeared at the militia station of Kielce, and said that he had been held captive by Jews for two days, that he could identify the place of his detention (the Jewish Committee's house), that he had been kept in a cellar, and that he had seen other Christian children murdered there by the Jews, presumably for ritual purposes.

The story was hair-raising, but the commander of the militia accepted the testimony of the boy without any doubt and ordered his militiamen to go to the committee's house and surround it. As a crowd began to assemble, the boy repeated his story, with no sign of disapproval by the militia, to an incensed audience. The crowd became a mob, a priest appeared on the scene and did nothing to calm them, and soon the attitude of the mob toward the occupants of the house became threatening.

Kielce was little more than a transit point for the Jews, and there were then no more than about two hundred Jews in the town of 50,000. In the committee's house, there were at that time staff members of the committee and a group of youngsters who were preparing to leave Poland at the next opportunity.

At about 11:15 that morning the crowd, including the militiamen, attacked the building. The defenseless youngsters were dragged outside and a number of them were brutally murdered. The mob then pillaged the house and, finding very little of any value there, turned to the office where the committee staff was assembled. The mob dragged them out and in the courtyard, the Jews were murdered with bricks, knives, and clubs. In the meantime, workers from nearby factories joined the crowd, and other Jews were attacked and killed in other parts of the town. When evening came and relative calm was restored, forty-one Jews were dead, and many dozens injured.

The murder of forty-one Jews in the pogrom created, once again, an acute feeling of vulnerability. The reaction of Polish Jewry, which now included tens of thousands of repatriates from the Soviet Union, was an immediate and overwhelming desire to leave Poland as quickly as possible, and a mass movement out of Poland began. Thousands fled by every perilous route into Czechoslovakia, on to Austria and, via Salzburg, to Germany.

With the aid of Rabbi Philip Bernstein, the supreme commanders' special advisor on matters affecting Jewish refugees, approval was granted for the entry of forty thousand Jewish refugees into the American zones of Germany and Austria. Later, their number was raised to one hundred thousand. Captain Nowinski informed me that we would be assigned additional transit camps. I took the camps over formally and was entrusted with the selection of their civilian staffs.

Very soon, seven transit camps were under the jurisdiction of the Brichah for the transient Jewish refugees from the countries of Eastern Europe. They were:

Mulln—our first transit camp. Capacity: 250.

Herzl—in the "Franz-Josef" barracks. Capacity: 2,000.

Bialik—previously army warehouses. Capacity: 3,000.

Trumpeldor—previously occupied by Nazi prisoners-of-war and criminals. Capacity: 1,500.

Yehudah—in Ridenburg camp. Previously, Yugoslavian refugees were sheltered there. Capacity: 3,500.

Israel—in the village of Puch. Formerly occupied by Nazi prisoners. Capacity: 1,500.

Saalfelden—in the city of Saalfelden, near the border of Italy, between the American and French zones of Austria. Previously occupied by non-Jewish refugees. Capacity: more than 3,500.

The ever-present benevolence of Captain Nowinski greatly eased the work of the Brichah in Salzburg. Thanks to him, we could enlist the support of other American officers. One day, the army issued an order restricting the movement of Camp Mulln refugees to a three-mile radius. This was not at all to our taste. The indomitable Nowinski, with the help of one of his fellow officers, got us exempted. We were all armed with passes to circulate freely throughout the entire American zone, as people working for the United States forces.

On August 17, 1946, I went with Nowinski to see Colonel Linden, acting, in General Collins' absence, as supreme commander in the American zone of Austria. He thanked me for our cooperation in the army's work with Jewish refugees assembled in the Salzburg area. Without our help, he confessed that he would have had a great deal of trouble, and he undertook that his officers would continue to co-operate with us.

That day, two Brichah members were married at Camp Mulln, and two special guests were present, Captain Nowinski and Rabbi Eliezer Silver.

Rabbi Silver was born in Lithuania, in the village of Abel. In 1907, he emigrated to the United States and became a leading spokesman for Orthodoxy on the American scene. He was president of the Union of Orthodox Rabbis and president and founder of the Agudath Israel of the United States. When the refugee Yeshivah pupils reached Vilna in 1939-40, following the Nazi invasion of Poland, he founded the *Va'ad Ha'hazalah* (rescue committee), and during the ensuing years this body worked to rescue European rabbis, scholars, and students.

Rabbi Silver came to Salzburg, after a visit to Eretz Israel, as an official representative of the United States government to assist the refugees. At the wedding, I made a speech thanking Captain Nowinski for all that he was doing for the

Jewish survivors. Rabbi Silver expressed his strong feelings about our friendly links with the American army, and on his return to the United States, he wrote the following in the New York-based Yiddish newspaper *The Day*:

> ...One day, L., a pleasant Jewish captain, came along and told me that Aba, the Brichah commander, would be coming to one of the camps and wished to have an interview with me. Among the refugees, Aba is a sort of Ataman, a king of the indigent, the "boss" of the disorganized Polish Brichah. Aba is a legendary figure, something like a Jewish Robin Hood. He wields more authority than the leader of an established army. I promised to go. That evening, two refugees were going to be married. I imposed a single condition: as far as possible, everything had to be kosher, according to Jewish ritual. Aba gave his word. After talking for several hours with the leader of the largest Jewish exodus, of which the least said the better, I gave a speech to the relatives and guests.

I smiled at his hyperboles, "Ataman," "Robin Hood," "legendary figure." But I could understand. He was not referring to me in person, his words were the perfect definition of how the refugees regarded the Brichah and its members, whom they considered as their angels, as envisioned in the Bible: "Behold, I send an angel before thee, to keep thee by the way, and to bring thee into the place which I have prepared." What was more natural than that its men be highly respected by the refugees, as the heroes of many a wonderful and thrilling tale?

Rabbi Silver's visit in Salzburg was an important contribution toward the further strengthening of our friendly relations with the army. It was also an excellent opportunity for me to consult with him about two essential issues facing us. First, the issue of Kashrut and Sabbath in the camps. Second, the problem of marrying young couples who did not have in their possession proper documents to prove they had not been married before. The rabbi understood our difficulties with Kashrut and Sabbath, and was satisfied with my promise to preserve it as far as it was possible.

As to the difficulties of marrying refugees, who were recently freed inmates of concentration camps with no documents whatever, he strongly emphasized that witnesses were a must. "The more the better," he said, "but at least two."

A few days after Nowinski's meeting with Rabbi Silver at the wedding, I came to him and proposed a representative body for the Brichah transit camps, asking that the army provide a headquarters from which we could supervise them. This meant official status and a proper office for the Brichah. The UNRRA building would suit admirably. Could the army turn it over to us, and move the UNRRA elsewhere?

Yes, it could and, on August 27, once again thanks to Nowinski, who handed me the official document recognizing me as its chairman, the "Committee for Assistance to Jewish Refugees" (CAJR) was born, and a bright new era had begun. Nowinski was so considerate as to have an army telephone installed in the private room we kept, enabling us to get into direct touch with Germany or anywhere in Europe with an American garrison. In those days, this was an incalculable advantage.

Later, Nowinski equipped me with a new document as chairman of the CAJR, but, this time, my photograph on it showed me in military uniform, an indication of enormous value to me. The Joint did likewise, and Arthur added a certificate that my committee was the local branch of an institution, with headquarters in Paris, which handled refugee affairs. Signed by a "Colonel," it made an impression on Austrians and Americans alike. When I went to see Nowinski for the first time in my uniform, he did not conceal his friendly amusement at my military style.

You might say that the Brichah was by now a sort of illegal organization with official status to the degree that, more than once, the Americans sought our aid to get certain people, in whom they were interested, across the frontier. For instance, one day I was invited to dine with Major Lifshitz, a good Jew and an ardent American, who was in charge of the O.S.S. activities in Salzburg. He asked me to move to Germany, over the pathways of the Brichah, a certain Scheinfeld, who had to testify at the Nuremberg trials of the Nazi war criminals—which, of course, we did.

XVIII.

GOD'S COVENANT WITH ABRAHAM

Early in the morning of December 9, 1946, wearing the uniform of a British officer, I left Salzburg on the "Heidelberg Express" for the Zionist Congress in Basel. I took with me a mass of "homemade" documents for the Brichah meetings with representatives of all the centers in Europe, under the chairmanship of Efraim Dekel. He was in command of the European Brichah, replacing Surkis.

It was the first Zionist Congress to be held after the Holocaust and in the very hall where the founding congress was convened by Theodor Herzl forty-nine years earlier. Herzl had been Paris correspondent of the Vienna *Neue Freie Presse* during the 1894 trial of Captain Alfred Dreyfus, an Alsatian Jew in the French army, accused of espionage for Germany. Against all the evidence, Dreyfus was found guilty and his appeal dismissed. Clearly he was a victim of that same ideology which was to destroy millions of Jews in the Nazi gas chambers half a century later.

The trial convinced Herzl that as long as Jews remained a minority, prisoners of circumstances and policies they could not control, their constant lot would be discrimination or worse. For him, then, the solution was the fulfillment of the age-old dream, of the yearning of thousands of years: the Return to Zion.

In 1896, he published his book *Der Judenstaat (The Jewish State)*, in which he articulated his ideas. They were not new. They had been inherent in Judaism since God made His Covenant with Abraham. They had been the theme of the first Jews who went into exile: "By the rivers of Babylon we sat and wept when we remembered Zion," and of Israel's prophets and visionaries throughout the centuries.

The Jewish people remained faithful to the Land of Israel in the centuries of their dispersion, never ceasing to pray and hope for their return and the restoration of their national freedom. In the Diaspora, in prayer, a Jew turned eastward to Jerusalem, and all the synagogues were so oriented. In the daily liturgy, morning, afternoon, and evening, Jews prayed to return to the Land that God gave to Abraham, Isaac, and Jacob.

The Jewish people enjoyed self-rule in Eretz Israel for some two thousand years. With the destruction of the Second Temple in the year 70 A.D., the Romans interrupted Jewish sovereignty, and from that time until 1948 the country was never independent. The Romans, however, only shattered the Jewish state, they did not destroy the Jewish presence in Eretz Israel. Jews in larger or fewer numbers lived on there, holding themselves always to be the representatives of the whole exiled nation. And the unbroken stream of home-coming Jews from East and West into Eretz Israel kept flowing.

But it was Herzl who, in 1897, crowned the concept of the Jewish National Home with primacy. In his diary, Herzl wrote, "In Basel I have founded the Jewish State," and predicted that "the State would be accomplished, if not within the following five years, for sure within the next fifty years." Herzl's prediction came true. In 1948, the Jewish state was reborn. The renascent Jewish state sprang from the destruction of our people by disciples of that diabolical ideology that had brought Dreyfus to trial and transformed an assimilated Jewish journalist into the visionary of Jewish national revival. Herzl proudly declared, "We accept the word Jew, ostensibly a term of abuse, and shall turn it into an honorific."

In 1917 Britain, in the Balfour Declaration, made known its sympathy with the idea of a Jewish Home. Foreign Secretary Arthur James Balfour wrote on November 2 to Lord Rothschild that "His Majesty's Government view with favor the establishment in Palestine of a national home for the Jewish people and will use their best endeavors to facilitate the achievement of this object."

The Balfour Declaration marked a decisive diplomatic victory in the contemporary chronicles of the Jewish people. It was the turning point. It also heralded a British military campaign which, a month later, led to the liberation of Judea from the Turks.

On the first day of Hanukkah, the Feast of Dedication that commemorates the triumph of the Maccabees over the Greco-Syrian king Antiochus IV, Epiphanes, who sought to extirpate the Judaic faith, General Allenby entered Jerusalem. Among his troops were three Jewish battalions, the *Gdudim*, fighting units of volunteers from England, the United States, Canada, and of sabras, the native-born, led by Zeev Jabotinsky and Joseph Trumpeldor.

Even the Arab leaders welcomed the Balfour Declaration. On March 3, 1919, the day after Dr. Chaim Weizmann had presented the Jewish case to the Paris Peace Conference, Emir Feisal, representing the Arab case there, wrote to Felix Frankfurter, a prominent American Jew, "We Arabs, especially the educated among us...wish the Jews a hearty welcome home....We are working together for a reformed and revised Near East and our two movements complete one another. The Jewish movement is nationalist and not imperialist. Our movement is nationalist and not imperialist. And there is room for us both".

In 1920, at the San Remo Conference of the Allies, the Palestine Mandate was finally settled, and Lloyd George, Britain's prime minister, parted from Chaim Weizmann, president of the Zionist Organization, with the words, "Now you have your state. It is up to you to win the race."

The right of the Jewish people to national revival in their own country was reaffirmed in 1922 by the League of Nations, which gave international recognition to the historic connection of the Jewish people with Eretz Israel and their right to reconstitute their commonwealth.

At the 1946 Congress in Basel, I could instantly feel the nervousness and confusion prevailing in Jewry in the aftermath of the Holocaust. Few of the delegates expected the British to keep their promises and obligations, and it was plain that the objective would not be attained by conventions, demonstrations, or discussions.

A majority trend crystallized that favored activism and the necessity to fight against the British authority in Eretz Israel for the independence of the Jewish people in their own land, for the establishment there of a Jewish state. The intensification of *Ha'apalah*, "illegal" Aliyah, was held to be one of the most important and rewarding strategies. The congress decided that it was essential to bring the remnants of European Jewry to Eretz Israel, above all, its youth, as a potential fighting force.

We left Basel determined to carry on with the Brichah activities in defiance of the mounting British fury. Until the gates of Eretz Israel could be thrown open to mass immigration through Jewish statehood, the Brichah must continue to play its part in the struggle to establish the Jewish state.

On my return to Salzburg, our American friends wanted details of the proceedings and the progress made toward solving the problem of the Jewish refugees living in the DP camps. I told them that the great day was drawing near, the day when we should see Eretz Israel as our own.

At Passover, in the company of Jewish and Gentile American friends, we celebrated the Seder, the anniversary of the exodus of the Jewish people from Egyptian slavery. The *Haggadah*, the "Telling" of that emancipation, is recited, and then comes a festive meal and traditional songs are sung. On the table stands a brimming cup of wine, "Elijah's cup." Reflections on past deliverance awaken hope of final redemption, and the prophet Elijah, the herald of the Messiah, is welcomed. Toward the end of the Seder, the door is opened to show that this was a "night of watching," on which Israel knows no fear.

I used the opportunity of the Seder to tell our American friends the history of our people, to help them to understand and feel that all the business of Brichah, all the illegalities that they were condoning, were not just the dream of a handful of youngsters who called themselves *Brichah'nikim*, barrier breakers. When we ended the Seder with the cry "Next year in Jerusalem," there was a glint in their eyes. They sensed that they were sharing in a sacred task, helping the scattered Jewish people to return to the land of Israel, the land of their forefathers.

XIX.

APPEASEMENT AT OUR EXPENSE

The American army provided for the refugees 1,500 calories per person per day in the camps, and supplied the rations in accordance with the lists of refugees forwarded by the camp commanders. The camp commanders received those lists from the civilian directors of the camps, who were nominees of the Brichah. Since 1,500 calories were insufficient, we did not report to the camp commanders the real numbers of refugees we were moving out of the camps and we thus received more rations. The more ration cards of refugees we had, the more food was received, with subsequent improvement in nutritional conditions in the camps. For instance, if we took one hundred people out of a camp and sent them to Italy or Germany, we told the army that only seventy had left. The "angels" were the rations received for those thirty refugees who were no longer in the camp.

The army finally discovered the existence of the "angels," and army head-quarters summoned me and demanded an explanation. I gave the reasons and they accepted them, but they asked me to keep the percentage of "angels" below twenty-five percent. At one of the camps, Camp Bialik, the American military camp commander was not known for his sympathy toward the Jews and he suspected we were not keeping that percentage at his camp. The camp's UNRRA director, also an American, and his staff, an Englishman and a German, did their work for Jews reluctantly.

They decided to dismiss the camp's storekeeper, a nominee of the Brichah, and offered a candidate of their own in order to have better control over the food rations. We informed the camp commander that if our storekeeper were dismissed, the camp population would at once go on a hunger strike. Faced by the ultimatum, the commander put off the change of storekeepers until after midday, and a Colonel Wootton summoned me for a talk. The camp commander, the UNRRA director and his aides were present, and they all complained about the Brichah people in the camp. They charged them with breaches of discipline, disobedience of orders, and non-cooperation.

"If UNRRA found it proper to dismiss a camp employee as being untrust-worthy," they said, "the Brichah must abide by its decision."

I rejected all their complaints. I told them that I knew very well about their anti-Semitic attitude toward the refugees, and had enough evidence of insulting expressions used by them, like, "Don't be a Jew!" I added that the English officer of the UNRRA must have forgotten what Benjamin Disraeli had said in Parliament when being taunted as a Jew, "Yes, I am a Jew, and, when the ancestors of the

Right Honorable Gentleman were brutal savages on an unknown island, mine were priests in the Temple of Solomon."

Our storekeeper in Camp Bialik stayed on, but there was a worse incident at Camp Yehudah. The war was over, but one could feel anti-Semitism in Austria wherever one went. One day, as a local bus passed by Camp Yehudah, a Jewish refugee seeking to alight, was rudely pushed off by the conductor. The refugee hit back. A crowd gathered, Austrian police and American military police came along. The refugees scattered, and an attempt by Austrian police to enter the camp and make arrests was held off. The military police detained Lippa Skolsky, chief of the Jewish police in the camp, Haim Max, of the Brichah, and two youngsters, on suspicion of participating in the rioting. The refugees at once organized a demonstration demanding that all four be freed.

General Collins went to the camp in person to calm feelings, and the prisoners were set at liberty. But the Austrian authorities demanded action against the refugees and anti-Semitic outbursts multiplied all over the city, often provoked by Austrian police. One could sense how some Austrians hated us and resented the Nazis' failure to complete their ghastly design. The Americans, although usually pro-Jewish, gave in to Austrian pressures and arrested five refugees, Skolsky among them, who would be put on trial.

We asked the Americans to order the release of the obvious scapegoats, but they would only promise that the army would see to it that they were properly defended. Once again, Jews were a political pawn. The Americans were anxious to placate the Austrians. We had to pay for it.

The defense lawyers wanted Captain Nowinski and me to appear as witnesses for the accused. I knew Lippa Skolsky well. I had met him in the town of Varena while tracking down war criminals. Skolsky, a survivor of the Holocaust who had been an anti-German partisan during the war and, after the liberation, exacted bloody vengeance on Nazis and their collaborators, was now to be tried in Salzburg for "not finding the culprits" in the reprisal against Austrian anti-Semites.

I was cross-examined, speaking in German. My answers were translated into English by an interpreter whose frequent attempts to twist my words I had to watch. Here is a sampling of the prosecutor's questions and my answers:

Q: Who chose Skolsky to be police chief of the camp?
A: I chose him.
Q: What duties do the police perform in the camp?
A: They keep order inside it.
Q: Why did the police intervene in a riot outside the camp, in a fight between Austrians and Jews?
A: The Jewish police are perfectly within their right in arresting a Jew, even if he is beyond camp limits, and that is precisely what they did. When the fight began, they wanted to arrest all the Jewish refugees involved and get them inside the perimeter again.

Q: The Central Committee of the Jews promised General Collins that they would try and find the culprits. Why did they not find them?

A: The Central Committee spent all the time looking for witnesses and for means of setting free refugees wrongly charged. This was much more important for us than anything else, once five innocent refugees had been arrested barely two days after General Collins' talk with the Committee.

Q: Did Skolsky find the culprits?

A: No.

Q: If Skolsky could not find them, he is a bad police chief, is he not? How can you have such an inefficient man in such a responsible position?

A: I never saw any previous evidence that he was inefficient. This is his first failure. That is why, when I returned from Italy and heard what had happened, I decided to dismiss him. (Laughter in court.)

The verdict: Skolsky was sent to jail for six months, two being conditional; two others likewise, but with four months conditional; and two acquitted. It was blatantly unfair. The army people knew that the object was to appease the Austrians, with not a word said about the anti-Semitic behavior of the Austrian police. It was not our last experience of appeasement of the Austrians at our expense.

The American army decided to close down Camp Herzl without consulting the Brichah. The people in it were ordered to leave for another camp, but they refused to go. The army decided to liquidate the camp by force and, at the appointed time, two hundred soldiers appeared to carry out the order. The inmates—men, women and children—barricaded the doors. The American soldiers tried, but failed, to get them to leave, whereupon the "Stars and Stripes" was lowered from the flagstaff as a sign that the camp was no longer under American protection. As far as the army was concerned, it no longer existed.

The soldiers tried to break their way in using tear gas, but that did not work either. They broke down the doors but could not get by the makeshift barricades. The scenes were heartbreaking. The American soldiers were not gentle but there was no surrender. In the end, the Americans left a small guard at the entrance, cut off the water and electricity, and prevented the delivery of provisions sent by the Joint. Everybody who went in or out was searched, and, if so much a bottle of water was found, it was confiscated.

Colonel Linden came to the camp and formally handed it over to Austrian officials. He notified the refugees that they were now trespassers and the Austrian authorities would issue orders that had to be obeyed.

The army appealed to the Brichah for help in closing down the camp. We said no, and the thirty daily rations of food that we had been getting and our quota of petrol were suspended as punishment. I told our American friends that this conduct was immoral and would quickly be regretted. One of them retorted that if the camp were not liquidated, Brichah work in Saalfelden would suffer, hinting that the passage of refugees to Italy would be obstructed.

Conditions at Camp Herzl became alarming. A hunger strike was declared in all the Salzburg camps; street demonstrations were organized. Eventually the Americans realized that closure of Camp Herzl by force was impracticable. Provisions from the Joint were readmitted and water and electricity reconnected until Rabbi Bernstein could appear as mediator.

When he arrived, Rabbi Bernstein met with us, accompanied by his aide, Major Heyman. The rabbi told us that the army had blundered in neglecting to inform him of its intentions, but it would make no more such errors. He said that he could not prevent the closure as it was now a matter of army prestige, of "face-saving." We should give up the camp before the situation worsened. Otherwise, he said, the affair would be publicized in the United States to our grave injury. We might forfeit public sympathy, our enemies would exploit the incident to their own advantage. Stubbornness on our part would give the anti-Semites an opportunity to strike. They could say, "You see? We've given them everything. We defend them and they don't obey but resist and beat up our soldiers." And not only gentiles, but also certain Jews would think so.

When I said that to win the public sympathy, we could divulge that the army had cut off the refugees' water and electricity, Major Heyman replied, "You are naive, Aba. The American press will give more space to a dog falling between two walls in New York than to the conditions of the Jewish refugees in Salzburg."

We saw no alternative to yielding and very soon we realized that the behavior of the Americans in the Camp Yehudah and Camp Herzl incidents reflected a change also in the American attitude toward the Brichah.

I went to see Colonel Hill, the new head of the DP Bureau of the American Zone Command in Austria. Colonel Hill confirmed that there was a new policy: the Austrian frontier was sealed, the camps would be under close control, the number of refugees found in each would be taken as its definitive capacity, and not another soul could be added, not one refugee more could enter Austria; entry into the American zone of Austria was strictly forbidden. I asked whether departure, too, was banned, and was told that it would not be. It was the shortest, and least satisfactory, conversation that we had ever had.

A short time after this very unpleasant meeting with Colonel Hill, a member of the United States Secret Service asked for an urgent meeting with me. His people wanted to interrogate the Jewish refugees in the camps and thus uncover Communist infiltrators among them. He recited a long list of complaints against the Brichah as obstructing his work. The Brichah people, he said, lately stopped offering him interpreters and began making technical difficulties for him in other ways, not giving him rooms to work in, not providing him with desks.

I said that as far as technical difficulties went, I was not at all surprised, but it was untrue that the members of the Brichah obstructed his work. They might not instruct the refugees to collaborate with American agents, but they were not opposed to the American Secret Service. Each refugee determined his own attitude. If he wished, he spoke, if not, he held his tongue.

Why, my visitor asked, was I not surprised about technical difficulties put in his way? "They do so on my orders," I answered, "and for a very simple reason: relations between the Brichah and the army have been less good lately. Some officers have been putting pressure on us in a variety of matters. So we try to respond in kind, negative tit for negative tat; and since we see a chance to impede this work, we do it unhesitatingly."

I also asked him why his agents were questioning the refugees about the Brichah, the papers we use, the irregular routes our transports follow into Germany, and so on. "Why were the Americans harassing us?"

Grateful for my frankness, he promised to stop the interrogations. The Americans, he said, were not making things difficult out of spite. On the contrary, they admired our work. But there was a political angle. The British were being unfriendly and complained of the American army's help to the Brichah, so the army put on an occasional show of interference, intercepting our transports, for example. After each such obstruction, however, the army would aid us generously by way of indemnity.

A few days later, another friend in the Secret Service told me that the British were preparing to send a group to the Brichah unit in Krimel, a new place that we had discovered in the mountains, very suitable for smuggling refugees, especially youngsters, from the American zone of Austria into Italy.

He had stopped that manoeuvre at the last moment by declaring that he was positive that the Brichah did no frontier-smuggling there. According to him, the refugees were themselves responsible for our secret leaking out. They wrote letters from Camp Saalfelden to kin and friends abroad, the letters were censored, and someone in the Secret Service passed the information to the British. My friend advised me to do my utmost to prevent the leaks of such details. But there was nothing that we could do. How could we order the refugees not to write about this and that? Did they ever ask us if they might? And if they did, would they listen?

At the same time, a French colonel from the Displaced Persons Bureau confided to us that, while they were not opposed to our sending small groups, they could not help us with the larger ones as the British had to be given proof that things were being made hard for the Brichah. However, we could not limit ourselves to small groups and, because of the British, we got into trouble with the French.

One day, we entrained a transport of two hundred and fifty refugees to Innsbruck. At the border, it was halted by the French even though the guide had a transit permit purporting to be issued by the French liaison officer in Salzburg. The French took the transport to a railway station siding and tried to send it back. The refugees, although tired and hungry, did not stir. The French asked for the papers again but by then, since the guide knew his orders, they had vanished. I went to the frontier and asked the commander of the French troops for permission to see the prisoners. He was very correct and drove me to them in his own car, explaining that the governor of Kitzbuhl was responsible. At my instance, the governor called up Colonel Thibault, in charge of refugee matters in the French zone, with headquarters in Innsbruck.

After an hour of conversation and inquiry, the governor told me that, this time only, they would admit the refugees to Innsbruck, on the express condition that no more such transports would be sent. I agreed, of course, and he wrote down his official instructions and conditions. This was an excellent opportunity to procure a replica of his seal. There was a double "rr" instead of a single "r" and "n" ("gouve<u>rr</u>ement" instead of "gouve<u>rn</u>ment"), a vital detail, for the French must know of this flaw in their original seal.

As difficulties on that frontier grew, we decided to force our way into the French zone: five hundred refugees were taken at night in two groups and given instructions to resist the police if a hold-up were tried. If French troops arrived, there was to be no physical resistance, but in no circumstances, even if a French general were to appear, were they to return to the American zone. If they were overwhelmed, they must demand the presence of a Jewish chaplain for negotiations.

The French stopped the transport and wanted to send it back. Arthur arrived from Vienna and went to the border as a press reporter, asking questions. No one dreamed that he was the author of the whole affair. I went into action with our American friends. We had to be absolutely sure that they would not readmit the transport. And they duly advised the French that they would not. These refugees were not originally from Austria but had only been in Austria in transit. They warned me that it might be unavoidable to take them back, as an agreement had been signed with the French to accept any refugee who crossed the border illegally from the American zone.

The five hundred refugees were taken to the DP camp at Gnadenwald, near Innsbruck, and were strictly guarded by French soldiers. We thought that we had won again. The next day, however, I was informed that the Americans had agreed with the French that, if they succeeded in moving the people from Gnadenwald, they would bring them to Camp Saalfelden and the Americans would pay the cost of transport to the camp. I got in touch with Arthur at once. He advised us to sprinkle the highway with broken glass to hold up the convoy.

Two hundred French soldiers with armored cars and tanks surrounded the refugees, who did not budge. The soldiers broke down windows and doors, tried to infiltrate their ranks, and vainly attempted to force the people onto the vehicles. The boys of the youth movements, and especially the girls, threw themselves in front of the oncoming tanks and cars, within a hairbreadth of death. The struggle and hunger strike lasted two days.

The refugees slept two nights in the open fields. Only the children were given shelter. The hardships which they underwent were indescribable. Finally, the soldiers succeeded in dragging the refugees out and forcing them into military trucks. It had been a tough battle. The soldiers belabored the refugees brutally to smother resistance. All five hundred refugees were brought back to Camp Saalfelden.

The brutal behavior of the French in this case was not the rule. Generally, they were helpful to us, and we learned afterward that a high ranking officer, unaware of all the circumstances, had taken a strictly formal line. When he sensed the blunder, he sent envoys to our people in Paris with contrite explanations and a promise that, if possible, he would try to repair the damage he had unwittingly done. In the meantime, the British, who did all in their power to undermine the Brichah activities, could claim a certain success. They couldn't, however, stop us.

Framed

The U.S. Holocaust Memorial Council
hereby expresses appreciation to
<u>Stanley Nowinski</u>
for valiant service during the 1944-45
liberation by Allied forces of Naze concentration camps.
International Liberators Conference
Oct. 26 through 28, 1981
The United States Department of State
Washington, D.C.

"The conference serves as a stark reminder of what transpires and will strengthen our resolve to prevent mankind from sinking into that horizon again."

Ronald Reagan, President of the United States

"We will tell, awake, and repeat over and over again without repute to the very end."

. Eli Wiesel

XX.

OUR UNFAILING AMERICAN PROTECTOR

On May 10, 1947, a farewell party for Captain Stanley M. Nowinski, who was returning to the United States, was held on the Brichah premises in Salzburg. Efraim Dekel, Brichah head in Europe, Arthur Ben-Nathan, the head of the Brichah in Austria, people of the Jewish Agency and the Joint, and also American officers who were in close contact with us, were present.

Arthur spoke, eulogizing the work of Captain Nowinski and his invaluable collaboration and help to us. Efraim spoke on behalf of the central Jewish institutions in Eretz Israel and, adding their praises, announced that the Brichah had planted thirty-six trees in Nowinski's name in the forests of Keren Kayemet L'Israel, the Jewish National Fund, as a token of thankfulness for his unforgettable aid. The letters that form the Hebrew word *Chai*, which means "alive," also stand for the number eighteen, so that we were wishing Nowinski "Long life!" twice over.

I presented him with a letter of appreciation and profound gratitude in the name of the Committee for Assistance to Jewish Refugees, the body he had helped form as cover for the Brichah work in Salzburg. I also gave him a photograph showing all the people there, together with five American officers, Brichah's closest friends: Captain Nowinski, Captain Mikelson, Lieutenant Seibert, Lieutenant Morley, and Rabbi Eugene Cohen. Indeed we regarded them as full members of the Brichah.

We bade farewell to Nowinski as to a dear friend, a truly righteous person, our unfailing protector in all our troubles and mishaps, who had undergone so much, had risked his career and endured vilification for his humanity. Even after he had been reduced in responsibility at General Headquarters and given a lesser job because of his intimacy with the Brichah, his dedication and friendship did not decline and he continued to stand at our side unhesitatingly.

No words of mine can adequately describe the value and extent of his efforts on our behalf. Whenever we got into a tight corner, he would appear like an angel out of the blue and extract us. I endeavored to reach out to him as little as possible, but he was always ready to lend a hand, to lighten the hardships of the refugees and get them with the least possible delay to where a happier life awaited them, though he was fully aware that these contacts might do him professional harm.

We never publicized Nowinski's intervention, nor did he wish for publicity. We trusted him implicitly; except that we withheld one secret, though he may well have guessed the truth himself, our use of "homemade" American seals.

He was slandered by certain American officers. Some accused him of becoming rich through the Jews, of having amassed a fortune, of collaboration in our illegalities for no other reason. The gossip had undermined his morale. We of the Brichah were deeply disturbed by this wicked campaign of a handful of anti-Semites. Their falsehoods and denigrations were the outcome of their hatred of Jews. So why not, also, a devoted friend of the Jews?

Who knew better than I that Nowinski had never had a cent for his help, that he did all out of compassion and kindness, wishing only to help the refugees? He had a good heart, and there is nothing finer than that. He was a religious man and believed in God. The gossipers, his maligners and traducers did not have God in their souls.

Nowinski expected no rewards from us. He considered it his duty as a human being to do his utmost for the survivors of a people that had lost six million of its sons and daughters, sadistically assassinated by the bloodthirsty German Nazis and their criminal accomplices in other lands. We remember Nowinski with overflowing love and grateful affection, and all Americans who will read these words and note my homage to Nowinski may be proud of him and thank him for rendering a service to the United States. By helping those survivors, Nowinski was sharing with the American people the merits of his noble attitude, gallantry, friendliness, and magnanimity.

One day, we sent a transport of one hundred and fifty refugees to Germany on a permit issued by the CAJR with my signature on it. The frontier guards did not always distinguish between the seals of the different authorities dealing with the refugees. So they let them through. A few days later, I learned that Nowinski was going to be reprimanded because of this transport. I went to see Major Schutz and said, "I know that Captain Nowinski is going to be punished on our account. I want to know the truth."

Schutz replied that Nowinski had exceeded his competence in the signing of permits, for instance, for the transport of the hundred and fifty. I asked why Nowinski was under suspicion of signing that permit, and was told that army command in Germany had so reported. I then said to him, "That is not true, and I can prove it. I can tell you a few things that you do not know until now. I hope that you will not use my disclosure to harm the Brichah in any way."

I pulled out of my pocket military traveller permits stamped with the CAJR seal and official transport-dispatch forms with our seal on them, all filled in and stamped by ourselves. Schutz was astounded. I continued, "As you can see, we were the ones who beguiled your soldiers, but we did not sign your name. True, we would mention names of your officers at times to convince the guard that you knew all about it, and more than once our drivers spoke of you, Nowinski, and others. But there was nothing more to it than that."

Schutz again checked the forms that I had shown, and I got the feeling that I had convinced him. He asked me to leave him one copy so that he, in turn, might convince his superiors, but begged me to stop that sort of business. He gave me his word, "I will only show it to friends. God forbid that I let others see it."

I then offered him an official exchange of one thousand refugees with Germany. Those who went to Germany would stay there; those who came to Austria would be moved to Italy after a few days. The American army in Austria would be the gainer by being rid of one thousand refugees. I added that, instead of the thousand declared, we would actually pass some hundreds more into Germany, and still only bring back one thousand to Austria.

Schutz went into Colonel Hill's office and, reappearing, said that the main problem was in Germany. The Americans in Austria agreed to the exchange, but we must win over the U.S. General Staff in Germany. He reminded me again that they were under orders not to help the Brichah, and would not protect us any longer. But he said that there were no orders to obstruct our work, whereupon I said to him, "Major Schutz, you have no way out but to help us, for you will be helping yourselves. Take care never to decide to hinder us, for even if you do, there will be no halting the tidal wave of our people. We will break through all barriers. The refugees must reach Italy to embark in the ships that will carry them to Eretz Israel. The ships are waiting for them and they will get there. With your assistance they surely will."

"What will you do if we decide to harass you?" Schutz laughingly asked.

I answered, "We will make up a transport of one thousand refugees from the concentration camps with numbers tattooed on their arms, bring them to the frontier and forcibly cross over. The American soldiers will not dare to shoot or strike them. The dignity of America would not allow it."

"Things would never get that far," he rejoined with a smile, and gave me a warm handshake.

He was right. Things never got that far, although, after Nowinski's departure, we had troubles now and then. Generally, Nowinski's efforts bore fruit, and we could always find American officers and men ready to uphold his wonderful tradition. A short time after Nowinski's departure, a farewell party was held in Vienna for Arthur. The speeches evoked the happy period during which Arthur had headed the Brichah, by many called the "fifth (occupying) power," and his invaluable contribution to it.

Events were recalled from the days of his arrival in Eretz Israel in 1938 with Aliyah Beth and his surreptitious disappearance to work in the Brichah and track down Nazi war criminals. He had left for Italy one night on an Aliyah Beth ship after it had secretly landed immigrants on the shores of the Promised Land. Then, in the uniform of the Jewish Brigade, he had gone to Villach in the British zone of Austria. In Villach, he doffed his uniform and arrived in Vienna, where he acted as a reporter from Eretz Israel, with the letters PR (for Public Relations) on his car's license plate.

Arthur won the trust of everyone he met. His courage and determination could surmount any obstacle, and his companions praised his persuasiveness, remembering various episodes. I recalled the case in which Arthur was summoned to travel to Bremen without an instant's delay in connection with the departure of an

Aliyah Beth ship. This meant traversing the British zone of Germany and he did not have the necessary papers. The only thing we could do was to resort to our American friends, explain the urgency of Arthur's journey, and ask them to help.

Arthur persuaded my friend in the Secret Service to give him a prisoner escort pass, and certify him on it as both prisoner and escort. Such a document permitted the holder to go anywhere, including the United States!

I took a week's holiday in Italy, stopping on my way at Brichah points in Saalfelden, Innsbruck, and Merano. From Saalfelden, the people went to Italy either through Innsbruck or directly across the Alps. Innsbruck was the easier route and we often managed to get the refugees across by train, our people having reached an "agreement" with the train conductors. This was most useful, especially for the aged, women, and children; others went by night, over farmland and hills.

Direct passage to Italy was much more difficult, indeed out of the question for any but young persons. It meant climbing a steep, 1,600-metre high mountain, along narrow tracks only wide enough in some places for single file passage, and then an eight-kilometre ravine, a second mountain twice as high as the first. It was very rough going, and ropes had to be used to hoist up the climbers from point to point. Only those whom the Lord called a "stiff-necked people" could make it.

In Innsbruck, I witnessed the nocturnal preparations of a transport for Italy: aged, weak and ailing people, pregnant women, children and babes. A similar group had crossed the frontier the night before, by a new route. They were told what they might expect, but they were in high spirits all the same, and the expression on their faces was of certainty that this would be their threshold to the port whence they would sail to join the ingathering of exiles in the longed-for land. I was reminded poignantly of Ezekiel's vision of the resurrection of dry bones.

"...The hand of the Lord was upon me, and the Lord carried me out in a spirit, and set me down in the midst of the valley, and it was full of bones; and He caused me to pass by them round about, and, behold, there were very many in the open valley; and, lo, they were very dry. And He said unto me: 'Son of man, can these bones live?' And I answered: 'O Lord God, Thou knowest.' Then He said unto me: 'Prophesy over these bones, and say unto them: O ye dry bones, hear the word of the Lord: Thus saith the Lord God unto these bones: Behold, I will cause breath to enter into you, and ye shall live....Then He said unto me: 'Son of man, these bones are the whole house of Israel...prophesy, and say unto them: Thus saith the Lord God: Behold, I will open your graves, and cause you to come up out of your graves, O My people; and I will bring you into the Land of Israel.'"

Only a higher power could have given these old and frail people, and expectant mothers, the will power, the strength, and the courage to endure the hardships of each stage of their journey.

I crossed the frontier to Italy with the group. When I reached Merano I went to see the frontier post for the mountain track from Saalfelden. Undoubtedly, the Brichah work there was exceptional. The job was actually done by the Italians themselves, and thanks to the friendly behavior of the kind Italians, thousands of Jews were able to enter Italy without trouble.

The frontier post was 1,621 metres up in the Alps, and some of the Brichah boys lived in the hut of the frontier guards. One hundred metres further on was an Italian dwelling to which the refugees from Austria, detained by the Italian frontier guards, were taken. The Italians would notify their superiors that a group of so many people had been held while trying to cross the frontier and lodged in the dwelling.

When the order came to return the refugees to Austria, the guard commander would send a token handful back, turning the rest over to the Brichah boys, who saw about getting them to Merano or straight to Bolzano, and from there by train to Milan. The Brichah trucks were parked opposite the hut of the guards. Even the token handful were only taken to nearby woods and set free. Needless to say, they did not return to Austria, but went back to the dwelling.

In Merano, on July 27, we learned that the 4,500 refugees who had sailed on the *President Warfield*, world-famous afterwards as *Exodus 1947*, were being returned to France. Three thousand five hundred adults, four hundred of whom were pregnant women determined to give birth to their babies in Palestine, and one thousand children were involved. In June the Brichah had taken them to France from the German refugee camps and handed them over to our colleagues of the Aliyah Beth.

One of the easiest ways for our transports from camps in Germany and Austria to reach the Mediterranean coast had been to provide them with "homemade" Bolivian, Cuban, or other such visas. As the ship drew near the shores of the Promised Land, it was attacked by British warships, bombarded with cannon fire and gas. Behind a smoke screen, destroyers surrounded the ship and boarding parties scrambled over its rails. Hundreds of British soldiers in full combat gear used clubs, pistols, and grenades against wretched refugees. There was hand-to-hand fighting between refugees and the unfeeling troops. One crew member and several refugees were killed by British gunfire, many more were wounded. After resistance collapsed, the ship was towed to Haifa and the refugees were transported by British destroyers back to France. At Port du Buc, the refugees would not land. The French were prepared to offer asylum to any refugees who sought it, but emphatically objected to accepting refugees forced to disembark. When the French advised the English that they would not permit forcible debarkation of refugees on French soil, the British decided to take them to the camps in the British zone of Germany. Anger and indignation swept the inmates in the German and Austrian camps for the refugees being shipped back like animals in their wire cages to DP camps in the one country that symbolized the graveyard of European Jewry. Hunger strikes were declared, protest meetings held.

In the meantime, the tide of refugees from Romania was rising. It was called the "hunger escape." It was a headlong flight precipitated by the insecurity of crossing the Black Sea. In our camps in Vienna there were already 11,000 Romanian refugees. Rabbi Bernstein asked us to avoid transfer from Vienna to Linz by the Brichah routes, as an official transport for three thousand was in the offing. But conditions in the camps were unbearable; 11,000 people were crammed within three camps with a normal capacity of one thousand. Despair, hunger and disease were rampant. This could not go on.

Despite our desire to yield to Rabbi Bernstein and not incur the disfavor of the American army, we could not stand by passively. We must assume the guidance and undertake the organization of the transfer. To start with, groups were moved to Linz, and from there to camps in the American zone. The army did not supply rations for them, but the Joint filled the gap, and the "angels" came in handy.

Once in Austria, the Romanian refugees began to press us to take them on to Italy. They were firmly convinced that they could then reach Eretz Israel without trouble or delay. One evening, a group came directly to the Brichah offices in Salzburg with that instant demand. We pointed out that it was impossible. First they would have to enter a camp and wait their turn. But they squatted opposite our premises and would not go. Darkness fell and it grew cold. They lit a fire and huddled around it, shivering in their light clothes. At three in the morning, one of us went and begged them to come in, at least to get warm. But they would only cry out, "No, you don't want to help us! You don't want to take us to Italy!"

The next day was no different and it was not until after long negotiations that they agreed to enter a Salzburg camp. Finally, we started sending groups of them to Innsbruck for Italy.

In Innsbruck, too, they had to wait their turn, which again created problems and, on September 27, a terrible thing happened there. In the small hours of the morning one hundred armed men, most of them Romanian Jews, entered the premises of the Brichah there, killing Eitan Avidov, from Eretz Israel, and gravely wounding two other members of the Brichah. It is, of course, conceivable that the crime was not premeditated, and I am sure that its authors regretted it. It was the result of wild and unwarranted agitation by a few hot-heads of the Zionist Revisionist Party who denounced the Brichah's alleged political partialities and accused it of discrimination. The unhappy circumstances of the Romanian refugees were only too easily inflammable.

The murder was a grim parallel of the political squabbling in Eretz Israel. The death of Eitan was a direct outcome of the senseless internecine strife that was developing there and gravely endangering the fight for independence. It inflamed the camps in Austria and Germany, and there were many who asked for revenge. But when Eitan's father, Yani Avidov, active himself in Aliyah Beth, arrived in Innsbruck to take his son's body back for burial in his native village of Nahalal, standing by the coffin, he appealed for moderation and conciliation, so that the sacred work might go on safely.

It was difficult to explain a crime with a background of internal politics to the French and Americans, to whom ideological differences between Jewish organizations were an enigma. The British exploited the incident and the danger was very real that a frontier, indispensable for our work, might be closed. It took desperate efforts and all our contacts in Paris to persuade the French to forgo orders that would have made Brichah activity in Austria much more difficult.

XXI.

A WOMAN OF VALOR AND PIETY

On October 21, 1947, Rabbi Abramowich, a chaplain in the American army, and Rabbi Bohm, a refugee from Hungary, officiated at my wedding to Frida Szmulowich. The ceremony and wedding dinner were held at an American club in Salzburg, placed at our disposal by the U.S. Army. The Brichah once again used the opportunity to give evidence of its friendship with the Americans. Among the guests were all the officers, and there were many of them, who in one way or another were connected with our work.

In jest, we remarked that members of the Brichah never had enough leisure to get married, and on the very day of my wedding, a large transport of refugees was detained at the Austrian-German frontier. I had to stay with them until they were permitted to proceed, and it was at the very latest statutory hour that I could take my place beneath the nuptial canopy.

Frida Szmulowich was born in Lida, near Vilna. Her father, Jacob, had been a respected businessman. Her mother, Liba, was active in many charitable organizations. Like so many Jewish families of the time, the Szmulowiches lived in comfort before the war, with no foreboding of imminent disaster. When the country was divided between Germany and the Soviet Union, the Red Army entered Lida on September 18, 1939.

Large enterprises were at once confiscated, and Frida's father, together with her elder brother, Samuel, fled to still-free Lithuania, making their way safely across the perilous frontier. The mother and her two other children, Eliezer and Frida, were to follow. In the midst of their frantic preparations for flight, at 2 A.M. on the fateful 13th of April, 1940, there came a clamorous knocking on their door. "Militia order, open up!" What choice was there? In burst men of the N.K.V.D. to search, as they said, for arms. Of course, no arms were found. Thereupon, the raiders told the Szmulowiches that they had come to deport the family, and that all three must be at the railway station at 4 A.M.

They wept and begged, but the leader of the group cut them short. Their pleas and tears were utterly useless; they must be realistic and understand that they were being sent very, very far away. They should take everything that they could carry and hasten; delay could only harm them.

So, they packed up and left amidst their neighbors' lamentations. They met other families in the station. Hundreds of Jews and Poles were bundled into freight cars, packed like sardines, to be sent to Siberia in inhuman conditions. For three days the freight cars stood in the station, more and more deportees being brought in. The train left in the afternoon. Fifty-two people were in the wagon in which the Szmulowiches traveled.

On their way, the deportees discussed what they might expect. Some believed they would be sent to work, others considered themselves lost. One named Zusl insisted that when the Russians came to deport him, he should have hanged himself to be buried among his own people. Zusl later died in Siberia and was buried in a cemetery where Jews and Christians lie together.

During the trip, from time to time the Russian soldiers counted the exiles according to lists, to make sure no one had escaped. After some days of traveling, the deportees began to complain about the lack of water and air. They were allowed to leave the train every day with buckets for water, and to answer nature's call, near the train, in the presence of the guards. It was humiliating. They traveled seventeen days, and that included the entire Feast of Passover.

"I had my prayer book, and I prayed to God all the way, reciting *Halel* (a group of psalms read on festivals) with tears in my eyes," Liba told me.

On arrival in Siberia, the entire transport was brought to a station called Tokushy, and the occupants of each car were sent to a different *kolkhoz*, a Russian collective farm. Shortly after their arrival at the farm, the women exiles were given the option of becoming seamstresses at the Tokushy cooperative. Liba grabbed the opportunity and moved with her children to Tokushy. Frida, too, joined the cooperative, and Eliezer went to work at the grain elevator.

There was some industry in Tokushy, supported by the large railroad station and, among others, there was a large compound with several grain silos. At the time, the grain in the silos started to ferment and, to save it, groups of exiles, men and women, were drafted to air the grain. They had to shovel the grain down the bottom of the silos by throwing the three stories worth of grain from one side of the silo to the other. After seemingly impossible, grueling labor, they were taken to a tremendous room where they slept on the floor in their wet clothes.

From Tokushy the Szmulowiches later moved to Petropavlovsk. Eliezer was drafted to work in the mines. Frida worked during the day as a clerk, and in the evening she went to school. Mother stayed at home. They remained in Siberia until 1946, when, thanks to the Polish-Russian agreement for the repatriation of Polish citizens from Russia, they returned home. There the Jewish repatriates were welcomed with violence and threats that death would be the end of those who had survived Hitler. The Szmulowiches could not remain in Poland and joined the stream of refugees making their hard way to the American zone of Germany. Thus they arrived at the refugee camp in Bad Reichenhall, where I met Frida.

From the day I first met my mother-in-law, I have felt she was an extraordinary person and, as time went on, I heard from various people who were with her in Siberia, about her goodness, friendliness, and hospitality, as well as about her bravery under Stalin's tyrannical anti-Jewish regime. In spite of the threats, she organized, in her small one-room apartment in Tokushy, a Friday night and Sabbath *minyan*, the requisite number of ten males for congregational worship. When she was arrested, during a year in jail she stayed kosher, and lived only on water, bread, onions, and garlic. Not a morsel of unkosher food was brought into her home during the entire six years of exile.

She was loved and respected by all the exiles and, if anyone had a problem or troubles, the first name that came to mind was Liba, who always had a clear and reasonable presence of mind. She never became excited, angry, or despairing. She was always level-headed, logical, and smart, and had a calming effect on those who met her. She opened her home to everyone, whether wanderer, exile, or refugee. No one left hungry, having a baked potato, a slice of bread with onion, or a bowl of soup.

She never said an unkind word about anyone. In her righteousness, she could not see any bad characteristics in anyone and, when I once made a comment to her about her always-outstretched hand to whoever needed help, she was surprised and did not understand how it could be otherwise.

While the mother with her younger son and daughter languished in Siberia, the father and the older son were wandering in another part of the world. As long as Lithuania was free, they could live there at ease and hoped to be joined by the other members of the family. But when the Russians occupied Lithuania in 1940, it became a deadly risk for them to stay. They were on the "black list," likely to be exiled to Siberia also. In Kovno, they learned of the possibility of getting a Japanese transit visa for Curaçao. They were among the lucky 5,000 Jewish refugees who arrived safely in Japan.

They converged in Kobe, where most of Japan's Jews lived since the earthquake of 1923. With the help of the Joint and other Jewish relief organizations, many of the transients were able to move on to the United States, Australia, and New Zealand. Some, granted certificates, went to Eretz Israel. The Szmulowiches were not so fortunate. In 1942, after the outbreak of war between Japan and the United States, they left for Shanghai where they lived until 1947, when a relative secured visas for Mexico for them.

Once in Mexico City, they arranged papers for the mother and daughter. The son Eliezer had married in the meantime and had smuggled himself into Eretz Israel via Marseilles. But by the time the Mexican visas arrived, Frida and I had decided to marry and go to Eretz Israel. Her mother, having shared such arduous years with Frida, was reluctant to be separated and, despite her ardent longing to be reunited with her husband and son, she made up her mind that the family reunion must take place in Eretz Israel and not in Mexico. She would join Frida and myself on our "illicit" vessel's journey to Eretz Israel rather than go legally and comfortably by plane to Mexico.

Once in the Holy Land, my mother-in-law advised her husband in Mexico that she had reached her final stop, that she had unpacked her valises and would no longer wander. Let him join her in Israel. He did, and they settled happily in Haifa on Mount Carmel. Samuel married in Mexico and remained there.

After both my mother-in-law and father-in-law had passed away, I met Mrs. Dina Gabel, formerly Shapiro, the widow of Rabbi Shimon Gabel from New York. She was deported from Lida with her mother in the same transport as the Szmulowiches, and she was in the group of eighty women and forty men who were drafted to work on the grain elevator in Tokushy. Dina told me that considering the indescribable difficulty of the work, due in large part to the clouds of moldy dust they were breathing and swallowing twelve hours a day, she doesn't know how she could have survived if not for Liba's help and support. The meals of the draftees were water for breakfast, hot water and bread for supper, and a bowl of watery cabbage soup with a sliver of bone in it for lunch.

Since Dina gave the unkosher soup away to a Polish woman, she was left with nothing for lunch. "Liba brought me a homecooked meal every day," she said, "though she hardly had enough for herself and her children." Liba helped her and her mother, Dina added, to find an apartment in Tokushy and lent them the large sum of money requested for the month's rent in advance. When Dina received a draft card to the coal mines in Karaganda and was in shock and despair, it was Liba who saved her from the disaster.

When Dina was in hot water again with the N.K.V.D., and escaped from Tokushy to Petropavlovsk, Liba, who had moved there with her children earlier, took her and her mother into their tiny one-room apartment. At that time the apartment shortage had made finding a place of their own impossible, and going back to Tokushy meant walking straight back into the lion's den.

Dina concluded her description of my late mother-in-law with the following words, "I cherish Liba's memory and I am eternally thankful for her motherly concern during my nightmarish encounter with Soviet slave labor, and for her invaluable help in saving my life, both from the coal mines and later from the N.K.V.D. During all these years I have been carrying in my heart deep respect and admiration for the remarkable woman of valor who was your mother-in-law."

PART FOUR

JEWISH STATEHOOD REGAINED

XXII.

WITH TRUST IN ALMIGHTY GOD

My wife and I left Salzburg for Eretz Israel on November 25, 1947. We went first to the refugee camp in Bad-Reichenhall, where we were joined by my mother-in-law, and then to Munich. On November 29 we left for the refugee camp in Bergen-Belsen. Before leaving Munich, we heard the news about the debates at the U.N. General Assembly regarding the proposal of its Special Committee on Palestine (UNSCOP) to divide Eretz Israel into Arab and Jewish states.

The UNSCOP was appointed by the General Assembly in May 1947, after Britain had submitted the Palestine problem to the U.N. The committee consisted of eleven members, representing the governments of Australia, Canada, Czechoslovakia, Guatemala, India, Iran, The Netherlands, Peru, Sweden, Uruguay, and Yugoslavia. Asked to study the problem of Palestine and submit recommendations for a solution, the committee heard oral testimonies, received written materials from individuals and organizations, and visited Palestine, neighboring countries, and the camps of displaced persons in Germany and Austria.

The displaced Jews, who at first presented a moral and humanitarian problem, became an ever-stronger political factor. When the UNSCOP members met with them, they saw the anguish and agony of those refugees; they saw with their own eyes the suffering of the people, and were moved by their talks with many of them. They realized from their discussions that not only were the Jews determined to immigrate only to Palestine, but that tens of thousands more Jews were waiting in their native lands to go to Eretz Israel.

Thus the Brichah work, the concentration of the 250,000 Holocaust survivors in the occupation zones of Germany and Austria, directly influenced the committee in its report of August 1947. The committee unanimously resolved that the British Mandate should be terminated and, while the minority proposed the establishment of a binational federal state, the seven member majority recommended the partition of the country into an independent Jewish state, an independent Arab state, and a "corpus separatum" consisting of Jerusalem and its environs as an international enclave.

The UNSCOP report occupied center stage when the General Assembly met in New York on September 16, 1947. Just when they were discussing at the U.N. the establishment of a Jewish state, the murder of Eitan Avidov occurred in Innsbruck. We were afraid that it might affect the chances of that resolution to be approved, our enemies arguing that the Jews, with their deadly squabbling in Eretz Israel and in the refugee camps, were not yet ready for independence. All night, on the train from Munich to Bergen-Belsen, we were not too heartened, the chances were unsure. There was the fear that, for one or two votes, the partition proposal might collapse.

To our joy, on arriving the next day, we were welcomed by inscriptions on the walls of Bergen-Belsen: "Long live the Jewish state!" "Long live Ben-Gurion!"

The General Assembly adopted the UNSCOP report by a vote of 33 in favor, 13 against, and 10 abstentions. In the refugee camp of Bergen-Belsen, the people embraced and kissed each other.

In Eretz Israel, the joy in the streets burst all bounds, and crowds danced the whole night through. But the joy of liberation was soon darkened when celebrants in the early hours learned of the first victims, murdered by Arabs as they traveled in a bus from Netanya to Jerusalem. There was now an outbreak of Arab terrorism. Roads were mined, villages isolated, convoys ambushed. Seven Jews were killed in the first few hours. By the end of the first week, one hundred and five Jews had perished. Apartments in Jerusalem were blown up and more than fifty men, women, and children were killed. Thirty-five Hebrew University students were massacred on the road near Jerusalem. The Jewish Agency's building was bombed, with heavy casualties. A convoy was set afire on the road to the Hadassah Hospital on Mount Scopus, and in that outrage seventy-seven Jewish doctors, nurses, and scientists met their death.

While the Jews accepted the United Nations resolution, which Ben-Gurion called historic justice, the Arabs rejected it and resolved to oppose it by force. The British refused to play any part in implementing it. The gates of Eretz Israel were still barred to the refugees, and the Brichah would have to continue its work until the Jews won free access to Eretz Israel.

My wife, my mother-in-law, and I still had to reach Eretz Israel clandestinely. We landed on February 24, 1948, with what was then called *Aliyah Daled*, each of us with the passport and name of someone else; only the photographs were ours. My mother-in-law traveled as Bertha Halpert, my wife as Paula Lehrer, I as Menashe Klein.

Less than two months later, the United Nations, confronted with a challenge to its authority, convened a second special session of the General Assembly on April 16, 1948, to vote on a new partition plan. The United States delegation at the U.N. voted in favor, in accordance with President Harry Truman's instructions overruling the position of his State Department. Veteran American diplomats were unreconciled, however, and soon after the partition resolution was adopted, supporters of the Arab cause, missionaries, oil lobbyists, Arabists, organized a powerful committee to demand its nullification.

The U.N. Security Council proved impotent to cope with Arab pressure and belligerence, and the United States proposed the establishment of a "temporary" trusteeship for Palestine. But this attempt to block the establishment of the Jewish state failed. Events in Palestine moved faster than diplomacy. The British withdrew their forces in anticipation of the end of the Mandate and the Haganah forces in combat with Arab armies and irregulars secured well-organized Jewish political authority over a substantial part of the country.

Defying the Holocaust

On the afternoon of May 14, 1948, my wife and I stood amidst an enormous crowd in front of Government House in Haifa, waiting for the dream of two thousand years to come true. Sir Alan Cunningham, the British high commissioner, left the soil of Eretz Israel that day with the last of his staff. From a cruiser outside territorial waters, he signalled the end of the Mandatory era and, at that historic moment, on the top of Government House, a banner now fluttered, bearing in giant letters the words so long in everyone's yearnings: "The State of Israel is born."

It was four o'clock in the afternoon and, simultaneously, in a short ceremony at the Museum of Tel Aviv, two hundred and forty men saw a new page written in Jewish history, as David Ben-Gurion read the Proclamation of Independence of the newly-born state; a young state, but of an ancient people dwelling on its national soil from which Jews had been driven by force at times, but toward which that people had ever turned its heart, its longings, and prayers for thousands of years; a state that is both the ancestor and the heir of a great universal tradition.

The governing paragraph in Israel's Proclamation of Independence reads:

> Accordingly we, the members of the National Council, representing the Jewish people in the Land of Israel and the Zionist Movement, have assembled on the day of the termination of the British Mandate for Palestine, and, by virtue of our natural and historic right and of the resolution of the General Assembly of the United Nations, do hereby proclaim the establishment of a Jewish state in the Land of Israel, to be known as the State of Israel.

Following the last words of the proclamation, "With trust in Almighty God, we set our hands to this Declaration, in the City of Tel Aviv, on this the Fifth Day of Iyar, the Fourteenth Day of May, One Thousand Nine Hundred and Forty-Eight," its signatories advanced to the table each to give it his sanction.

The Hebrew benediction was recited, "Blessed art Thou, O Lord our God, King of the Universe, Who has kept us alive and preserved us and enabled us to see this day," and all filed out into the sun-drenched street. Eleven minutes later, President Truman granted *de facto* recognition by the United States, to the dismay of the U.S. State Department. After two days, the Soviet Union granted *de jure* recognition. In the ensuing U.N. debates, the Soviet Union and the United States both supported Israel, while the British delegation remained aligned with the Arab states. The Jewish state was finally established not by the U.N. partition resolution, which was only one important link in a chain of events that brought the state into being. Under international law, Israel became an independent state when it proved its viability as a legal unit in meeting the four cumulative conditions: nation, territory, government, and independence, which emerged from the throes of its War of Independence.

For as speedily as joy and satisfaction, difficulties began. An armed invasion was launched against Israel by seven Arab states. From the north came the Lebanese army; from the northeast, the Syrians; Jordan's Arab legion and the Iraqi forces attacked at the center; and from the south, the Egyptians moved up, supported by bomber planes. Units from Saudi Arabia and Yemen, too, joined the invaders.

Jewish manpower was meager and the weaponry pathetically inadequate, and the Arab forces surged with impressive vigor, attacking the isolated Jewish settlements, as well as the Jewish sectors of the cities with mixed populations. As Jewish dead began to pile up, it seemed that the miracle of the rebirth of the Jewish state, rising out of the very ruins of our people, would not be realized; that the threshold of statehood would never be crossed.

XXIII.

NO SECOND MASADA!

"Independence is never given to a people," said Chaim Weizmann, Israel's first president. "It has to be earned and, once earned, must be defended." Ours was both earned and defended.

When the infant State of Israel was invaded from all sides by Arab armies, the secretary-general of the Arab League, Azzam Pasha, boasted in Cairo, "This will be a war of extermination and momentous massacre which will be spoken of like the Mongolian massacres and the Crusades."

The United Nations, in Abba Eban's view, behaved then like the alligator that, according to zoologists, gives birth to its young with great tenderness and then devours them with calm apathy. Self-reliance became the inevitable posture for a people for whom no one outside would risk any blood, even when destruction stared it in the face.

There was, however, an exception: the *Machal*, Jewish volunteers from abroad, mainly from the United States and Canada. They were war veterans, and they poured into Israel to fight for its independence.

I was living in Haifa. Most of the city's 70,000 Arabs responded to the call of their leaders and fled to Lebanon. Five days after the Proclamation of Independence, I was sent to work at the port, which was considered a vital position to defend, and I was mobilized into the paramilitary unit established there. The War of Independence lasted more than thirteen months, including sixty-one days of continuous combat, and was won.

It was in the ghettoes, in the forests, and in the extermination camps that the spirit of Jewish heroism was ignited, to reach its greatest incandescence in that war and in the other wars that Israel has had to fight since then.

When the fighting ended, Israel's frontiers were not those recommended by the United Nations. Israel's authority extended over the whole of Galilee; the entire coastal strip, except for the Gaza salient in Egyptian hands; the whole of the Negev; and West Jerusalem, with a sizable corridor to the coast. Its area of jurisdiction was more than 8,000 square miles. Judea, Samaria, and East Jerusalem, including the Old City, were under Jordanian control.

The war ended officially on July 20, 1949, with the signature of the armistice agreement with Syria. Similar agreements had been signed earlier with Egypt, Lebanon, and Jordan. Iraq, whose troops were in heavy concentrations on the West Bank of the Jordan River, refused to sign an agreement with Israel.

Israel's casualties were 4,000 soldiers and 2,000 civilians. Israel mourned with feelings of praise and pride its beloved and faithful sons and daughters who gave up their lives in the flower of their youth. They are forever engraved in the nation's heart.

One of the outcomes of the War of Independence was the Palestinian refugee problem. When the war broke out, the leader of the Palestinian Arabs was the mufti of Jerusalem, Haj Amin al-Husseini, a fanatical supporter of Hitler. He had organized the anti-Jewish terror in Eretz Israel and then had flown to Germany, where he met with Hitler, broadcast appeals to the Arabs to overthrow the British, organized espionage squads, recruited Moslems in East Europe to the Nazi ranks, and supported the Nazi efforts to wipe out the Jews.

Al-Husseini visited the death camps to learn the grisly techniques of extermination. He asked the Nazis and was promised that a representative of Eichmann should arrive in Jerusalem to serve as his, the mufti's, personal adviser, when he himself returned there after the victory of the Axis powers. At a rally in Berlin in November 1943, he declared, "The Germans know how to get rid of the Jews."

When the independence of the State of Israel was proclaimed, the mufti exhorted the Arabs of Palestine to take brief refuge in the neighboring Arab states so that nothing might hinder the advance of the invading Arab armies. He promised that they would return soon, to pillage and plunder, after the Jews had been thrown into the sea. Broadcasts from Cairo and Amman, from Damascus and Beirut, promised that "Any Arabs who did not withdraw from Palestine would be hanged as collaborators with the Jews."

Thus the Arab states set in motion the events out of which the Arab refugee problem developed. Their aim was to thwart the establishment of the Jewish state, but it came to naught. Israel's statehood was reborn and confirmed.

If the Arab states had cajoled or coerced more than 550,000 Palestinians into exodus, they terrorized 650,000 Jews into fleeing Arab lands where they had lived for centuries as loyal citizens. In utter destitution, stripped of all they possessed, most of these Jewish refugees were welcomed and integrated by Israel. It was an exchange of populations. Jewish refugees from Arab lands went to a country with a Jewish majority. Arab refugees from Israel moved to Arab countries: an internationally accepted transfer.

After the end of World War II, exchanges of populations took place in various parts of the world: four million Moslems passed from India to Pakistan; about the same number of Hindus moved from Pakistan to India; three million Sudeten Germans were expelled from Czechoslovakia; two million settled in West Germany and Austria; one million in East Germany.

In 1949-1961, there were in West Germany 2,739,000 refugees from East Germany; 6,750,000 Germans left the territories annexed by Poland. More than one million French or pro-French Arabs left Algeria for France. When Vietnam was divided, 800,000 North Vietnamese passed to South Vietnam. More than one million refugees from North Korea settled in South Korea. More than one million refugees from Communist China arrived in Hong Kong. Masses of refugees were settled from Nigeria, Biafra, Ethiopia, Eritrea, Cyprus, Cambodia. More than sixty million persons became refugees since the Second World War, and most were settled and rehabilitated in the countries where they sought refuge. The civilized world has expressed the concept of resettlement and absorption of refugees in international laws and regulations.

The Arab states, however, with all their wealth and space, will not absorb the Arab refugees, who are akin in blood and faith. They rejected Israel's offer to open peace negotiations and, on humanitarian grounds, to discuss the refugee problem as the first item on the agenda. They denounced Israel's proposal to convene an international conference on the problem, with a view to working out a five-year plan of solution, even before peace talks.

While Israel gave the Jewish refugees a new home, the Arab states have perpetuated the Arab refugee problem. They have kept the Palestinian refugees in camps and used them as tools in their war against Israel. They have kept the refugees in quarantined ghettoes, forbidden resettlement, denied integration into the economies of the host countries, using them as political pawns. In arithmetic textbooks, they teach the children in the camps: "In a concentration camp there were 1,000 Jews; the Arab Police of the camp killed 850 of them; how many remained alive?"

They insist that the Arab refugees return to Israel. Abdel Nasser of Egypt did not hesitate to reveal his purpose: "If the refugees return to Israel, Israel will cease to exist."

For Israel to let the Arab refugees return would be suicidal, giving the Arab terrorists a choice of deciding whether to shell Israel from across the borders or to destroy it from within. National suicide, however, is neither an international nor a moral obligation.

True, one of the most dramatic suicide episodes in Jewish national history was enacted in the rock-fortress of Masada, overlooking the Dead Sea. There, 960 Jews refused to succumb, preferring death to surrender in 73 A.D. They chose to die by their own hands rather than yield to the tyranny of Rome, and the farewell words of their leader, Eleazar ben Yair, recorded for posterity by Josephus Flavius, are among the finest ever spoken:

> All men are equally destined to death; and the same fate attends the coward as the brave. Can we think of submitting to the indignity of slavery? Can we behold our wives dishonored and our children enslaved? Let us die free men, gloriously surrounded by our wives and children. Eternal renown shall be ours by snatching the prize from the hands of our enemies, and leaving them nothing to triumph over but the bodies of those who dared to be their own executioners.

But the State of Israel, the legitimate successor of the kingdom of Judea, whose last stand was at Masada, is determined that there will be no second Masada in the chronicles of Jewry. Israel prefers to be blamed for insisting on survival rather than praised for committing suicide, and Masada will not fall again!

With the War of Independence won, there was a general conviction that the national aims were worthy of sacrifice.

"The graves that had been dug, the tears that had been shed because of them, the griefs that had been suffered, the perils that had been surmounted, the inexpressible hopes that had been kindled, would all live on deep in the mind and heart of Israel so long as any memory of the past endured," writes Abba Eban, "and from the war's dust and havoc a new tomorrow was waiting to be born: Israel was now free to build its future."

In the Haifa Port, I saw how the gates of Israel swung wide open to the hundreds of thousands of Holocaust survivors who poured into the country. In the first four months of Israel's independence, when the country's fate was still in the balance, some fifty thousand immigrants reached her shores. By September 1948 the stream had become a flood. Within three years, between May 1948 and December 1951, 687,000 newcomers had landed in Israel. Earlier, it had taken thirty years, under British mandatory rule, for the Jewish population to increase by 650,000.

On May 11, 1949, Israel became a full-fledged member state of the United Nations. When it took its seat as the fifty-ninth member of the U.N., it had secured its place in the international community as a partner equal in rights to all others. Said Foreign Minister Moshe Sharett, in reporting to the Knesset, Israel's parliament, "Israel amongst the nations! A sovereign Jewish state secure within the international family."

While I was working at the Haifa Port, Asher Ben-Nathan—Arthur—became a senior official at Israel's Foreign Ministry, and he invited me to enter the diplomatic service and go on a mission to Rome. In May 1950, I left for Rome as attaché at Israel's embassy. A month later, my wife joined me, together with our year-and-a-half old daughter, Ruhama, a name given in memory of my mother, may she rest in peace. In Rome, a son was born to us, Meir, named in memory of my father, may he rest in peace.

Israel's first foreign minister, Moshe Sharett, asked that all Israeli diplomats change their names to Hebrew ones, and so, instead of Weinstein, I became *Gefen*, the Hebrew word for vine. In Rome, we saw the Arch of Titus that marks the Roman victory, two thousand years ago, over the Jews, the conquest of Jerusalem, and the razing of the Second Temple. A panel is carved on the Arch showing the carrying of the Menorah (the seven-branched candelabrum) as part of the spoils in the triumphal procession following the subjugation of Judea.

After the U.N. General Assembly had approved the partition of Palestine, thousands of Jews assembled at the arch in Rome for a thanksgiving prayer that the Jewish state, destroyed two thousand years ago, had been rebuilt. When the State of Israel was to establish its emblem, it decided on a menorah patterned after the one carried by the Romans.

Italy was one of the European countries where Jews had been saved thanks to a friendly population. The number of Jewish victims in Italy was estimated at about 7,500 out of a Jewish population of about 35,000. Many Jews were hidden and given false documents. Sympathetic Christians supplied their needs for shelter, food, and documents. Money facilitated survival.

Approximately 2,000 Jews fought against the Germans and Fascist forces in the Italian Resistance Movement. There were no all-Jewish resistance units in Italy, and Jewish partisans fought in integrated units, both because Jews were proportionately few in Italy and because they were totally assimilated.

More Jews survived in Italy than in other countries also because of the fact that the Holocaust in Italy began late in the autumn of 1943, and by September 1943 most Italians had heard about the deportation of Jews, although they did not believe rumors of extermination. Also by September 1943, after German routs in Russia, North Africa, and Sicily, Hitler's total defeat seemed likely. Italian Jews could hope that they would not have to hide for long. While liberation did not come as quickly as many expected, the danger period was shorter for Jews in Italy than for those in most other occupied countries.

Yet the Holocaust occurred in Italy. Its roots lay in the racial laws imposed upon a reluctant people by their Fascist dictator. Mussolini was ready to collaborate with the Nazis in the extermination of the Jews, and many Italian Jews were deported to the death camps. During the German occupation of Italy, thousands of Italian fanatics endorsed the extermination of the Jews. Most were intimidated, but courageous individuals saved thousands. As in other countries, the Holocaust in Italy was sustained by a terrorized, preoccupied, or indifferent majority.

At the end of the war, about 29,000 Jews remained in Italy, and a further 26,000 refugees, originating mainly from Central and Eastern Europe, were added to this number. Italy was a main gathering place for refugees en route to Eretz Israel, legally or illegally. A certain number settled permanently in Italy.

When we arrived in Rome, we could distinguish three groups of Jews in Italy: the Jews of Rome, the great majority of whom were born there, who partly still lived in the old ghetto, in modest conditions, and with strong bonds with Jewish tradition; other Italian-born Jews, widely scattered geographically, with tenuous links to Judaism, and hence more open to social contacts with non-Jews, mixed marriages, and rapid assimilation; and Jews born abroad, with greater social cohesion, but inclined to adopt the habits and customs of the less vital groups of Italian Jewry.

During our four-year stay in Rome, I studied at the university. In 1955, I returned to Rome to present my thesis, "Israel and its Declaration of Independence," and the Faculty of Political Sciences conferred a doctorate on me.

While we were in Rome, on the night of July 22-23, 1952, a group of Egyptian officers, led by Lieutenant Colonel Nasser, seized control the of country without bloodshed. King Farouk was forced to abdicate and he left the country unharmed. A new government was set up, headed by General Naguib, considered by the Egyptians as a hero of the Palestine war. Nasser, too, had fought in several battles in the war. The change in Egypt was no doubt a turning point in the history of the entire Middle East.

I had a very painful experience in Rome, when a Jew of my acquaintance residing there was arrested in Israel for being a spy for the Egyptians. He was sentenced to fourteen years imprisonment. He was, in fact, a triple agent. He worked for the Israelis, the Egyptians, and the Italians.

Years later, the Israeli security discovered a pro-Syrian espionage and sabotage network, and among those arrested were Jews, known for their extreme left-wing views and believed to have pro-Chinese Communist leanings. The suspects went to Damascus via Europe, received training in arms and sabotage, and passed information to the enemy. A traitor was tried in Israel for having given out secrets on Israeli atomic installations, and another one, not yet caught, had disclosed secrets of the Mossad, Israel's Intelligence organization.

This recalls a case of treason which I witnessed during my activity in the Brichah. As the work of the Brichah in Austria grew more intense, so did the counteraction of the British Intelligence Service. The British sent agents from all corners of the empire, even from Palestine. At times, informers would be recruited from among the refugees themselves, ready, for cash, to divulge what went on in the camps, and more than once the betrayal meant that our transports were stopped.

One day, we caught a Jew who had left Romania with the "hunger escape," passing information about the Brichah to the British. He confessed to collaboration with the secret agents in the British zone in Austria, especially naming a Captain Forley. He confessed to having entered the American zone of Austria, having been suborned by the British to contact an American lieutenant. The password was "Forley." He confessed, also, to informing the British of a convoy from Vienna to the British zone of two hundred and fifty people who were detained and returned to the Russian zone.

For his spying, he received ten American dollars a week from Captain Forley, besides canned food and cigarettes, plus a pass. He was to find out who were the Salzburg members of the Brichah. He admitted that during his short stay in the American zone he had gathered much information, for example, that all the work of the Brichah in Salzburg was being carried out under the protection of American officers.

During the Nazi occupation, too, some Jews were renegades, not for material gain but to survive, only to be murdered by their German masters in the end. True, some members of the councils were traitors, but to generalize is to distort history, for many members were upright and honest people.

My friend Jeanette Nestel told me what happened in Stanislawow ghetto in September 1942. She was coming back to the ghetto from work. On her way, she met a friend who told her that the Judenrat was asked by the Germans to deliver up all the infants. If not, they would pay with their own lives. Jeanette at once took her baby from the ghetto to the home of a Gentile friend. The next day she learned that the members of the Judenrat, having refused to deliver up the infants, had been hanged from the lamp-posts all along the Belvederska Street. They hung for a whole week, for the Jews to see what would happen to anyone who did not collaborate with the Nazis.

In my own town, Simna, the Judenrat acted as the liaison between the Germans and the community, but never did a wrong thing, never gave the Germans any information that was not public knowledge, or hid anything that they knew from the community. On that catastrophic day in September 1941, when the remaining Jews of the town were summoned to the barracks, the chairman of the Judenrat, Faivel Perechansky, passed from door to door handing everybody the summons in person, adding that this was very bad news. He might not have another opportunity, so he came himself, in this darkest hour, to ask forgiveness from each for any harm he might have done. This was a righteous man in a world where every vestige of civilization had vanished. It is Israel's good fortune that we have had fewer traitors than other nations. But the case of the triple agent in Rome is additional proof that there is no immunity.

While in Rome, we also learned of the hair-raising anti-Semitic developments in the Soviet Union, which began in 1948. Headlines in the Soviet press announced that "Jewish volunteers were going to settle in Birobijan." It was the beginning of Stalin's deportation plan. That year, the arrests and liquidations began, including the murder of Solomon Mikhoels, director and star of Moscow's Yiddish State Theater. This was quickly followed by the liquidation of the Jewish Anti-Fascist Committee, set up during the war under the chairmanship of Mikhoels, with the aim of stimulating global Jewish support for the Soviet war effort.

In Stalin's last years, with the advent of the Cold War and official Russian nationalism at its zenith, the image of the Jew as an alien and a "cosmopolitan," took permanent form. In 1952, Yiddish writers were executed. A year later, the Jewish doctor was represented as a foreign agent who, under the cloak of medical science, was murdering Soviet leaders. In February 1953, after a bomb placed by a fanatic exploded in the courtyard of the Soviet embassy in Tel Aviv, the Soviet Union broke off diplomatic relations with Israel.

Although relations were restored a few months later, expanded Soviet support to the Arabs at the U.N. indicated a distinct change in policy and encouraged the Arabs to strain every nerve to defeat Israel by political and economic pressure, constantly threatening a "second round" of war.

The author addressing the Jewish Community in the Great Synagogue of Rome on Hanukkah, 1953. Looking on is Dr. Elio Toaff, Chief Rabbi of Rome

XXIV.

PRIMARY RESPONSIBILITY

The Arab states had laid down their arms in exhaustion and defeat, but there was no disarmament of their spirit or purpose. While Israel regarded the armistice agreements as the end of the war and as a virtual peace settlement in embryo, the Arab governments saw them as a temporary phase in a continuing war which they had never renounced. The Arabs rejected the hand of friendship held out to them by Israel in Paragraph 17 of its Proclamation of Independence:

> We extend the hand of peace and good neighborliness to all the states around us and to their peoples, and we call upon them to cooperate in mutual helpfulness with the independent Jewish nation in its Land. The State of Israel is prepared to make its contribution in a concerted effort for the advancement of the entire Middle East.

The Syrians, Jordanians, and Egyptians very soon began to disturb Israel's internal life. Without risking total war, they resolved to drive Israel out of its collective mind by the constant torment of piecemeal violence. Syria interfered with Israel's irrigation projects in the northern demilitarized zone and opened fire to stop Israeli development work. They attacked Israeli fishing boats and patrol vessels in the Sea of Galilee. They called for the destruction of the "Jewish cancer."

Lebanon, too, called for the liquidation of Israel. The Jordanians began harassing Israel's frontier villages. Numerous attacks were carried out on Israeli civilians and soldiers by infiltrators and Jordanian troops. The infiltrators attacked Israeli buses, killed tens of people, and returned to Jordan where they had a safe haven. Legionaries fired from the Old City walls, killing Jews in Jerusalem.

The Egyptians sent bands of terrorists into Israel, organized from among the Palestinians in the Gaza Strip. The infiltrators, known as *fedayeen* (suicide fighters), penetrated deep into Israel territory. The fedayeen gangs infiltrated Israel every night from all sides: from the Gaza Strip, from Jordan, and from Syria and Lebanon. In Gaza a Palestinian army was formed, well-trained and equipped with the best arms, whose purpose was, in the words of Egypt's Nasser, to "liberate Palestine." The Egyptians tried to make the Negev uninhabitable.

Egypt also intensified its blockade of Israel in the Suez Canal and confiscated cargoes destined for Israel, in spite of a ruling by the U.N. Security Council against maritime interference or active belligerency against Israel as being "inconsistent with the letter and spirit of the Egyptian-Israeli armistice agreement."

Egypt occupied the uninhabited islands of Tiran and Sanafir in the Red Sea at the entrance to the Gulf of Akaba. Later it established a garrison at Sharm el-Sheikh, interfered with Israel and international shipping to and from Eilat, and banned planes from flying over the Straits to or from Israel.

The years 1954-56 were nightmare years for Israel. Raids by Arab armies and terrorists took a heavy toll. It was becoming unsafe to live in an Israeli border settlement and to attempt to go about one's business in the interior of the country. The Israeli public was hot with anger and Israel's army reacted with heavy reprisals, which led to disagreements between Prime Minister David Ben-Gurion and Foreign Minister Moshe Sharett.

Ben-Gurion was a born national leader and fighter, a man who believed in doing rather than explaining, and who was convinced that what would always matter in the end would be what the Israelis did and how they did it, not what the world outside Israel thought or said about them.

"The first question Ben-Gurion always asked himself about almost any issue that came up in those days," writes Golda Meir in her memoirs, "was whether it was in the long run good for the State of Israel....He believed that, ultimately, history would judge Israel on the record of its deeds, not its statements or its diplomacy."

Ben-Gurion rejected the permanent self-questioning by some: "What will the Gentile think or say?" Sharett, on the other hand, was a diplomat and negotiator, concerned with how policymakers elsewhere reacted to Israel and what was likely to make the Jewish state look "good" in the eyes of foreign ministers or the U.N. What he really wanted most for Israel was that it be viewed as a progressive, moderate, civilized European country of whose behavior no Israeli, least of all himself, ever need be ashamed.

Until the 1950s, Ben-Gurion and Sharett worked together despite the differences in their basic personalities, but the question of Israeli retaliation for terrorist acts became a major area of conflict between them. Sharett was as convinced as Ben-Gurion that the incessant incursions across Israel's frontiers by gangs of Arabs had to end, but they disagreed sharply on the method that should be used.

Sharett believed that the most effective way of dealing with this acute situation was to put maximum pressure on the great powers so that they, in turn, would pressure the Arab states to stop aiding and abetting the infiltrators.

Well-worded protests to the U.N., skillful and informed diplomatic notes, and clear, repeated presentation of our case to the world would, he was sure, eventually succeed, whereas armed reprisals by Israel could only result in criticism and make our international position even less comfortable than it was.

But Ben-Gurion still saw his responsibility not to the statesmen of the West or to the U.N., but to the ordinary citizens who lived in the Israeli settlements that were under constant Arab attack. The duty of the government of any state, he believed, was to defend itself and to protect its citizens, regardless of how negative the reaction abroad might be.

There was another consideration of great importance to Ben-Gurion. The citizens of Israel, that conglomeration of people, languages, and cultures, had to learn that the government, and only the government, was responsible for its security. It would have been simpler to permit the formation of anti-terrorist vigilante groups, close an official eye to private acts of retaliation and vengeance, and then disclaim all responsibility for the resultant "incidents." But that was not his way.

The hand extended in peace to the Arabs would remain extended, but at the same time the children of Israeli farmers in border villages were entitled to sleep safely in their beds at night. If the only way to accomplish this was to strike back mercilessly at the Arab gangs, then that would have to be done.

In the meantime, a defense treaty between Iraq and Turkey, linked to one between Turkey and Pakistan, was signed in Baghdad on February 24, 1955. Britain and Iran joined it. The United States did not formally adhere to the pact, but its spiritual father was John Foster Dulles, the American secretary of state, with the main support in arms and money coming from the United States.

The pact was part of Dulles' policy of containing Soviet expansion in the Middle East. Nasser interpreted it as an effort by Washington and London to divide the Arab world into rival blocs corresponding to the East-West division. His position as leader of the Arab world was being challenged, and he responded by an arms deal with the Soviet Union via Czechoslovakia. The Egyptian-Czech massive arms transaction was followed by a Syrian-Czech one. Weapons of destructive capacity poured into Egypt and the region at a rate beyond all previous experience. Large quantities of tanks, artillery, jet planes, submarines were on their way to Egypt.

Israel saw itself now faced with dangers far greater than those presented in the daily border attacks. The border conflicts were threatening Israel's short-term tranquility, while the pursuit of Arab favor by the powers was undermining its long-term security. The actions of the major powers were destined to appease the Arabs, rearming them under defense pacts and arms deals. These powers, however, gave no clear reply to Israel's appeals for arms to redress the balance.

Israel had neither an assured source of arms nor a guarantee of its security, and a wave of anxiety swept the country. Israelis from all walks of life came forward spontaneously with donations of cash and jewelry for the purchase of arms.

On July 26, 1956, Egypt announced that it had nationalized the Suez Canal. Although this Egyptian action had arisen from the decision of the United States not to finance the Egyptian Aswan Dam scheme, it was Britain and France who were under threat. Both countries now found themselves with a growing anxiety over the danger posed by Egyptian control of the Suez Canal to their supplies, communications, and interests.

While the United States still refused to sell arms to Israel, it consented to France supplying Israel with advanced Mystère aircraft. Large quantities of French heavy armaments were sent and unloaded in secret. Once French and Israeli policies *vis-à-vis* Nasser had converged, Britain, too, joined them.

The London newspaper *Daily Sketch* described the feeling in London in those days: "The time has come for Israel to do for the West what the West had not done for Israel." London and Paris finally realized that Nasser was a mad dictator and that they must crush his ambitions with force, and the sooner the better.

Britain and France went forward with military warnings and preparations. On October 17, 1956, Egypt and Syria signed a military pact. On October 25, after an election victory for pro-Nasserist elements in Jordan, that country joined the Egyptian-Syrian military pact. The three armies were placed under the command of Nasser and a military alliance against Israel was announced.

At the U.N., Israeli Ambassador Abba Eban tried to explain his country's predicament. No one in the world community was in Israel's position: hundreds of its citizens killed by the action of armies across the frontier; its ships seized and their cargoes confiscated in international waterways; it was surrounded by hostile armies on all its land frontiers; it was subjected to savage and relentless hostility; exposed to penetration, raids, and assaults by day and by night; threatened by neighboring governments to accomplish its extinction by armed force; overshadowed by a menace of irresponsible rearmament; embattled, blockaded, besieged. The noose was tightening around Israel's neck.

If resistance were not made now, a future decision to make it might be too late. The nation's security, interest, honor, and morale could not indefinitely withstand the forward surge of Nasser's arrogance. Moreover, for the first time, there was a prospect that if Israel struck out in her own defense, she might not be alone. Others would understand her, would regard her action as legitimate and salutary, and perhaps give her aid.

The tension and disagreements between Ben-Gurion and Sharett reached a climax. Sharett had to leave. Golda Meir was named foreign minister and the road was open for the Sinai Campaign. On October 27, Ben-Gurion submitted to the cabinet a proposal for a large-scale operation to demolish the bases of the fedayeen and the Egyptian army in the Sinai Peninsula and the Gaza Strip and to occupy the shore of the Gulf of Akaba in order to safeguard navigation.

Israel mobilized its forces and, on October 29, its troops moved into Sinai, capturing vital points on the peninsula, and threatening the Suez Canal. Israeli fighter planes established air superiority over the combat areas. On the afternoon of October 30, Britain and France issued an ultimatum calling on both sides to stop fighting and withdraw to ten miles on either side of the Suez Canal. That evening they vetoed a U.S.-sponsored resolution in the Security Council calling for immediate withdrawal of Israeli troops. Israel accepted the Anglo-French demand, but since Egypt rejected it, its advance continued. In five days the Israeli army captured Gaza, Rafah, Al Arish, and thousands of prisoners and occupied most of the peninsula east of the Suez Canal. Israel suffered one hundred and ninety killed.

The British and the French invaded Egypt after bombing its airfields. But their invasion went slowly and did not achieve its goals. Soviet-American pressure forced the British and French to withdraw. Who can understand the logic of President Eisenhower and Foreign Secretary Dulles in supporting the Soviets to humiliate Washington's allies?

Heavy Soviet-American pressure was also put on Israel to withdraw, and they threatened her with sanctions. The General Assembly of the U.N. called on Israel, on November 2, 1956, to withdraw her forces from Sinai and Ben-Gurion stated that Israel would withdraw its forces from Egyptian territory when arrangements had been made for a U.N. emergency force to replace British and French troops, who had seized part of the Suez Canal.

Ben-Gurion delayed the withdrawal until he had assurance that the U.N. emergency force would be stationed within the borders of Egypt to prevent raiding from either side and to maintain free navigation in the Gulf of Akaba. A force of 4,500 men took over its task in December. Israel withdrew from Gaza in March. Israel's achievements in the Sinai Campaign were: the Egyptian army had been demolished, the fedayeen gangs in Gaza destroyed, the maritime blockade broken, the Red Sea opened to navigation, the threat to Israel's existence removed, unfortunately, only temporarily.

*Left to right: Aba Gefen, Frida Gefen, and Count Henrik Potocki
(Lima, Peru, 1958)*

*Aba Gefen greets Peru's president, Dr. Manuel Prada,
at the Presidential Palace in Lima (1957)*

XXV.

SANCTIFICATION OF THE DIVINE NAME

After two years in the Research Division of the Ministry of Foreign Affairs in Jerusalem, in the spring of 1956 I was appointed first secretary at our embassy in Moscow. But I thought it would be dangerous for me to go to Moscow, since I had left the Soviet Union illegally, and I was considered by the Russians as a deserter. A few months later, therefore, I was appointed first secretary at our embassy in Lima, Peru.

We arrived there in November 1956. From the airport we were taken to the Hotel Bolivar, and there I got my first shock. When I asked the clerk at the information desk for advice on where to buy what I wanted, I was told to try a store on the nearby Matajudíos ("Kill the Jews") Street! True, the name had been changed, but people had not forgotten the old name and still used it.

Our daughter, Ruhama, was eight years old at the time and became friendly with a neighbor's child her age. One day, invited to the neighbor's home, Ruhama saw for the first time in her life a painting of the Last Supper. Her friend's mother, noting that Ruhama was a stranger, inquired where she came from. Ruhama replied, very proudly, "I am Jewish, I am from Israel!"

"Jewish?" exclaimed Ruhama's young friend, "*Los Judíos son diablos.*" "The Jews are devils!"

It was a bitter episode, but not surprising. After all, Lima is called the City of the Inquisition. When I accompanied our ambassador on his way to present his credentials to the president of Peru, we traversed a street along which, some four hundred years ago, Jewish martyrs, *los Marranos*, nominal converts from Judaism to the Christian faith, were dragged to the stake.

Since Peru was a Spanish colony, a regional inquisitional tribunal was opened in Lima in 1570, although an active episcopal inquisition had been in existence since 1539. Between 1569 and 1620, fifty-nine "heretics" were burned there. The Jews perished sanctifying God's name: *Kiddush Ha-Shem.*

Those Marranos, who went on living their clandestine lives in Spain, heroically handed on their Jewish traditions in secret from generation to generation, subjected to the horrors of the Inquisition. The Inquisition in Peru was finally abolished by the South American liberator, San Martín, in 1822.

After the unrest in Germany and Austria, which followed the revolution of 1848, a new period of Jewish life began in Peru. Ten years later, around 1880, Sephardi Jews, mainly from North Africa, began to arrive in Peru, and as early as World War One, some Sephardi Jews from Turkey and Syria went to Lima as merchants. After the war, more arrived from the ravished Turkish Empire. As early as World War I, Ashkenazi Jews began to arrive in Peru, most of them refugees from Bessarabia, especially from the Romanian border town of Novoselitsa. For many years Peru was a sort of America for Bessarabian Jews, who came there to make a few dollars peddling, and then return home to their *shtetl*. After the war, it became increasingly difficult to live in the stifling anti-Semitic atmosphere of the East European countries, nor was there much impulse to return to these lands which were in the throes of economic depression. Letters to friends and relatives in their native countries attracted many to come.

When we arrived in Lima, there were more than 4,000 Jews in Peru, most of whom lived in the capital, Lima. A small number lived in remote areas among primitive natives, and tiny Jewish communities could be found all through the interior. The Jewish communities in Lima were united through a central committee, and the presidency was regularly alternated among the three *kehillot*. There were then three rabbis: a Sephardi, a German, and an East European, and the Israeli ambassador and I prayed in all three synagogues.

We found in Lima a very good Jewish school for our children. Its enrollment included a number of non-Jewish children who were taught the Hebrew part of the curriculum along with the others. The Jewish school is named after the Marrano, Leon de Pinelo, who was a poet, theologian, student of colonial culture, as well as historian. He wrote a history of the Incas.

We soon learned that many descendants of the Jews, now no longer part of the Jewish people, often sought the occasion to meet Jews and talk of their common origin, sometimes with longing and regret. We were told that at the time of the creation of the State of Israel a number of aristocratic families in Peru stated that they were descendants of Jews. They considered it preferable to be of Jewish descent than of Indian origin, or to stem from Spanish conquistadors.

The German immigrants found that the surviving descendants of the Marranos had been absorbed into the indigenous population. These immigrants established a rudimentary form of community structure—a free loan fund (*gemilat chasadim*) and provision for the sick (*bikur choilim*), and on Rosh Hashanah and Yom Kippur they prayed in the Masonic temple. It was only in 1870, when an English-Jewish engineer who built the railway across the Andes contributed land for a cemetery, that the German-Jewish community was officially registered in Lima.

XXVI.

TO HOLD FAST TO THE BIBLE

In 1959, we left Lima a bigger family. Our son Yehudah was born in the Peruvian capital, and we named him after my youngest brother, may he rest in peace.

We found a different Israel. In the period before the Sinai Campaign, many in the world still doubted Israel's durability. In 1959 no one doubted it any more, and the people of Israel looked to the future with vitality and optimism. In the international arena, however, Israel often found itself entirely alone. France continued to be an ally and a good friend, and a few other European countries were sympathetic to us. Though the Americans became more alert to the danger of neglecting Israel's security risks, our relationship with the United States continued to be strained; with the Soviet bloc it was worse than strained.

In Asia, our campaign against Egypt had evoked disapproval, though it had also inspired respect. In spite of having established diplomatic missions in some of the Asian countries, we were misunderstood and unpopular, while the Asian Moslem states were openly hostile to us. We were among the first nations to recognize Communist China, but the Chinese did not want an Israeli embassy in Peking and, at the conference of Asian and African nations in Bandung in 1955, they joined the anti-Israel bloc of states.

The so-called "Third World," where the leaders of India, Nehru, and of Yugoslavia, Tito, played decisive roles, looked toward Nasser and the Arabs and away from us. Describing our position at the U.N. in the years 1957 and 1958, Golda Meir wrote:

> I used to look around me and think: we have no family here. No one who shares our religion, our language, or our past. The rest of the world seems to be grouped into blocs that have sprung up because geography and history have combined to give common interests to their peoples. But our neighbors and natural allies don't want to have anything to do with us, and we really belong nowhere and to no one, except to ourselves. We were the first-born of the United Nations, but we were being treated like unwanted step-children, and I must admit that it hurt.

Still, the world was not entirely made up of Europeans and Asians; there were also the emerging nations of Africa, then on the verge of achieving their independence. Israel believed there was much it could offer to those black states-in-the-making. Israel's experience was unique because it had been forced to find solutions to problems that wealthy, powerful states had never encountered. Israel couldn't offer Africa money or arms but, on the other hand, it was free of the taint of the colonial exploiters. All that Israel wanted from Africa was friendship. True, it had another motive, which wasn't trivial. It wanted votes in our favor at the U.N. but that was not the most important aim.

A separate department for relations with Africa was formed at the Ministry of Foreign Affairs, and I was attached to it. I worked in the department only six months and was transferred to head the director-general's office, but I followed with admiration the wonderful work and achievements of my colleagues in Africa. Between 1959 and 1973, thousands of Israeli experts in agriculture, hydrology, regional planning, public health, engineering, community services, medicine, and scores of other fields had been sent to Africa. Thousands of Africans were trained in Israel during those years. In the wake of the Yom Kippur War, most of the African states broke off their relations with Israel.

From the director-general's office I was moved to the Information Department, and one of my first functions was to accompany a very important guest, a European diplomat, on his visit to the Holocaust Chamber, next to David's Tomb on Mount Zion, dedicated to those who had died under the Nazis, and to Yad Vashem, the Martyrs' and Heroes' Remembrance Authority. The task of Yad Vashem, as defined in the 1953 law establishing it, is "to gather in material regarding all those Jewish people who laid down their lives, who fought and rebelled against the Nazi enemy and their collaborators, and to perpetuate their memory and that of the communities, organizations, and institutions which were destroyed because they were Jewish...and for research and documentation." A memorial hall, a synagogue, a museum of the Holocaust and the Hall of Names containing the names of the victims, collected through testimonies from relatives in Israel and abroad, were set up as well as facilities to provide for ceremonies of communion, memorial gatherings, and documentary exhibits.

It is the general opinion that diplomats are prudent and careful people, and that even the harshest things are pronounced by them in "diplomatic language." But when I accompanied my European colleague to the Holocaust Chamber and Yad Vashem, I learned that diplomats, too, are mortal, and cannot stand calmly in face of such things. Our guest forgot the rules of caution, which he had himself studied and which he had taught his disciples, facing the jars of Zyklon B gas used by the Germans to poison their Jewish victims in the extermination camps, and the soap sold by the Germans and their collaborators with a label on it saying "it was made of pure Jewish fat."

He saw the yellow badge and the shirt, shoes, and purses made of the parchment of the Holy Scrolls; he faced the prayer-shawl and the bloodstained Holy Book of the Law, which the victims did not abandon even when death was in full sight.

When he saw all that, he forgot that in a few days he was to go to Germany for commercial negotiations, and he said, "The Germans are a mixture of talent and brutality, and whoever did such things once might do them again." It was July 1960, a short time after Adolf Eichmann was captured in Argentina and was going to be tried in Israel, unfolding day by day in gory detail, for two years, the mystery of man's infinite degradation that had so shocked our diplomat guest.

Eichmann, living in Argentina as "Ricardo Clement," was abducted in Buenos Aires while walking home from a factory where he worked. His trial was exemplary in its dignity and judicial precision. The court of three judges heard hundreds of witnesses whose stories were so macabre and agonizing that the whole nation was stunned by a new flow of grief. But of far greater gravity than the justice meted out to a single odious monster was the electrifying effect of the trial on world opinion and on Israel's young generation. A bright light was thrown on the Jewish people as history's most poignant victim. One of the underlying motivations of Israel's struggle for freedom and security was brought into clear view.

Eichmann's secret arrest in Argentina by Israel's Security Services, his transfer to Israel, his trial and hanging in 1962, presented, however, a danger of worsening Israel's relations not only with Argentina, but all the Latin American bloc. Argentina asked that the Israeli ambassador be recalled and brought a complaint to the U.N. Security Council. But the irregularity of the capture struck most of the world as secondary to the greater drama: here was an arch-criminal, an assassin of Jewish masses, brought to trial in a Jewish homeland.

The countries of Latin America understood Israel's motives and sympathized with them. But as long as the issue with Argentina was not settled, they were on Argentina's side, no matter who was right. Israel, therefore, did everything possible to restore its relations with Argentina to normalcy and, accidents and unpleasantness notwithstanding, things began to improve.

In 1963 a new Israeli ambassador, General Joseph Avidar, was appointed to Buenos Aires. As time passed, relations with Argentina returned to their traditional cordiality, as they did with the other countries of the region. The Latin American bloc had played a decisive role in the 1947 deliberations at the U.N. when it was decided to create the Jewish state and, since then, full diplomatic relations have been established by Israel with every Latin American country and have developed satisfactorily in all fields: political, cultural, economic, and in the sphere of technical and scientific cooperation.

At the same time, Israel has continually strengthened its brotherly ties with the Jewish communities there, a total of 750,000 souls in those days, identified unconditionally with Israel and its supporters in all possible ways. Latin American gentiles consider the links of their Jewish fellow-citizens with Israel as natural and normal. Indeed, in all democratic lands, non-Jews look favorably upon the ties between their Jewish fellow-citizens and Israel, almost to the extent of regarding them as Israeli "colonies." This point of view is especially understandable in Latin Americans, who are attached to a motherland, of their own, Spain, and to a religious spiritual center, the Vatican. They comprehend that for Jews, similarly, Israel is both motherland and religious spiritual center.

In November 1963, after having served for a short time as our Foreign Ministry's spokesman, I was sent to our embassy in Buenos Aires as first counsellor.

There were times in Argentina when many Jews held fast to the Bible, when Jewish colonization began there and the immigrants came accompanied by their ritual slaughterers (*shochatim*) and rabbis. In time, isolation and lack of Jewish education caused a decline in religious life. On the other hand, many of those who settled in the cities, especially those who arrived after the abortive Russian Revolution in 1905, were immigrants to whom religion had little meaning.

Unofficially, there are historic traces of the Marranos who fled the Inquisition. Buenos Aires was a free port and the Marranos sought refuge there. Some historians credit the Marranos with being pioneers of Argentine development. Officially, however, Argentina's Jewish community, which is the largest in Latin America, came into being in 1860 when, on November 11, the first Jewish wedding was solemnized in Argentina. In 1862, the first Jewish congregation, the Libertad Synagogue, was established. Its founders were mainly Jews from Alsace-Lorraine.

Pogroms in Russia in 1881 brought many Jews to Argentina. But large-scale immigration began in the late 1880s, when echoes of Argentina's prodigious efforts to attract immigration reached eastern Europe. A government agent was appointed to invite Russian Jewish immigrants; this decision produced vehement anti-Semitic attacks in the press. Most of the immigrants were Ashkenazim (Yiddish-speaking, from eastern Europe), but a small number of Sephardim (Ladino-speaking) came from the Ottoman Empire and North Africa.

Immigration increased after the Jewish Colonization Association was established in 1896 by Baron Maurice de Hirsch. The Jewish agricultural colonization in Argentina was a byproduct of Jewish love and yearning for the land of Israel. In July 1889, before Baron de Hirsch began his plan for Jewish colonization in Argentina, an attempt had been made by a group of Russian Jews to make their way to Palestine to become farm workers there. The one hundred and thirty families in this group were marooned in Germany, en route, without funds to make their way further.

The Alliance Israelite Universelle, based in Paris, took an interest in them but, instead of sending them on to Palestine, diverted them to Argentina. Arrangements had been made there for the purchase of certain stretches of land. Upon their arrival, they found the fields barren, and they suffered from starvation. More than sixty children died of exposure and hunger during that first season.

It was in the ensuing months, when the Jewish world rose up on alarm over this tragedy, that Baron de Hirsch, created the Jewish Colonization Association to assist Jews to emigrate from Russia into countries where they could develop freely and become productive persons through labor on the land.

Jewish colonization in Argentina did not attract the masses, but despite the movement into the cities, the Jewish colonies have remained to this day the special pride of the Jewish community. I witnessed it when I attended, in 1965, the celebration of seventy-five years of Jewish colonization in Argentina, held in the village of Moisesville.

Moisesville is the oldest Jewish agricultural colony in Argentina. It was the glory of Argentine-Jewish colonization; in its "golden age" it was considered the "Jerusalem of Argentina."

Argentina's Jews are proud of their educational system, made possible by the economic rise of the community. Within years, the former peddlers became owners of factories and were integrated into the Argentine economy. Utilizing their vitality, energy, and contacts abroad, they built up important industries, especially during the world wars when Argentina was neutral. Jews developed the furniture and leather industries, and weavers from Lodz and Bialystok built factories and developed a great textile industry.

What were small and primitive free-loan funds grew into large Jewish banks, and the old Chevra Kadisha, whose sole function was to bury the dead, became a centralized *Kehilla* (community) with facilities and personnel embracing all aspects of Jewish life, education, culture, and philanthropy in Argentina.

When we arrived in Buenos Aires, we realized that the number of children receiving Jewish education was between twenty and twenty-five percent of the total. The increasing number of drop-outs each year was illustrated by the fact that in 1967, our last year there, in all the schools run by the Jewish community, only five hundred pupils finished elementary and one hundred graduated from high school. It was estimated then that only twelve percent of Argentina's Jewish youth was active in community organizations.

During our stay there, for four years, there were two newspapers in Yiddish: the *Presse* and the *Yiddishe Zeitung*. The second and third generations, with very little exception, no longer speak Yiddish. We were told that the majority of the cultural and educational leaders of Argentina's Jewish communities are the children and grandchildren of the colonists. Their education and training in the environment of the colonies imbued them with a sound and healthy spirit which brought new blood to the cities and made valuable contributions to Jewish community life.

When my wife and I were in Moisesville, we went to the cemetery which is a memorial of the sufferings and martyrdom of the Jews who came as colonists to Argentina. There stand many of the graves of the pioneers of Moisesville who were murdered by the half-savage natives years ago. While some historians insist that the murders of Jewish settlers in the colonies resembled incidents between gauchos and settlers of other origins, there are others who describe the events as anti-Semitic.

From 1933 onward, anti-Semitic activity increased, encouraged by German diplomatic institutions and by the local branch of the Nazi Party until it became a central problem for Argentine Jewry. Their worsening security compelled, in 1939, all factions, Ashkenazi and Sephardi, to unite and form a common organization, the D.A.I.A. (the Delegation of Argentine Jewish Institutions), which began to fight for the right of Jews to be free from persecution.

Juan Peron's rise to power, in 1946, prompted fears among the Jewish population because he had been aided by the Fascist organization, *Alianza Libertadora Nacionalista* and was known to sympathize with the Nazi government in Germany. Buenos Aires became a center for anti-Semitic publications and neo-Nazi activity on a large scale. Jewish immigration was stopped entirely, while Argentina welcomed thousands of Nazis and their collaborators escaping from Europe. The overthrow of Peron, in 1955, was accompanied by an increase in anti-Semitic activities, especially by *Tacuara*, the racist pro-Nazi terrorist group. These activities were further expanded after the capture of Adolph Eichmann and his execution in Israel.

After June 1966, when General Carlos Onganía seized power, anti-Semitic organizations became adherents of the new regime and, by 1967, when we left Buenos Aires, despite the placatory declarations of the government, Argentina continued to be a center of anti-Semitic activity. Of the 313 anti-Jewish incidents recorded in the world in 1967, 142 occurred in Argentina.

Between 1963 and 1967, our period of service in Argentina, the anti-Semites were aided by representatives of the Arab League there. The increase of these operations heightened the efforts of D.A.I.A. Among its activities was the annual ceremony commemorating the Warsaw Ghetto Uprising. At the ceremony in 1963, which I attended and addressed, 20,000 people were present.

Aba Gefen speaking at the 21st anniversary commemoration
of the Warsaw Ghetto Uprising (Buenos Aires)

XXVII.

CRITICAL EVENTS

Important internal political changes took place in Israel as a result of the security "mishap" of 1954. An ill-conceived operation by Israel's Intelligence Service, it was marked by explosions in Cairo calculated to embroil Egypt with the western powers. It led to the execution of some Jews in Egypt and the prolonged imprisonment of others. The uncertainty about the initiative for these acts led to the resignation of defense minister Pinhas Lavon, considered responsible for the operation. In the second half of 1960, Pinhas Lavon claimed that new evidence, recently disclosed, proved that he had not been responsible for the security "mishap" that had led to his resignation.

In the meantime, he had been appointed secretary-general of the *Histadruth*, Israel's Federation of Labor, but his further progress in the political field was blocked by the memory of the old affair. Lavon's efforts to clear his name developed into a bitter controversy with Ben-Gurion and his supporters, coming to a climax in Lavon's removal from his Histadruth post. At the same time, a second aspect of the controversy emerged: the decision of a cabinet committee clearing Lavon. Ben-Gurion denounced this decision as a misuse of authority and a miscarriage of justice, and he decided to fight this matter to the very end and to rectify it.

Gradually, Ben-Gurion lost the unchallenged authority he had enjoyed before. His position with the public as well as in his Labor Party was deteriorating and, in June 1963, he resigned. Levi Eshkol, then finance minister, replaced him as prime minister.

Six months after our arrival in Buenos Aires, in May 1964, almost a year after he had taken over as prime minister, Eshkol was faced with the establishment of the so-called "Palestine Liberation Organization" headed by Ahmed Shukeiry, and the adoption of the "Palestinian Covenant," in which the Palestinians negate absolutely the right of existence of the State of Israel. They declare that only the Palestinian Arabs possess the right of self-determination and that the country belongs to them alone, while the Jews have no right whatever to sovereignty or political independence there.

The Palestinian Covenant was to serve as an ideological basis for the struggle against Israel. The document states that the Palestinians will struggle for the liberation of all of Palestine and that armed warfare against Israel is legal, while Israel's self-defense is illegal. According to the covenant, only those Jews who lived in Palestine before 1917, the year of the Balfour Declaration, will be permitted to live in "liberated Palestine."

The covenant rejects any solution except for the "liberation of Palestine by the Arabs." The previous demand for the "return of the Arab refugees to their homes" is replaced by the demand for the "restoration of the legitimate rights of the Arabs in Palestine." The "Palestinian Covenant" is the basic document of the PLO, and in its name, Arab spokesmen swear to eliminate Israel.

Two Arab summit conferences of 1964 and 1965 both sought to postpone armed conflict, but in fact, to keep its prospect alive in policy and rhetoric and to stir enough irritation to prevent any long-term tranquility. On July 11, 1965, Nasser said, "The final account with Israel will be made within five years if we are patient. The Moslems waited seventy years before they expelled the Crusaders from Palestine."

A year later, however, Nasser grew impatient and, certain that the Arabs could achieve Israel's elimination, a Joint Arab Command was established under Egyptian General Amer to plan an eventual military assault, while the *Fatah*, the military arm of the PLO, developed the ideology of a "people's war" and engaged in continual terrorist activities within Israel's territory.

The constant terrorist activities carried out by Fatah from Syrian territory were fully supported by the Syrian Ba'ath regime and created ever-growing tension. The revolutionary Ba'ath regime in Syria, established in 1963, sought to appear as the main champion of the Palestinians and the most extreme in its hatred of Israel. Syria became Moscow's favorite ally.

On November 3, 1966, Egypt and Syria signed a war pact. The raids into Israel continued and there was a chain of mutual commitments among Syria, Egypt, and the Soviet Union to keep Israel under murderous harassment while protecting Syria from reprisals. After several terrorist raids, the Syrians attacked Israeli farmers in the Sea of Galilee area. The exchange of fire escalated from machine-guns to artillery and from artillery to aircraft.

In an air encounter on April 7, 1967, six Syrian MIG aircraft were brought down, two of them in the territory of Jordan. The extent of the Syrian defeat was unexpected even in Israel.

The leaders in the Kremlin were furious. This debacle might completely undermine the Arab states' trust in Soviet protection. The Soviets were afraid to participate directly in the fighting, which might have invited a confrontation with the United States, so they prodded the Egyptians to rescue Syria from its self-inflicted humiliation, and supplied Cairo with false information that Israel was concentrating massive armed forces on the Syrian border. It was, of course, a gross lie, and Israeli Prime Minister Levi Eshkol invited the Soviet ambassador and his attachés to get into a car, without prior notice, and search for the "massive Israeli concentrations" they said were lurking in the north. The ambassador replied that his function was to communicate Soviet truths, not to test their veracity. At the same time, however, the secretary-general of the U.N. reported publicly that no exceptional Israeli troop concentrations existed at all.

On May 15, 1967, Israel's Independence Day, Nasser began dispatching, with conspicuous publicity, large numbers of Egyptian troops into Sinai, and convoys were routed through Cairo's busiest streets on their way to Ismailia. That day,

Egypt demanded the withdrawal of the U.N. Emergency Force (UNEF) from the Gaza Strip, from Sinai borders, and from Sharm el-Sheikh. Israel had agreed earlier to withdraw from the Sinai Peninsula after satisfactory arrangements had been concluded for the deployment of the UNEF on the borders between Israel and Egypt, and Israel had been given assurances by the U.N. as well as by the United States that the dangerous situation to its security on its border with Egypt would never repeat itself. These assurances were null and void ten years later.

Confronted with Nasser's demand, U Thant, U.N. secretary-general, replied that any such request would be regarded as a demand for the UNEF's complete withdrawal. Nasser then officially requested the evacuation of the Force and, on May 19, the UNEF Commander, General Rikhye, told Israel that it would cease to function on that day.

On May 22 Nasser took the fatal step of blockading the Straits of Tiran against Israeli ships and on ships carrying cargoes to Israel. Egypt brought up 90,000 troops facing Israel's southern region, concentrated nine hundred tanks and their advanced force within swift striking distance of Israel, and occupied the entrance to the Straits of Tiran. Nasser declared he was now prepared to wage total war on Israel. Radio Cairo announced, "The existence of Israel has continued too long. The great hour has come. The battle has come in which we shall destroy Israel."

In Israel, a sense of renewed vulnerability was coming to the surface. Here was the specter of genocide again and the destruction of everything that Israel had achieved in its nineteen years of existence as an independent state. The Jewish population in May 1967 was almost two and a half million, and now in danger of extinction, as the surrounding Arab states thundered that they would destroy Israel and divide its territory among themselves.

Egypt no longer pretended to present its actions as meant to protect Syria. It spoke openly and clearly of its preparations for the destruction of Israel, and Ahmed Shukeiry, the head of the PLO, when asked by a French television reporter what they would do with the Jewish children after that destruction and dismemberment, replied, "This they would decide after the victory, if any children survived." For Shukeiry murder of one and a half million Jewish children by Hitler was not enough. Israel prepared for the worst.

Under the looming shadow of war, the organization and training of the reserve units was brought up to highest pitch, while older men, women, and schoolchildren helped to keep services going. Many worked overtime without pay to bring in the harvest, keep up supplies, and fill export orders. The government announced that ample supplies of food were available and kept the warehouses open until late at night so that shops could replenish stocks. The country anxiously awaited a government decision to end the uncertainty, and army leaders pressed for action.

Widespread demands were made for the establishment of a government of national unity to strengthen public confidence and, specifically, for the appointment of General Moshe Dayan, who had been Israel's chief-of-staff in the Sinai Campaign of 1956, as defense minister.

On May 30, King Hussein of Jordan arrived in Cairo, signed a military pact with Egypt, and placed his forces under Egyptian control. Five days later, Iraq followed Hussein's example. Egyptian, Saudi Arabian, and Iraqi troops were sent to Jordan, and Iraqi, Algerian, and Kuwaiti forces to Egypt.

On June 1, Dayan was appointed Defense Minister, enhancing national morale. With the inclusion of Menachem Begin, the opposition leader and previous chief of the Irgun Zvai Leumi, in the government as Minister without portfolio, the government of national unity was complete. On June 3, Radio Cairo quoted an order of the day by General Murtaji, commander of the Egyptian Forces in Sinai, hailing "the Holy War to restore the rights of the Arabs which have been stolen in Palestine, and to reconquer the plundered soil of Palestine."

The world's reaction was, unfortunately, the same apathy and deplorable indifference that had cost the lives of a third of the Jewish people in the Holocaust, and the Jews saw the State of Israel, which had become the symbol of Jewish survival, in danger of destruction. The Jewish state, founded and built up in part by the shattered remnants who escaped the gas chambers and by refugees from Europe and Arab lands, was now threatened with annihilation. There were those who tried to differentiate between the State of Israel and the Jewish people, between Jews and Zionists, but during the days of May 1967, Jews all over the world saw Israel, reborn as the child of them all, in mortal danger, and themselves jeopardized with it. The Jews are not only a religion, as are Catholics or Protestants. Judaism is both a nation and a creed. The Jews have been a nation for thousands of years and in the Land of Israel.

"We have guarded the Book for thousands of years and it has guarded us," said David Ben-Gurion. "It is a Jewish duty, therefore, to hold fast to the Bible."

Surrounded by Arab forces likely to attack at any moment, Israel could delay no longer. On the morning of June 5, the Israel air forces attacked Egypt's airfields and destroyed most of its planes on the ground. In less than three hours, Israel achieved complete superiority in the air and the Israeli government conveyed, through the U.N., a message to the king of Jordan, expressing the hope that he would remain outside the conflict, promising that Israel would attack nowhere unless it was attacked.

Hussein, however, made his fateful mistake. Almost immediately, his forces launched a destructive and unprovoked assault all along the armistice line, occupied U.N. headquarters in East Jerusalem, and indiscriminately shelled the Jewish areas in the city, killing scores of its citizens and wounding hundreds. Israel repelled the attack and on the same day destroyed the Jordanian air force and inflicted heavy casualties on the Syrian and Iraqi air forces.

By dawn on Friday, June 8, all of the Sinai peninsula was in Israel's hands and its forces were encamped along the Canal and the Gulf of Suez. The Gaza Strip had been taken and Israeli naval forces had captured Sharm el-Sheikh. All of Judea and Samaria were won, including the Old City of Jerusalem, which was taken by a paratroop unit. When Moshe Dayan paid his first visit to the Old City of Jerusalem, on June 7, he said, "We have unified Jerusalem, the divided capital of

Israel. We have returned to the holiest of our holy places never to depart from it again."

With the fighting over in the south and the center, the Israel air force attacked the heavily fortified artillery positions on the Golan Heights and in two days Israeli soldiers reached the town of Kuneitra, on the main road to Damascus. The Security Council called for a cease-fire and, with its acceptance by Israel, Egypt, Jordan, Lebanon, and Syria, the Six-Day War came to an end. Israel's casualties in the war were 777 killed and 2,586 wounded.

Israel's soldiers fought heroically, buoyed up by the knowledge that they were not alone, that they had an uncompromising ally in Jews all over the world. They were an inspiring source of fortitude for the people of Israel, partners in a victory that averted a second Holocaust. How different had been feelings of the abandoned Jews under Nazi occupation!

The unusual tension felt by world Jewry during the Six-Day War and the tremendous relief that followed Israel's victory, inspired Jews all over the world. We were then still in Buenos Aires, except for our daughter Ruhama. On reaching the age of eighteen, she had left for Israel to enrol in the armed services, and in March 1967 she joined the navy.

In Argentina, there were then over half a million Jews, including many old Socialists, and I remember one of them telling me that he was ashamed of being a Socialist when the "Socialist" Soviet Union was inciting the Arabs to destroy Israel, and that he was ashamed of being a man when humanity did nothing to prevent a new genocide. The one thing he was not ashamed of, he said, was being a Jew, because now it was a great honor, more than ever, to be Jewish.

The outcome of the Six-Day War was a bitter setback to those who had been its prime instigators. Israel held 26,476 square miles of territory previously in Arab hands: 444 square miles on the Golan Heights; 2,270 square miles in Judea and Samaria; 140 square miles in the Gaza Strip; and 23,622 square miles in Sinai. All those areas, except for Jerusalem, were to be administered under the cease-fire agreements by the Israeli military government.

In Jerusalem, the nineteen-year-old barriers between its eastern and western parts were removed, and the City of God, spiritual shrine and center for all the Jews on earth, was again united. A law was passed by the Knesset extending the limits of Jerusalem and the jurisdiction of Israel law to the eastern part of the city, which had been sundered from it during the War of Independence. It had been occupied by Jordan and, for nineteen years Jerusalem the Golden, the City of Peace, of which the Talmud says, "Ten portions of beauty descended to the world, of which Jerusalem took nine while the remaining tenth was distributed to the rest of the world," had been bisected by barbed wire and concrete barriers.

Arab soldiers, along the artificial frontier through the heart of the city would open fire at will, wounding and killing Israelis. The Jordanian government forbade Jewish identity. The Jewish Quarter of the walled city was practically destroyed and scores of synagogues there were laid waste. The ancient Jewish cemetery on the Mount of Olives was desecrated and partly demolished. In its dishonoring of a solemn obligation in the armistice agreement Jordan had signed with Israel, no Jews in Israel or from anywhere in the world were allowed access to their most sacred shrine, the Western (Wailing) Wall, or to any place, beyond the artificial frontier, steeped in Jewish history, religion, and tradition.

The Moslem Arab citizens of Israel were not permitted to make their personal devotions in the territory under Jordan's rule. In May 1967, the Temple Mount became a camp for the Jordanian militia.

Throughout history, Jerusalem has known many rulers. But for the Jews, only three times has it been the capital of the nation living in this land. Until the destruction of the First Temple it was the capital of the kingdom of David and his successors. Until the destruction of the Second Temple it was once more the capital of the Jewish people. In 1948, it became again the capital of the Jewish state. At all other times, Jerusalem was ruled by foreigners: Babylonians, Greeks, Romans, Byzantines, Persians, Arabs, Crusaders, Ayyubids and Mamelukes, Ottomans and British and, between 1948 and 1967, a part of the city was ruled by Jordan from the Hashemite capital in Amman.

The Jews of Jerusalem today are the inhabitants with the longest unbroken historical association with it. Their memory of Jerusalem is recorded in the Bible, the Mishnah, and the Talmud, in prayer and poetry. Once every year on the ninth day of the month of Av, the Jewish people fast and mourn the destruction of Jerusalem. On festivals, they bless each other as they do on the night of the Seder of Passover, "Next year in Jerusalem!"

The Psalmist sang of Jerusalem, "If I forget thee, O Jerusalem, let my right hand wither! Let my tongue cleave to my mouth if I remember thee not, if I prize not Jerusalem above all my joys." These dramatic words are no empty verbiage for the Jewish people, but a living reality, a part of their daily awareness. All the occasions of life, of rejoicing and of sorrow, are marked by the anguish of the destruction of Jerusalem. No joy is ever total. A wedding ends with the groom breaking a goblet of glass underfoot to remind the guests that no Jewish bliss can be perfect because of the ruin of Jerusalem. That ruin was more than the devastation of the holiest of the holy places of Judaism, of the national capital. It struck at the very existence of the people.

This bond of Jewish memory of Jerusalem is engraved upon its ancient stones and structures now being uncovered by archaeologists. Remnants have been revealed of the City of David, of the days of the First Temple, and of the Second Temple. The Western Wall of the Second Temple has stood as a focus of Jewish longings for over nineteen centuries. The Jewish attachment to Jerusalem under alien dominion is an unremitting struggle to preserve a Jewish presence, never allowing the link to be broken.

The Babylonians destroyed the city. Seventy years later the Jews were rebuilding it. The Romans destroyed it and changed its name to Aelia Capitolina, and the Bar-Kochba revolt, which cost half a million Jewish lives, was a last desperate attempt to oust the Romans and free Jerusalem. The Byzantines denied Jews the right to live in Jerusalem. The Crusaders massacred its Jewish population. Yet, despite embargoes and duress, Jews maintained a continuous presence in Jerusalem.

The Christian link with Jerusalem is the traditional association of many places in the city with the life and death of Jesus of Nazareth. But for no Church does Jerusalem represent its world center. For the Catholic Church, Rome is that center. Jerusalem's first encounter with Islam was in the seventh century and it was also its first encounter with the Arabs who acquired a vast Islamic empire from the Persian Gulf to the Atlantic Ocean. Arab Moslems refer to Jerusalem as *Al-Quds*, the "Holy." It is not the holiest of Moslem cities; Mecca and Medina outrank it. But since the Dome of the Rock was built there, it has become centrally associated with Islamic tradition in that region. It is said that the Dome of the Rock was built at the order of Abdul Malek Ibn Marwan, the Umayyad Caliph of Damascus, because "when the Caliph saw the Holy Sepulchre, which is revered by the Christian world, he was afraid that this church would win the hearts of Moslems and so he decided to build a sanctuary even more beautiful."

But for the Jews, Jerusalem is the place where the Lord chose to establish His Name, and it is here that His eyes and His heart dwell eternally. Therefore, for 3,000 years, Jerusalem has been and still everlastingly is, for the Jewish people and for no other, the focus of their faith and nationhood, and now has been the center of government of its state for more than forty years.

Yet Israel is deeply sensitive to universal interests and does not claim exclusive jurisdiction over the holy places of Christianity and of Islam in Jerusalem. It is Israel's policy that Moslem and Christian holy places should always be the care and responsibility of those who hold them sacred. Today there is complete freedom of movement within the city, to it and from it, for members of all faiths, including nationals even of countries still claiming to be at war with Israel.

Jerusalem is today, and will remain, an open city under the authority of a single administration, which is indigenous, not foreign, a city where religious freedom and the protection of holy places are guaranteed, a city where all the denominations are free to worship in their own way.

Aba Gefen confers with Israel's late Prime Minister, Levi Eshkol

XXVIII.

MISSED OPPORTUNITIES FOR PEACE

Three weeks after the end of the Six-Day War, Jordan's Hussein met secretly in London with Ambassador Yaacov Herzog, special emissary of Israeli Prime Minister Levi Eshkol. Hussein's first secret talk with Herzog also took place in London in September 1963, three months after Eshkol had become prime minister. Hussein held two more secret meetings, in 1964 and 1965, with Ambassador Herzog and Ambassador Ehud Avriel, respectively. At those meetings, agreements on the use of common water resources were reached and border security arrangements made.

In September 1965, Eshkol sent Foreign Minister Golda Meir to Paris to meet the king there. Golda Meir proposed to him the signing of an Israeli-Jordanian Peace Treaty within the then-existing Israeli borders, each side committing itself to respect the territorial integrity and independence of the other, and with guarantees by the major powers.

Hussein ignored the fact that Nasser had called him "an imperialistic lackey," "a treacherous dwarf," and "the Hashemite harlot." He also ignored what was clear to anyone, that, although the PLO's intention was to fight Israel in the undefined future, its wish was to destroy Hussein in the more immediate present. Hussein rejected Israel's extended hand for peace, its generous offer with the best imaginable conditions for Jordan.

At that meeting, Hussein committed his biggest error. He missed the opportunity of signing a peace treaty with Israel. If not for that historical neglect on Hussein's part, wars would have been prevented, many thousands of lives saved, and developments in the Middle East would have been completely different.

At the July 1967 meeting in London, it was Israel's turn to disregard the opportunity for signing peace. Hussein proposed a peace agreement based on significant border changes. He was willing not to oppose the emigration of the majority of the Arab refugees to distant countries, was ready to solve the problem of the Moslem holy places in the framework of a unified Jerusalem, and asked to meet personally with Moshe Dayan. Dayan strongly believed in the possibility of signing a peace agreement, which the king could present as a "reciprocal and honorable arrangement," as Hussein was offering.

Eshkol, however, refused to meet with Hussein and did not allow Dayan to do so, either. The government of Israel had not yet clarified its policy about the future of the territories, while Menachem Begin's position was to retain every inch

179

of them. Eshkol feared internal political strife, especially since the general view was that, regarding Jordan, time worked in favor of Israel.

Hussein's readiness for the above-mentioned compromises very soon disappeared and, at the next secret talk with Herzog in November of the same year, Hussein agreed only to very minor border changes. He said he would not concede the Mount of Olives or even one Arab village and announced that Jerusalem was not negotiable.

In the meantime, an Arab summit meeting had convened in August 1967, in Khartoum, Sudan. The conference resolved that there would be no peace with Israel, no negotiations, no recognition. There isn't the slightest doubt that these three "no's" of Khartoum became the biggest obstacle to peace between Israel and her neighbors. The question is: Why such Arab intransigence?

We recall the U.N. Partition Resolution of November 29, 1947; the admission of the State of Israel to membership of the United Nations in 1949; the recognition of Israel by a great majority of the nations of the world, and Israel's network of diplomatic relations with states on all five continents.

All efforts to persuade the belligerent Arabs to enter into meaningful peace negotiations with Israel were ineffective. Peace opportunities offered following the fighting disappeared, the Arab governments believing that a lost war was only a temporary setback, to be redressed by the next round of fighting.

An interesting interpretation of the Arab attitude was given by the Lebanese intellectual and author, Cecil Hourani. He wrote after the Six-Day War:

> We Arabs have a psychological weakness: that which we do not like, we pretend does not exist. Therefore at every debacle we regret that we did not accept a situation which no longer exists. In 1948 we regretted that we had not accepted the 1947 partition plan; in May 1967 we tried to go back to pre-Suez; today we would be happy, and are actually demanding at the U.N., to go back to things as they were before June 5th. From every defeat we reap a new regret and a new nostalgia, but we never seem to learn a lesson.

Others see the basic Arab position in regard to Israel as an integral part of Islam's attitude toward the Jew and of its perception of peace with the enemy. On a whole, the Arab attitude toward the Jew is negative, one of distrust, suspicion, contempt, and animosity. Throughout history, Jews have known hatred and persecution at Moslem hands. Mohammed expelled or killed Jews who would not accept Islam. Islam relegates Jews to second-class citizenship and, among the restrictions imposed upon the Jews, was the requirement to wear distinctive clothing, including a yellow badge. The evidence of a Jew was not accepted in court against that of a Moslem, and they were confined to special ghettoes.

While there were periods of Arab-Jewish cooperation (notably the "Golden Age" in Spain during the tenth and eleventh centuries), there were many periods characterized by massacre, pogroms, and expulsions. On the occasion of Mohammed's birthday, one can hear even now in the mosques, "The most splendid thing that the prophet Mohammed did was to drive the Jews out of the Arabian Peninsula...Jerusalem is our property. We shall retrieve it from the hands of those of whom it is written in the Koran: they will be brought low and made wretched...."

As for the Moslem perception of peace, its rule is not peace *with* Islam but peace *within* Islam, and war against non-Moslems is a religious command. It is a command upon individual Moslems, upon the Moslem community as a whole and, therefore, upon all heads of Moslem states. The *Jihad*, the Holy War, is aimed at expanding the frontiers of Islam, and it is a constant command until Islam will achieve dominion over the world. According to Islamic law, peace with non-Moslem enemies is temporary and peace agreements with non-Moslems are not binding. Moslems are free to violate and nullify such agreements if they believe they have gathered enough force to prevail over the enemy.

No wonder, therefore, that, with the election of Yasser Arafat, leader of Fatah, as head of the PLO at the Khartoum Conference, he was promised the support and help of all Arab governments in order to carry on the war against Israel. The Arabs wished to take away our sovereignty, our land, its scanty water, our capital city, the safety of our homes and lives, gifts that other nations inherit at birth, but which to us were not given freely; they had to be earned by bitter fighting.

The PLO was given facilities to operate from Syria, Jordan, and, later, Lebanon. Saudi Arabia, Libya, and Kuwait promised Egypt and Jordan generous subsidies for the war. The Soviet Union undertook to rehabilitate the Egyptian and Syrian armies, initiating a vast airlift of planes, tanks, and other equipment to replace their losses, and sending thousands of Soviet advisers. They embarked on this dangerous process in flagrant violation of their own support of the U.N. Security Council's Resolution 242, adopted unanimously on November 22, 1967, which emphasized the need to work for a just and lasting peace in which all states in the Middle East can live in security.

Resolution 242 also calls for the withdrawal of Israeli armed forces from territories occupied in the Six-Day War, for the termination of all claims or states of belligerency, for respect for and acknowledgment of the sovereignty, territorial integrity, and political independence of every state in the area, and for their right to live in peace within secure and recognized boundaries, free from threats or acts of force.

Even as the resolution was being discussed at the Security Council, Fatah detachments, trained and organized in Syria, attacked the cease-fire lines, which were now much easier for Israel to defend, especially against the threat of a large-scale assault, with the Suez Canal and the Jordan River as "anti-tank ditches" and the increased warning time available before Egyptian aircraft could approach the populated areas. Most of the Fatah infiltrators were intercepted on or near the cease-fire line, but some sabotage was done and the situation deteriorated. Explosives planted near villages and in Jerusalem, Tel Aviv, and other places killed and injured civilians and damaged property.

On the Suez Canal, which Nasser blocked immediately after the war, Egypt began massive artillery shelling of the Israeli positions in September 1968. It was the beginning of the War of Attrition, having as its purpose to weaken Israel by border infiltrations, shelling, and terror. Israel paid a high price in the War of Attrition with seven hundred and twenty-one Israelis killed, but it wasn't weakened. Egypt was. The Israeli reprisals by land, sea, and air caused the destruction of the canal cities, the flight of their inhabitants, and many casualties. In August 1970, Egypt accepted a cease-fire.

On September 28, 1970, Nasser died, and Egypt's new president, Anwar Sadat, decided to exploit the cease-fire for the preparation of a new Jihad against Israel. When Islam doesn't have the force to successfully carry out war against the enemy, it postpones the Jihad by making a tactical step and agreeing to a truce in order to accumulate strength and, at the proper time, to strike again and defeat its enemy.

The author with former Israeli Foreign Minister, Abba Eban

XXIX.

AS RECITED IN THE HAGGADAH

A short time after the Six-Day War, I was appointed consul-general of Israel in Toronto, Canada. I arrived there at the beginning of September 1967, with my wife and two sons. A year later, after having concluded her military service, our daughter Ruhama joined us and entered the University of Toronto to study English language and literature. We were in Toronto four years. There Ruhama married Dr. Sol Goldstein, a Canadian-born Jew, and they named their first-born son Benjamin, after my brother, the fourth member of my immediate family killed by the Nazis, may he rest in peace.

During my four years of service in Toronto, Israel was struggling against an unholy alignment of elements, all opposed to each other yet all against the Jewish state. It was led by the Soviet Union, which had broken off diplomatic relations with Israel because of the Six-Day War, and it had a Canadian partner, the official publication of the United Church of Canada, the *United Church Observer*.

This publication trod the perilous path of encouraging Arab terrorism. If its editors did not openly uphold the terrorist deeds, they certainly did not shrink from condoning them. The *Observer* printed articles calling for unreserved aid to the terrorists and inviting support for Fatah, which was tantamount to subsidizing the terrorist groups.

The editor, the Reverend Al Forrest, supported the irrational Arab leaders, proclaimed a holy war against Israel, and identified himself with those who had confessed guilt of the worst atrocities. "You can't be long with these commandos," he told a reporter, "without sympathizing with their cause."

The wife of a United Church minister was moved to write to the editor:

> ...I am ashamed to be a member of the United Church of Canada....We let the Jew die alone in 1940-45 and, if it had been up to us, we probably would have let him die alone in 1967....All alone, Israel won a war against impossible odds. Jewish lives were lost to protect their own and our Christian holy places from shelling. Bad enough that you say nothing when the knife is at Israel's throat. But you bid her swallow the knife....If you are aware of Israel's efforts to make peace, why do you not report that? If you are ignorant of it, your ignorance is deplorable. If you are aware, your prejudice is intolerable. One hesitates to use

the word anti-Semitic but it seems to me that I see a subtle brand of it in the *Observer*.

The Canadian poet Irving Layton, responding to the anti-Israeli campaign of the editor of the *Observer*, wrote,

> In the Middle Ages it was the poisoning of wells. In the 1970s it's the whole world that Jews are threatening, according to that fine and upstanding United Churchman....With a stroke of the pen he promoted them from mere well-poisoners to world destroyers.

The general media criticized Forrest for making his Church publication an adjunct of Arab propaganda. An editorial in the *Toronto Telegram* read: "...His [Al Forrest's] problem is that he cannot understand that Canadian daily newspapers support the position of Israel because it is a just and reasonable one...." A former moderator of the United Church came to the rescue of his fellow churchman, protesting at great length that he and his friend were not anti-Semites. Yet he permitted himself to say, "Bad as has been the suffering of the Jews throughout history, blacks can indubitably claim that their lot has been worse and that their injustices have been unrelieved by corresponding periods of wealth and privilege."

Such words hardly suggested a rejection of anti-Semitic sentiments. They pointed to a deeply ingrained belief that the blood of six million Jews can be balanced by the riches of Jews of Canada or the United States and that Jews in the Diaspora are but second-class citizens whom their non-Jewish fellows graciously accord certain privileges.

It was further evidence that there was religious bigotry in Canada, and historians will long debate the reasons for restricting Jewish immigration to Canada when a more flexible attitude could have saved thousands of Jews from the Holocaust. Confronted with the Jewish danger at the time, the responses of government, the civil service, and much of the public were indifferent or hostile. Even when the outbreak of war brought evidence of an ongoing Nazi program for the total annihilation of European Jewry, Canada's response on immigration remained legalistic and cold.

From Ruhama's husband, I heard the following episode, recalling his childhood memories of anti-Jewishness. Christmas time in Quebec where he went to school seemed to be a charitable season and he cannot recall anything but sympathetic comments from his Christian classmates, who felt sorry that the Jewish boys did not enjoy a Christmas dinner or gift. But Easter was different. Then, for a few days, his "friends" would become "enemies," and he would be called "Christkiller." When school resumed, hostilities forgotten, a young girl friend approached him to say excitedly that she had talked to her parents who had said that it was okay. The Jews had not killed Christ, the "Hebrews" had done it.

With the Allies' victory, the remnant of European Jewish survivors found no welcome, no succor in Canada. Though the Holocaust was yet fresh in the public mind, the country still barricaded itself from the Jewish refugee question. When international pressure and economic self-interest compelled Canada to admit displaced persons, it took calculated steps to insure that there were as few Jews admitted as possible.

Jewish population growth in Canada has always been slow. Canadian Jewry until the 1850s was to a great extent the small Jewish community in Montréal. The years 1881-82, the years of the Russian pogroms, marked the beginning of Canada's Jewry in its present day composition. By 1892, there were synagogues in the cities of eastern Canada and even in the west.

Toronto's Jewish population grew steadily. In 1911 there were over 18,000 Jews, and by 1921, over 34,000. In the 1920s, Jewish immigration brought the number to 40,000 by 1931. In 1949 the population was nearly 50,000.

After World War II, the projects of the Canadian Jewish Congress and the needle trades brought numerous immigrants from the displaced persons' camps. In 1951, greater Toronto had 66,773 Jews. Refugees of the Hungarian uprising of 1956 brought more immigrants. The 1961 census indicated 88,648 for metropolitan Toronto. Then, Sephardi Jews from former Spanish and French Morocco arrived and established their synagogues and associations. When we left Toronto in 1971, the Jewish population there was estimated at 105,000, out of a Canadian Jewish total of about 300,000. An important development in Toronto since the end of the war was the growth of the congregational school and, more strikingly, the growth and expansion of the day school. Toronto was years behind Winnipeg and Montreal in establishing Jewish day schools, but began to catch up with them.

In Toronto, we found synagogues of all three religious streams: Orthodox, Conservative, and Reform. During my four years of mission there, I attended services in all of them. I was invited to address their congregants on political actualities. Such meetings were often reported in the news media thus serving as a platform for Israel's public relations.

In February 1970, the United Church of Canada sponsored a public meeting in Toronto on the Middle East crisis, and invited an Arab representative and me to present our positions. It was the second time that I was invited to such a confrontation. The first time was in Buenos Aires at the end of May 1967, on the eve of the Six-Day War. Egyptian and Israeli diplomats were invited to appear on a television program called *"Dos Caras de la Verdad"* ("Two Faces of the Truth").

We were to be asked the same questions in turn, but separately, and then, on the program, shown each other's answers. Both sides agreed to attend but, at the last moment, while I was already at the studio, a phone call came from the Egyptian embassy saying it would not take part. The station broadcast my answers, showing an empty chair for the Egyptian diplomat. The next day the Egyptian embassy protested to the Ministry for Foreign Affairs that the station had ridiculed it.

This time, in Toronto, the Arab representative came. It was the director of the Arab Information Center in Canada, Ibrahim Shukrallah, stationed in Ottawa. The news media were invited and part of the proceedings was televised. The auditorium was packed. It was the first time since the establishment of Israel that Arab and Israeli diplomats appeared on the same platform. When question time came, I found myself facing a hostile axis: Palestinian refugees, Canadian-born Arabs, and the editor of the *Observer*.

I rejected their hostile arguments and stressed that their attitude was pure and simple anti-Semitism. This is evident when a Jew as an individual is deprived of his civil rights, or when the Jews as a people are deprived of their right to corporate existence.

I denounced the existing anti-Israel unholy alliance, imbued with the ideology that led to the genocide of six million Jews. I emphasized that the hatred of Jews was the only thing common to Old Leftists in Russia or China and Neo-Nazis in England, South Africa, or the United States; to New Leftists in Germany and Neo-Fascists in Italy; to a black general in Uganda and a "Tacuara" racist in Argentina; to an anti-ecumenical Vatican spokesman, a nationalist Socialist bigot in Quebec, and a liberal United Church editor in Toronto.

I asked the audience why Christians were silent when Jewish blood was being shed, yet remonstrant if Arab metal was destroyed in an Israeli reprisal. I said that Christian apathy to the dangers that menaced Israelis disagreeably reminded one of ecclesiastical hand-washing in war-time Germany.

"The certain way for evil to prosper," I concluded, "is for good men to do nothing."

In those days, Israelis were being killed by merciless assassins in supermarkets, in apartment houses, in parking lots, in university cafeterias. Bombs exploded at Israeli embassies and business premises overseas, and there were threats of kidnapping. Envelopes filled with a deadly explosive were mailed from abroad to Israeli and Jewish individuals throughout the world, and a Greek child was killed at the El-Al office in Athens. Planes were being hijacked, and forty-seven defenseless passengers and crew were killed in a SwissAir plane over Switzerland.

When we returned to Israel in September 1971, the Arab terrorists were harassing Israel's border villages with mortar and gunfire from bases in a complaisant Lebanon. They had moved there after Hussein, finally realizing who his real enemy was, had liquidated their bases in Jordan. The fedayeen, expelled or fleeing from Jordan, found refuge in southern Lebanon, where several thousand concentrated in an area that became known as "Fatahland." From this haven they crawled forth from time to time to lay mines, dynamite Israeli houses or installations, and fire Russian rockets at settlements, villages, or towns in the north.

They killed children in a school bus traveling along Israel's northern frontier, and shelled the town of Kiryat Shemonah. An agricultural attaché at the Israeli embassy in London was killed, and twenty-seven civilians, most of them Puerto Rican pilgrims, were massacred at Lod airport by Japanese terrorists and then came the most atrocious murder, in September 1972, by the Arab "Black September" terrorist group.

Eleven members of Israel's Olympic team were assassinated in Munich, where the tactics and means were borrowed from the Nazis. The murderers blindfolded the helpless young athletes, bound them hand and foot and, after hours of agonizing despair, shot them down one by one. The Arab terrorists killed in Munich were given a state funeral by the government of Libya. Libya's Muammar

Qaddafi bestowed upon Fatah an award of $5 million dollars for the murder of the Israeli athletes, and the terrorist broadcasting station in Syria boasted, "Congratulations to you, members of 'Black September,' on your success. Your activity in Munich is a gold medal for the Arab people."

The Kuwaiti Defense Minister boasted: "The Arab brain that planned the Munich operation is a creative and inventive one," and Uganda's Idi Amin, ungratefully forgetful of the tremendous help extended to him by Israel, praised the bloodthirsty Arab terrorists who had murdered the Israelis. The entire world was privy to Amin's outrageous words, cabled openly to the secretary-general of the U.N. The entire world kept silent. It tolerated Arab terrorism, for which violence was means and end, and which threatened the fabric of international life. Innocent civilians lived in fear of attack by foreign murder squads; airlines worked in a constant atmosphere of vulnerability; international mails were violated by cowards whose malice knew no restraint.

Arab terrorism did not emanate from the minds of deranged extremists. The Arab terror organizations could not exist without the extensive support and participation of Arab governments, politically, financially, materially, militarily, overtly, and covertly. Many governments, however, found it difficult to grasp the significance of Yasser Arafat's declaration, that his aim was "the liquidation of Israel's existence," and the expressions of full support by Arab heads of state. The concept of the extinction of a sovereign state was strange to them. It was nothing new for Jews who judge threats against the background of another unique experience, whose like no other people has ever experienced.

Aba Gefen (second from right) accompanies Prime Minister Golda Meir

XXX.

ASSIGNMENT IN ARGENTINA

When we arrived in Buenos Aires, we found written on the wall of our assigned residence, "*Vida á Eichmann, muerte á Israel.*" "Life to Eichmann, death to Israel."

It was hardly a warm welcome. As our daughter Ruhama had learned six years before in Peru, our sons Meir and Yehudah would soon realize that there was no need for them to learn about anti-Semitism from history books. They lived it often, in place after place. Here a schoolmate would yell "Dirty Jew," there an anti-Semitic slogan on a fence of a Jewish school, or its windows broken as a Christmas Eve routine. Jewish boys were attacked as they played football in their own school grounds. There was the case of a Jewish hockey professional who was forced to quit by anti-Semitic taunts and insults.

There were times in Argentina when many Jews held fast to the Bible: when Jewish colonization began and the immigrants came accompanied by their ritual slaughterers (shochatim) and rabbis. Religious life in the colonies followed then traditional patterns. However, isolation and the lack of Jewish education caused a decline in religious life. On the other hand, many of those who arrived in the cities, especially among those who arrived following the abortive Russian revolution in 1905, were revolutionary-minded immigrants to whom religion had no meaning.

Unofficially, there are historical traces of the Marranos who fled from the Spanish and Portuguese Inquisitions. Buenos Aires was a free port and the Marranos sought refuge there. Some historians credit the Marranos with being pioneers of the Argentine revolution. Officially, however, Argentina's Jewish community which is to this day the largest in Latin America, came into being in 1860 when, on November 11 of that year, the first Jewish wedding was solemnized in Argentina. In 1862, the first Jewish congregation, the Libertad Synagogue, was established, its founders mainly West European Jews from Alsace-Lorraine.

Pogroms in Russia in 1881 brought a number of Jewish immigrants to Argentina. Large-scale immigration began only in the late 1880s, when echoes of Argentina's prodigious efforts to attract immigration reached Eastern Europe. A government immigration agent was appointed to attract Russian Jews, and this decision prompted vehement anti-Semitic attacks in the press. Most of these immigrants were Ashkenazim, but a small minority of Sephardim came from the Ottoman Empire and North Africa.

Arriving singly at first, Jews later came in groups. It seems that Jewish agricultural colonization in Argentina was a byproduct of Jewish love and yearning for the land of Israel.

The story is that in July 1889, an attempt had been made by a group of Russian Jews to go to the land of Israel to become farm workers there. The one hundred and thirty families comprising this group were stranded in Germany, en route, without financial means and without any way of making their way further. The Alliance Israelite Universelle took an interest in them, but instead of sending them on to Palestine, diverted them to Argentina, where arrangements had been made for an Argentine estate owner to sell them certain stretches of land.

Upon their arrival in Argentina, however, they were bitterly disappointed. They found the fields barren and they suffered from starvation. More than sixty children died of exposure and hunger during that first season. In the ensuing months, the Jewish world rose up in alarm over this tragedy, and Baron de Hirsch, who had been considering the possibility of large-scale colonization, created the ICA in 1896 which undertook to assist Jews to emigrate from Russia into countries where they could develop freely and become productive persons, earning their livelihood through labor on the land.

Jewish colonization in Argentina did not attract the masses. But despite the movement into the cities the Jewish colonies have remained to this day the special pride of the Argentine Jewish community. I witnessed it when I attended, in 1965, the celebration of seventy-five years of Jewish colonization in Argentina, which took place in the village of Moisesville. Moisesville is the oldest Jewish colony in Argentina. In addition to the well-merited reputation it acquired in the heyday of Argentine Jewish colonization, it was its crowning glory. During what they considered the golden age of Moisesville, they called it "the Jerusalem of Argentina."

Argentina's Jewry is also very proud of its educational system, made possible by the economic rise of the Jewish community. Over the years, the former Jewish peddlers became owners of factories and were integrated into the Argentine economy. Thanks to their vitality, energy, and connections abroad, they built up important industries, especially during the two war periods when Argentina was neutral. Jews developed the furniture and leather industries, and weavers from Lodz and Bialystock built factories and developed a great textile industry.

What used to be small and primitive free-loan funds grew into large Jewish banks, and the old Chevra Kadisha, whose sole function was to bury the dead, became a centralized Kehilla with facilities and personnel embracing all aspects of Jewish life, education, culture and philanthropy.

But when we arrived in Buenos Aires, we realized that the number of children receiving Jewish education was between twenty and twenty-five percent of the total. The increasing number of dropouts each year was shown by the fact that in our last year in Buenos Aires, in 1967, in all the schools run by the Jewish Community, only 500 pupils finished elementary school and 126 graduated from high school. It was estimated then that only twelve percent of Argentina's Jewish youth was active in community organizations.

During our stay there, for four years, there still existed two newspapers in Yiddish: the *Presse* and the *Yiddishe Zeitung*. But the second and third generations, with very little exception, no longer speak Yiddish.

We were told that the majority of the cultural and educational leaders of Argentina's Jewish communities are sons and grandsons of the colonists. The education and training they received in the environment of the colonies imbued them with a sound and healthy spirit. They brought new blood to the cities and made valuable contributions to Jewish community life.

When my wife and I were in Moisesville, we went to the cemetery, which is a living memorial of the sufferings and martyrdom of Jewish colonists in Argentina. There stand many of the graves of the pioneers of Moisesville who were murdered by the half-savage natives years ago. While there are historians who insist that the murders of Jewish settlers in the agricultural colonies resembled incidents between gauchos and settlers of other origins, there are others who describe them as anti-Semitic events.

It was the Russian Revolution in 1917 which increased the Argentine government's fear of similar revolutionary activity in Argentina and, since the Jews were generally identified as "Russians," anti-revolutionary fervor developed into overt anti-Semitism. From 1933 onward, anti-Semitic activity increased, encouraged by German diplomatic institutions and by the local branch of the Nazi Party, until it became a central problem for Argentine Jewry. The deteriorating security of the Jews compelled, in 1939, all factions, Ashkenazi and Sephardi, to unite and form a roof organization, the D.A.I.A., which began to fight for the right of the Jews to be free from persecution.

Juan Peron's accession to power, in 1946, brought serious fears to the Jewish population because he had been aided by the Fascist group, *Alianza Libertadora Nacionalista* and was known to sympathize with the Nazi government in Germany. Buenos Aires became a center for anti-Semitic publications and neo-Nazi activity on an international scale. Jewish immigration was stopped entirely, while Argentina welcomed thousands of Nazis and their collaborators escaping from Europe after the war.

The overthrow of Peron, in 1955, was accompanied by an increase in anti-Semitic activities, especially by "Tacuara," the racist pro-Nazi terrorist group. These activities were expanded after the capture of Adolph Eichmann and his execution in Israel.

After the revolution of June 1966, in which General Carlos Onganía seized power, anti-Semitic organizations became adherents of the new regime and, by 1967, when we left Buenos Aires, despite the placatory declarations of the government, Argentina continued to be a center of anti-Semitic activity. Of the 313 anti-Semitic incidents in the world recorded in 1967, 142 occurred in Argentina.

Between 1963 and 1965, our four years of service in Argentina, the anti-Semites were aided by representatives of the Arab League in Buenos Aires. The increase in anti-Semitism heightened the activity of D.A.I.A. Among its activities, was the annual ceremony commemorating the Warsaw Ghetto uprising. At the ceremony in 1963, which I attended and addressed, 20,000 people were present.

While in the first post-Holocaust decades anti-Semitism was considered disgraceful and unrespectable in cultured lands, the situation changed with the new generations that did not experience World War II and for whom the Holocaust is at most a subject taught at school. Perhaps the cardinal reason for the rise in anti-Semitic manifestations is the loss of shame felt by the post-Holocaust generation about this subject. The loss of shame brought skeletons out of the closet, and provided an opening for extremists of the left and right to engage in a campaign of denying the occurrence of the Holocaust. Its denial helped the Neo-Nazis in their attempts to cleanse the Nazi period of its stigma in order to consolidate their own political power. For the leftists, denying the Holocaust, which is perceived as the cause of the establishment of the State of Israel, helped the Palestinian movement to justify its struggle against Israel.

Faced with world apathy toward Arab terrorism, even after the Munich slaughter, and toward the increased anti-Semitic incidents on all continents, I have asked myself, "How many more Jews must be massacred before the world acts effectively to prevent a new genocide? What further price must Jewry pay to convince the world that the State and the people of Israel have an absolute right, as any other State and nation, to peace and tranquility?

XXXI.

ON THE MOST SACRED DAY

The Arabs continued to flaunt the banner of their three "no's" of Khartoum and express their commitment to fight and take the whole of Palestine. Egypt's President Sadat proclaimed, "Egypt is committed to the liberation of the whole of Palestine and the annihilation of the Jewish state politically, militarily, socially, and spiritually."

The Arabs continued intensive activity against Israeli and Jewish targets. At the end of 1972 and the beginning of 1973, Arab terrorists were caught with weapons and explosives in the United Kingdom, Greece, Cyprus, and Austria. These terrorists, as well as those who attacked Israel's embassy in Bangkok, had come from Lebanon, where the terrorists had their headquarters and maintained training camps for volunteers from Japan, China, Turkey, and Cyprus, as well as Arabs.

A further batch of letter-bombs was uncovered in Israel and an Israeli agent was murdered in Madrid. An Israeli merchant was shot dead by an Arab in Nicosia. An Italian employee of El Al was murdered in Rome and an Israeli assistant military attaché in Washington was shot dead outside his home. The El Al office in Athens was attacked, and five persons were injured by a bomb in the Jerusalem market.

In May, 1973, Israel learned of the reinforcement of Syrian and Egyptian troops on the borders, and there was some tension. Israeli reserves were mobilized for a while as a precautionary measure, but the intelligence circles thought it most unlikely that war would break out. Since nothing happened, the reserves were sent home. The terrorists, however, continued their attacks and Israel fought back by striking at their leaders and bases. Terrorist camps in northern Lebanon were hit and three top Fatah leaders were killed in an Israeli commando attack in the heart of Beirut.

The Syrian border was comparatively quiet until September, when tension was raised by a serious incident. An attack by Syrian aircraft on an Israel naval patrol some twenty miles off the Syrian coast began a series of clashes in which thirteen Syrian fighter planes were shot down on September 13. Despite this, our intelligence people were reassuring. It was most unlikely, they said, that there would be any major Syrian reaction. The continued Syrian build-up of troops was caused, they explained, by the Syrians' fear that Israel would attack.

Golda Meir, who had become Israel's prime minister in June 1969 following the death of Eshkol, said in her September 18 Jewish New Year message to world Jewry that there were signs peace was becoming "less remote." Two weeks later, on October 2, large concentrations of Egyptian troops and equipment were reported on the west bank of the Suez Canal, and of Syrian forces on the cease-fire lines in the northeast. Israeli intelligence staff continued to hold the opinion that no attack was to be expected.

I attended a meeting at that time of the Foreign Ministry's senior officials with the head of the Israeli military intelligence, General Eli Zeira. I heard Zeira assure us that there won't be a war "for at least another two years," in spite of the fact that President Sadat of Egypt continued to repeat the threats he had made since 1970 to resume the war against Israel. Sadat emphatically rejected the possibility of any negotiations, interim settlement, or separate arrangement with Israel.

On Friday, October 5, 1973, the Israeli Government received a report that the families of the Russian advisers in Syria were packing up and leaving in a hurry. This worried Golda Meir very much and she didn't like it, she writes in her memoirs, since it reminded her of what had happened before the Six-Day War. "Why the haste?" she asked those around her. What did those Russians know that we didn't know? Was it possible that they were being evacuated? Her advisors did not seem very disturbed and it did not change the military's assessment of the situation. Golda Meir was assured that there would be adequate warning of any real trouble and that sufficient reinforcements were being sent to the fronts to carry out any holding operation that might be needed. All that was necessary had been done and the army was placed on high alert, particularly the air force and the armored corps.

Chief-of-Staff Elazar urged a pre-emptive strike, but Golda Meir refused. She did not want Israel to appear to the world as the one who had struck first. She had forgotten what Ben-Gurion had taught her and what is written in the Talmud: "If a man means to kill you, strike first!" In that fateful moment, she preferred the concern: "What will the Gentile think or say?"

This was the first mistake. The second followed: she did not order a call-up. There should have been a full-scale mobilization.

The next day, the peace and calm of Yom Kippur, the Day of Atonement, was shattered by the piercing sound of the air-raid alarm. The massive and unprovoked simultaneous assault of the Egyptian and Syrian armies, prepared and planned by an Arab-Soviet conspiracy, had begun.

Yom Kippur is the most solemn and sacred day in the Jewish calendar. It is the one day in the year that Jews throughout the world, even if they are not very pious, unite in some observance, totally abstaining from food, drink, and work, praying and atoning for sins they may have committed in the course of the past year.

In Israel, Yom Kippur is a day when the country comes to a virtual standstill: there are no newspapers, no television or radio broadcasts, no public transport, and all schools, shops, restaurants, cafes, and offices are closed for twenty-four hours. By attacking when the Israelis were fasting and worshipping in their synagogues, when everyday routine life throughout the country gave way to spiritual reflection and prayer, the aggressors thought the Jews would not be ready to fight back.

They attacked our positions on the Suez Canal, crossed the Canal, and our forces in Sinai were battered. The Syrians penetrated in depth on the Golan Heights. On both fronts, the casualties were very high. Attacked without warning, Israeli forces were fighting on two fronts simultaneously and fighting enemies who had been preparing for years. Our forces were overwhelmingly outnumbered in guns, tanks, planes, and men, and were at a severe psychological disadvantage. Israel faced the greatest threat it had known.

The shock was not only over the way in which the war had started, but also because a number of Israel's basic assumptions had been proven wrong: the low probability of an attack, the certainty that we would have sufficient warning before any attack took place, and the belief that we would be able to prevent the Egyptians from crossing the Suez Canal. The circumstances could not have been worse.

But the assault was frustrated and repelled, and Golda Meir writes, "In the first two or three days of the war, only a thin line of brave young men stood between us and disaster. And no words can ever express the indebtedness of the people of Israel to those boys on the Canal and on the Golan Heights. They fought, and fell, like lions."

At the beginning of the war, as the Arabs advanced on the battlefield, Moscow supported them militarily and politically, and put obstacles to ending the fighting. But when it became clear that Israel was going to win, the Russians asked for a cease-fire. On October 22, the Security Council of the U.N. adopted Resolution 338 that called on both sides to stop the fighting.

When the cease-fire officially went into effect on October 24, the Arabs had been defeated again, and Israel's forces occupied some 1,000 square miles of Egyptian territory west of the Suez Canal and about two hundred and fifty square miles of Syria east of the 1967 cease-fire line. Israel's forward positions were about sixty-two miles from Cairo on the Suez-Cairo road and twenty-five miles from Damascus.

The Egyptian Third Army on the East bank of the Canal and the town of Suez were completely encircled. This situation was particularly intolerable for the Egyptians, whose Third Army faced a humiliating surrender. But Israel paid a very high price for its victory, 2,119 dead, 508 missing, including 293 presumed dead.

On January 18, 1974, Israel and Egypt signed the disengagement agreement, and on May 31, an agreement was signed between Israel and Syria.

After the war, Israel was isolated on the international scene as never before. Internally, it was faced with many problems, unlike after the brief wars of 1956 and 1967, arising from the prolonged mobilization of the reserves; the pay of the reservists and the care of their families; businesses abandoned at a moment's notice and threatened with ruin; and factories hampered by the absence of key technicians and managers.

There was an upsurge of disquiet, soul searching, and criticism. The public was deeply disturbed over the sudden transition from confidence in Israel's military might to uncertainty and apprehension, over Arab success in taking the army by surprise, over the indications of unpreparedness, and the agonizing loss of life. Despite the fact that Israel had won the most impressive military victory in her history after the initial setback, it was the shock of the first two days, the pain of bereavement, and the powerful international forces ranged against Israel that were uppermost in people's minds.

Demands were voiced in many quarters, including some supporters of the dominant Labor-Mapam Alignment, for the ouster of those responsible for the blunders and shortcomings revealed by the war. Prime Minister Golda Meir and Defence Minister Moshe Dayan had to go. Yitzhak Rabin, who was the chief-of-staff during the Six-Day War and Israel's ambassador in Washington during the Yom Kippur War, became, in June 1974, prime minister.

As a result of the country's development, aided by the Jewish people through the years, Israel's economy was able to withstand the Yom Kippur attack, and maintain the country's civilian life at nearly normal levels despite the interruption of many services and the mobilization of most of its manpower.

Following the Yom Kippur War, a period of significant economic aid by the United States began, in addition to American weapons and political support, to the point of using its veto in the U.N. Security Council to prevent decisions harmful to Israel. The continuing closeness with the United States aroused misgivings that Israel was dangerously dependent on the Americans and that her capacity to make independent decisions was being compromised. Not only opposition spokesmen but many government supporters felt that Israel had made unjustified concessions in the negotiations for the interim settlement with Egypt because of American pressure and the fear of weakening American support.

The interim agreement was signed in Geneva on September 4, 1974. The agreement, achieved through the shuttling back and forth between Israel and Egypt, of American Secretary of State Henry Kissinger, established that "the conflict shall not be resolved by military force but by peaceful means," and that "both countries were determined to reach a final and just peace settlement by means of negotiations."

The major significance of the agreement, therefore, was that it was political in nature: a contractual public agreement between Israel and Egypt to reach a just and final peace through negotiations, regardless of developments on other fronts.

This positive development in the relations between Israel and Egypt, however, did not change the attitude of the PLO. Its terrorists continued their outrages. Intensive and prolonged efforts were made, mostly from bases in Lebanon and some from Syria, to attack Israel towns and villages near the northern frontier, firing murderous rockets from time to time. A group of terrorists broke into a block of apartments at Kiryat Shemonah and killed eighteen people, including eight children and five women. Another group broke into a house at Ma'alot, three miles from the Lebanese border, shot a couple and their child, and then seized a school where more than one hundred children from Safad, on a school trip, were asleep. They held them and some of their teachers as hostages, demanding the release of twenty-six terrorists held in Israel. They threatened to blow up the school and kill all the children unless their demands were met.

Shortly before the deadline, Israeli troops stormed the school in a last-minute attempt to save the children. The terrorists opened fire on the children and flung hand-grenades among them. Twenty children were killed and about seventy wounded.

In August 1974, Archbishop Hilarion Capucci, head of the Greek Catholic Church in Jerusalem, was arrested and charged with smuggling arms and explosives found in his official car for the Fatah terrorists. In Tel Aviv on the night of March 5-6, 1975, eight Arab terrorists occupied the small Savoy Hotel on the seafront. Just before dawn, Israeli troops attacked the hotel, but the terrorists detonated explosives, demolishing part of the building. Eight civilians, three Israeli soldiers and seven terrorists were killed.

The 1975 U.N. General Assembly resolution, equating Zionism with racism, inspired Palestinian terrorists to increase their outrages abroad. The most famous of them was the kidnapping in Athens, on June 27, 1976, of an Air France plane on its way from Tel Aviv to Paris with 258 passengers, including over 100 Israelis, and 12 French crewmen. Seven Palestinian kidnappers took the plane to Entebbe, the capital of Uganda, whose president, Idi Amin, had been overjoyed with the murder of the Israeli athletes in Munich.

A week of almost unbearable tension followed, during which, at our Ministry in Jerusalem, a twenty-four hour watch was held to maintain contact with the Israeli embassies abroad as well as with the foreign embassies in Israel. My turn was the night between July 3 and 4, and it was my great privilege to send out to our embassies scattered on five continents, the news about the deliverance of the hostages by Israel's air force from the clutches of "the brute of Uganda."

When the good news broke, Israel overflowed with messages of jubilation and relief. It had never experienced anything of this sort before. People everywhere cheered the David who had dared Goliath. The frustrated dream of multitudes of decent people had come true. Gideon Rafael was then our ambassador in London, and he relates in his memoirs that shortly after the successful rescue mission in Entebbe, he met James Callaghan, Britain's foreign secretary, at the traditional festival of the coalminers of Britain. After the meal, Callaghan took him aside and said in a conspiratorial whisper, "When I heard the news [about Entebbe], I understood what you had meant when I asked you what your government would do and you had answered cryptically, 'It would put the fear of the God of Israel into the heart of that brute'."

Except for that most daring and successful operation, the Rabin Government was lacking in inspiration. Many Israelis had lost confidence and faith in the ruling Labor Party. In the Knesset elections of May 1977, Labor was defeated. The leader of the Likud Party, Menachem Begin, became prime minister, and he invited Moshe Dayan to take up the post of foreign minister, in spite of his membership in the Labor Party. Dayan accepted.

The new government formed in June was sharply attacked by the left-wing parties, which, during the election campaign represented Menachem Begin as a warmonger, who, if elected, would bring another war on Israel.

It was Nicolae Ceausescu, the president of Communist Romania, who thought differently. After having been disappointed in his 1972 attempt to arrange a meeting between Anwar Sadat and Golda Meir, he believed that Begin could do what Golda Meir did not, and he invited Begin to officially visit Romania. Thus, Ceausescu was the first foreign head of state to meet with Israel's new prime minister.

Begin arrived in Bucharest on August 25, 1977. In spite of the differences of opinion between Begin and Ceausescu about the solution of the Arab-Israeli conflict, a relationship of mutual respect and understanding arose during their long talks. Ceausescu became convinced that Begin sincerely wanted peace, and he invited President Sadat to come to Bucharest. Sadat arrived in October and, after a long talk with the Romanian president, he asked Ceausescu whether he was really convinced that Begin wanted peace and was able to sign a treaty.

Ceausescu answered both questions affirmatively, and then, as Sadat himself stated publicly, he decided he would go to Jerusalem. On November 19, 1977, Sadat arrived in Israel on a visit that initiated the peace process in the Middle East.

Dayan, with the approval of Begin, appointed me ambassador to Romania. After having served for six years as director of the Department for Cultural and Scientific Relations at our Foreign Ministry, I boarded an El-Al plane for Bucharest on January 25, 1978, with my wife. We left our two sons who were in the air force: Meir, an aeronautical engineer, and Yehudah, a fighter pilot.

Before my departure, the director-general of our ministry, Ephraim Evron, stressed to me the special importance of my mission to Romania following Sadat's visit to Jerusalem. He spoke of the serious challenge facing me as Israel's ambassador in the one Communist country that did not break its diplomatic ties with us, and emphasized the delicate framework of relations between our two countries, with the complexities of bilateral problems in political, economic, immigration, and other fields.

He said that he considered Romania "Israel's window on the Iron Curtain," a potential "bridgehead" for the renewal of relations with the countries of Eastern Europe, and asked me to devote attention also to what was happening around Romania. The hope of advancing our relations with the Soviet Union and its East European satellites, was one of the main reasons I accepted the appointment. Eli Rubinstein, the head of Dayan's office, while bidding me farewell, said, "Please, say the journey's prayer!"

XXXII.

KING, EMPEROR, OR GOD?

At the Bucharest airport, my wife and I were welcomed by the Romanian chief of protocol and by members of our embassy. On our way to the city, my attention was drawn to the women cleaning the streets, loading and discharging goods. We drove through pretty and well-cared-for streets, where residences of foreign ambassadors were. The residence of the Israeli ambassador was in a "nondiplomatic" area on a quiet street in an old residential area. Around the house were armed guards.

After the first night in our new home, I went to the embassy, also in an old residential area, not far from the city center. It was an old but attractive house, surrounded by a wall and around it, too, were many watchful guards. Whoever wished to approach the building had to identify himself.

January 26, 1978, was a festive day in Romania. Throughout the country, public assemblies were held to mark the sixtieth birthday of President Nicolae Ceausescu, and the local news media were full of descriptions of the event.

I was informed that my meeting with Romanian Foreign Minister George Macovescu for the delivery of my credentials had been fixed for January 30, so I prepared the text of the message I was to present to him on behalf of Moshe Dayan, Israel's foreign minister.

At my briefing session with Dayan before my departure, he spoke extensively about the visit of Sadat in Jerusalem. He considered the very coming of Sadat to Jerusalem as a major success, and said to me, "Imagine yourself, the same Sadat who had said, in the not distant past, that our generation was not ready for peace, that negotiation with Israel was out of the question, and that he was ready to sacrifice a million Egyptians in a war against Israel. The same Sadat who had declared that Egypt was committed to the annihilation of the Jewish state and the liberation of all of Palestine."

But Dayan was also very careful not to fall into the trap of wishful thinking. He understood that Sadat didn't consider our security as we did. Dayan believed that Sadat had recognized the need to assure Israel's security, but he spoke of guarantees and demilitarized areas, mentioning all this to prove that Israel did not need the occupied territories. Sadat's main goal was to get Israel out of the territories. Regarding Sadat's declaration that there would be no more wars, Dayan was of the opinion that Sadat could declare exactly the opposite the following day, and a million Egyptians would acclaim him again.

Dayan asked me to inform the Romanian foreign minister that, in his view, the solution of the administered territories was a "functional division, and not a line that would divide the West Bank." Instead of dividing the territories, there should be a division of control in the territories: a kind of federation or confederation, a condominium or an autonomy.

Annexation, the aspiration of the Likud, would transform Israel into a bi-national state, or would force the Jews to rule over another people. It was not the kind of territorial agreement that would lead to the establishment of a Palestinian state in that part of the territories from which Israel would withdraw.

When I met Macovescu, I presented him with my credentials, expressed my appreciation for Romania's independent position and for its contribution to the initiation of the peace process in our region, and delivered Dayan's message. He thanked me for my warm words and said, "Peace must be achieved in the region. Peace is necessary for Israel, for the Arab countries, and for Romania itself, as a close neighbor to the conflict area. We know that one could not expect the problems of the Middle East to be solved in a few dramatic encounters. There is need for long and tiresome negotiations, negotiations and not talks. It is necessary to put the cards on the table, and also to keep some of them in the pocket, but to negotiate. I consider the Israelis to be very good diplomats, and I am convinced you will find your way to it."

Macovescu told me that the president would receive me the next day for the presentation of my credentials.

When I met Ceausescu, I delivered a message from Israel's prime minister. Begin had asked me to transmit to Ceausescu his warmest regards and best wishes, and to thank him for his part in opening direct negotiations between Egypt and Israel. Begin also asked me to mention the Jewish community of Romania, to express our appreciation for the good attitude of the Romanian authorities toward the community regarding freedom of religion and Jewish education, and to convey our hope that the process of reunification of families (emigration to Israel) would be accelerated.

President Ceausescu thanked me for Begin's message and for my own words of appreciation, and said, "The relations between Romania and Israel are good, very good, and I wish that during the period of your mission, these relations should become even better, that the widest of horizons could be opened for relations between us."

Then, he repeated Romania's position for the solution of the Arab-Israeli conflict, stressing Israel's withdrawal from the occupied territories and negotiations with the PLO about the creation of a Palestinian state at Israel's side. "Were the PLO not in existence, you would have to create it," he said.

I explained our opposition to the idea of an independent Palestinian state, elaborating on the two main reasons for our position: the military dangers threatening Israel's existence and the dangers of Arab terrorism from the territory of a Palestinian state. I explained our refusal to negotiate with the PLO, which continued to cling to its proclaimed goal, the destruction of Israel. I reminded him that all the attempts by the Americans, and by some Arabs, to convince the PLO to adopt a more flexible stand had failed, and Yasser Arafat had only recently declared, "The decision in our region is in the hands of the Palestinian gun. The Palestinian state will arise by blood and fire."

I quoted Prime Minister Menachem Begin, that "everything was negotiable, except suicide," and asked the president to distinguish between the PLO and Palestinians worthy to be partners to negotiations.

The president thought for a while, and then replied, "Please transmit to Begin my following proposal. Instead of agreeing to negotiations with the PLO, let Israel declare its readiness to negotiate with the Palestinians and with any of their organizations which is ready to discuss peace with her."

I promised to transmit his proposal to Begin and with that our conversation ended. Before I said goodbye, he raised a glass of champagne and proposed a toast, wishing me success in my mission. I responded with a toast and wishes for his good health and happiness, and for the strengthening of the friendly relations existing between our countries.

On my way home, the chief of protocol noted the flexibility of the president in regard to the PLO issue, as expressed at the end of our conversation. He congratulated me on it and said, "You started your mission on the right foot."

A few days later, I had the opportunity to meet almost all the heads of the diplomatic missions in Bucharest. It was in the framework of an annual diplomatic "hunt" in the presence of Romania's prime minister and foreign minister. At this event, the newly-arrived ambassadors were obliged to lie down on a mattress outside, in the Romanian winter's cold, for the prime minister and foreign minister to "strike" them with a branch. The striking was accompanied by shooting to create the impression that the ambassadors were receiving real blows. It was a kind of "baptism," a ceremony by which the new ambassadors were admitted to the diplomatic corps.

On that day, I was one of fifteen newly "baptized" ambassadors, including also the Soviet ambassador. Imagine him lying on his belly in the bosom of nature, and bending over him Romania's prime minister with a branch in his hand, whipping his behind to the sound of shooting and laughter of one hundred foreign diplomats.

I arrived at the hunt without knowing a single person and I looked for a western diplomat to introduce myself to and with his assistance to meet other colleagues. I had to be very careful not to extend my hand to someone who would leave it hanging in the air, as had happened with the Polish ambassador in Buenos Aires after the Six-Day War, after Poland had broken off relations with us.

I finally approached a blond man and introduced myself. I was not mistaken. It was Norwegian Ambassador Per Borgen, who was warm and cordial. He introduced me to our colleagues, among them two from Communist countries, Cuba and East Germany. The Cuban ran away immediately after we shook hands, while the East German smiled at the behavior of his comrade, and continued to converse with me. He was very kind and, during my five years of service in Bucharest, we developed a very friendly relationship.

From one of the westerners I learned about the diplomats' conditions of life in the Socialist Republic of Romania. I had arrived at a time when, to use my colleague's words, the policy of the East European countries seemed to be, "Nothing that occurs inside should be known outside, and nothing that happens outside should be known inside."

He told me about the strictly controlled wall between the citizens of Romania and foreign citizens, diplomats in particular. The regime in Romania, he said, looked at diplomats from various countries, including Israel, with suspicion, and its security services checked the character of a new diplomat from the moment he arrived. They were looking especially for diplomats' weaknesses for women and employed "seduction-girls" [prostitutes] to serve as a sex trap for the purpose of extortion and to involve them in the spy rings of the local security services.

In Romania, an ambassador never felt himself alone. The employees at the ambassador's residence were agents of the security services and constantly spied. They checked every book, searched everywhere, photographed everything, and reported in detail. "They will know the color of your underwear," my colleague said to me. In Romania, there was no place for the expression, "Talk to the wall." A microphone was hidden in every corner and, when you talked to the wall, the microphones listened in all languages.

In the house of one of the ambassadors, his embassy's security people revealed hidden microphones in the telephones. So they dismantled them. Immediately, the telephones went out of order. The local technicians came, fixed the telephones and returned the microphones. They were dismantled again and the telephones went out of order again. The ambassador had no alternative but to make peace with the microphones and let them stay where they were.

In Romania, as in other Communist countries, an ambassador never went alone to the hospital. When a foreign diplomat needed surgery, he generally went to Vienna or to another western capital, out of fear that, while under anaesthesia, he might be interrogated, or a "bug" (which could be heard outside like a microphone) could be planted in his body. No wonder Romania was called "the regime of the Securitate," the security service.

"Securitate" wasn't the only defect of Ceausescu's regime. Romania, which in those days produced thirteen million tons of petroleum a year, imported fifteen million tons, with a negative effect on its balance of payments. Romania's debts to banks and governments in the west and to creditors in the Middle East were estimated at more than $12 billion, and she was unable to pay them. Bucharest had, therefore, difficulties in obtaining new loans, while the gap was widening in its commercial balance.

Moscow had assigned Romania the position of an agricultural resource, the "granary of the Soviet Bloc." But Ceausescu considered this another aspect of his country's dependence on Moscow, while his ambition was to achieve the greatest possible independence in all spheres. His dream was to transform his agricultural country into an industrialized one, and he diverted all means to this goal.

A rigid regime of saving was introduced and all basic products went to export, the income from which was devoted to the industrialization effort. The enormous efforts, however, and the heavy investments in industry had poor results. The aspiration to high technology was above the abilities of the Romanians and the most sophisticated machines imported from Japan and other countries lay like stones no one could turn over. Agriculture, in the meantime, grew old and unproductive. The work system was old-fashioned; they did not have the necessary agricultural tools, equipment, and pesticides, and the young villagers tried to seek their luck in the cities.

The general lack of efficiency; the absence of motivation; the excessive bureaucracy; the rigid ideology, which saw in economic centralization the answer to everything and proved to be wrong; the export commitments to the countries of Eastern Europe; and the existence of many who had adopted the Romanian saying, "If you will steal, God, too, will help you"—all this contributed to the tragedy of the country's economy.

Thus, Romania, upon whom nature had bestowed gold, coal, petroleum and natural gas, iron and timber; plants, rivers, streams and torrents, lakes and a sea, put a small stab of envy in the heart of an Israeli. Romania had become a country incapable of providing her people with the minimum of basic foods.

The Romanians have a sense of humor, and in those very difficult days, the shortages and industrial backwardness contributed to the introduction of many jokes: Three Romanian women agreed to meet at a certain place on a certain date; one, as the representative of the past; the second, as the representative of the present; the third, as the representative of the future. The representative of the present arrived late, and the two others asked her for the reason. She replied, "I was waiting in a queue for cheese." The representative of the past asked, "What is a queue?" The representative of the future asked, "What is cheese?"

Another disturbing defect of the Romanian regime was the incredible personality cult of Nicolae Ceausescu, difficult to imagine for someone who had not seen it. Ceausescu believed that during a certain period of their history, nations need a symbol. Once there were kings, emperors, and princes as images of leaders. In Romania it was Ceausescu. With my fellow ambassadors, I often saw Ceausescu watching artistic programs dedicated to him, in halls decorated with posters, slogans, and pictures of him only. The president himself applauded, extending his hands toward the crowd of thousands, as they rose to their feet and shouted, "Ceausescu, the beloved son of the nation! Ceausescu, the rising sun of Romania! Ceausescu, the embodiment of the Romanian nation! Ceausescu, Romania's lay God!"

He dreamed of being transformed into a still living legend. His wife, Helena, was no less ambitious, aspiring for glory. According to a joke of those days, the president returned home one day and told his wife that he had decided to proclaim himself king. Helena replied, "Excellent idea." The next day, Ceausescu came home and said, "King is not enough, I will proclaim myself emperor!" Said Helena, "I agree from the bottom of my heart!" A few days passed and Ceausescu informed his wife about his decision to proclaim himself God. She responded, "You can't do that. I am God."

His foreign policy, however, seemed very positive. His "all directions policy," which widened and deepened his country's relations with many countries, had made significant achievements. The Western world favored Ceausescu's foreign policy and his activities for peace and, on his visits to Western countries, he was received like a real king. When he visited the United States, he was received with the highest honors and President Jimmy Carter called him "the architect of Sadat's visit to Jerusalem." When he arrived in England, he was greeted with warmth, great honors, glory, and splendor.

Ceausescu showed a great degree of political wisdom, and was one of the few world leaders who had been received with open arms by the president of the United States, the queen of England, and the king of Spain, as well as by the rulers of China, Vietnam, and Cambodia. Ceausescu believed in his principles and was an efficient politician. He was a successful maneuverer, a superb manipulator, a sharp polemicist, and fantastically erudite on an enormous variety of international subjects.

He studied well the matters he was dealing with, and liked to be precise. He worked hard, considered every subject seriously, and omitted no detail. His attitude was didactic, his arguments supported by full knowledge of the facts, and his wording was businesslike. Ceausescu used to say that while he had become a Communist at the age of sixteen, he was a Romanian by birth, and his slogan was, "First Romanian, then Communist." Being a sober politician, who knew the rules of political games, he studied the tolerance level of the Soviet "Big Brother" well, and walked the tightrope between the "Big Brother's" supervision and his own wish to pursue an independent policy. He played only the cards that would not stir up Moscow's anger too much.

Romania's attitude toward Israel was in line with her "all directions policy," but it was also the result of Ceausescu's being a brave man. On the issue of Israel, I saw him as very courageous *vis-à-vis* the Soviets. Already in 1967, Ceausescu was the only Communist leader who had refused Moscow's demand, after the Six-Day war, to break off relations with Israel. A year later, he agreed to raise the status of the diplomatic representations in Israel and in Romania to that of embassies.

In spite of the differences of opinion between Romania and Israel regarding the Arab-Israeli conflict: the Palestinian problem, the PLO, the final status of the administered territories, the status of Jerusalem, and the International Conference, a fruitful political dialogue developed between the two countries. With his political wisdom, Ceausescu succeeded in encouraging the first blossoms of peace in our region with the visit of Sadat in Jerusalem, which the Soviets condemned. When the Camp David agreements were signed in October 1978 for the establishment of peace between Egypt and Israel, and for negotiations to solve the Palestinian problem, I received a message from Menachem Begin for Ceausescu.

In it, Begin described the talks and discussions to reach the agreements, and thanked him for his efforts, stressing that on various occasions he, Begin, had mentioned Ceausescu's contribution to the peace process. Ceausescu was very pleased with the message and, when I mentioned Moscow's rejection of the agreements, he suggested that we should ignore it, and said, "The Camp David agreements are a *fait accompli*."

When he was invited to Moscow a month later for a meeting of the heads of state of the Soviet bloc to condemn the agreements, he went but did not sign the condemnation. It was published with the signatures of only the Soviet Union, Poland, Czechoslovakia, Hungary, Bulgaria, and East Germany. Ceausescu's not signing the condemnation was a brave deed that merited praise.

On March 16, 1979, I received a message from Begin for Ceausescu on the successful results of the negotiations on the peace treaty with Egypt. Begin again thanked Ceausescu for his significant contribution to the historic peace process, and concluded his message with expressions of appreciation and friendship. Ceausescu asked me to transmit to Begin his congratulations on the signing of the peace treaty, and he welcomed it publicly, in spite of the Arab and Soviet condemnations.

On October 6, 1981, while I was delivering another message from Begin to President Ceausescu and discussing with him how to advance the peace process in the Middle East, Anwar Sadat was assassinated in Cairo. The PLO spokesman declared that he embraced the man who had shot Sadat. In Damascus, Tripoli, and Beirut there was dancing in the streets and shots of joy.

Ceausescu sent a cable of condolence to Egypt and went to the Egyptian embassy in Bucharest to sign the condolence book, never having made such a gesture before.

Ceausescu's friendly attitude toward Israel also was shown with regard to the emigration of Romanian Jews to Israel. Since the re-establishment of the Jewish state, Jews had been permitted to leave for Israel, under a quota. For instance, during my five years of service, about a thousand Jews could leave every year within the framework of "reunification of families."

On this subject, too, Romania's attitude was in marked contrast to that of the Soviet Union and the other Communist countries. In Romania, we witnessed a situation of coexistence between the Communist regime and the Jewish community. Jews were not afraid to declare their faithfulness to the Jewish people and their love for the Land of Israel. Romania was a unique case in the Communist world.

It wasn't so, however, in 1944, when Romania was liberated on August 23 by the Red Army and became communist. In those days Jews who were with the communist leadership tried to imitate the Soviets in everything. They wanted to solve the Jewish question by the Russian pattern. They formed a "Jewish Democratic Committee," whose leaders aspired to strangle any basis of Jewish nationalism, to keep only a symbolic Yiddish culture, and to deny any spark of loyalty to Zionism and to the State of Israel.

In their struggle against what they called "negative trends," the people of the committee would slip to the lowest levels, including slander which caused the arrest of hundreds of Jews who were suspected of being "unfaithful" to the new regime. Although the committee was dissolved in 1962, a positive change began in the mid-1950s. Chief Rabbi David Moses Rosen convinced the Romanian authorities that it was impossible for lay Jews, hated by their own people, to head the Jewish community whose main basis was religion.

When we arrived in Bucharest, I was told that there were 26,000 Jews in the country. These were people who defined themselves as Jews in the 1977 census. In the Jewish community I was told there were many who did not register as Jews. Before the war, Romanian Jews numbered more than 800,000, about half of whom were killed in the war. Most of the Jewish survivors immigrated to Israel, and those who remained in Romania felt that if they wished, they could preserve their Judaism in all its aspects while keeping their obligations as Romanian citizens.

During our mission there, the Federation of Jewish Communities supplied to Romanian Jews religious services and materials related to all aspects of Jewish life. A network of "Torah Learning" (Talmud Torah) institutions was created to bring children and youth closer to Jewish values and traditions. Since the remnants of Romanian Jewry were mainly adult and elderly people, special emphasis was placed on social welfare assistance: food, clothing, medical treatment and medicines, as well as some cash money. The needy ones, who received only partial pensions from the state, received a monthly allowance. During the year, they received parcels of food and, toward winter, money to buy supplies for heating.

Compared with the situation of Jewish communities in the other countries of the Soviet bloc, that of the Romanian Jews was relatively good. The community was affiliated with the World Jewish Congress, and its chief rabbi, who was also the president of the Federation of Jewish Communities in Romania, served as a member of Parliament. The community published a bi-weekly news journal in three languages: Romanian, Hebrew, and Yiddish, and sometimes with additions in English. It also published an annual calendar, in three languages, with information about Jewish laws and customs, traditions, prayers, holidays, as well as a report of the events of the past year in the community.

When my wife and I visited the Jewish Historical Museum in Bucharest, it was an emotional experience for me as the Israeli ambassador and as a Holocaust survivor. No less emotional was the visit to the Jewish State Theater, established one hundred years earlier. The first time, we saw the original performance of Sholem Aleichem's "Fiddler on the Roof." It was sad to see only twenty persons in the audience. During the summer, Romania is visited by tourists from Israel and by Jews from other countries, who come to the theater, providing an infusion of encouragement to the artists. Without tourists, the artists on the stage sometimes outnumber the people in the audience.

When we were in Romania, there were sixty-three organized Jewish communities outside the capital, each with a synagogue and a community office. Most of Romania's Jews were Ashkenazim, but in Bucharest there was also a Sephardic synagogue with a congregation of a few hundred people.

As a rule, the Israeli ambassador seeks to be in constant close contact with the Jews of the country of his mission. In a democratic country, the ambassador may meet with any Jew or Jewish organization anytime, anywhere, discuss with them everything, help them with fund-raising and other activities for Israel, and contribute to the strengthening of Jewish and Hebrew culture and education. All this with no interference from the local authorities. I did so as a member of our embassies in Italy, Peru, and Argentina, and as consul-general in Toronto.

But in Romania it was different. I could not meet in private with any Jew, since contacts between citizens and foreign diplomats were strictly forbidden. During my five years in Romania, I did not invite any Jew privately to my home and did not receive any invitation from a Jew to come to his home. The only exception was Rabbi Rosen, who had permission to exchange invitations and visits with the Israeli ambassador.

I was convinced that he had to report to the authorities about his conversations with me, and he had to be very careful not to mislead them. We knew there were microphones hidden everywhere.

But we maintained official contacts with the community as such. The Israeli ambassador and members of his staff had reserved seats in the first row of the Choral Temple. This was so for embassy staff wives also. The members of the Israeli embassy went to the synagogues on Sabbath and holidays and attended the memorial services. We Israelis were always called to the Torah, and the Chief Rabbi blessed the State of Israel at the Holy Ark.

On the eve of Passover and the New Year, the ambassador visited the Rabbi and brought to him, and through him the entire Jewish community of Romania, the greetings and blessings of the State of Israel.

On the first evening of Passover, the first Seder was held by the ambassador at the embassy building for the entire Israeli colony and the next day all the members of the embassy participated in the Second Seder at the community center. On the festivals of Purim and Hanukkah, receptions were organized every year at the embassy for the Israeli students studying in Romania. The leaders of the Jewish community and other Jews were invited to receptions offered by the Israeli ambassador, and the embassy staff attended all festivals and cultural events and receptions organized by the community. The community supplied the embassy with kosher meat, and the embassy supplied the community with prayer books, prayer-shawls, Megillahs, Haggadot, books for studies of Jewish education, and study books of the Hebrew language along with the spinning tops and noise makers for Purim.

My wife and I visited all sixty-three Jewish communities of Romania in that vanishing world of the last of our brothers there. I was the first Israeli ambassador to visit those communities, and our meetings with the Jews were a very emotional experience for us. Romania was considered a reservoir of Jewish creative force that was ended by the Holocaust.

During these tours, my wife and I traveled thousands of miles, and the trips were sometimes very tiring, but the glow of pride in the eyes of our brother Jews when they saw the Israeli ambassador and the Israeli flag; the great cordiality and affection they bestowed upon us, the happiness in their faces, made the visits to those communities an unforgettable experience. The Jews would go around my car, caress the flag, and say, "When we see this flag, our heart warms up."

They would make the benediction of *Shehechiyanu*, for having reached the moment when an Israeli ambassador finally came to their community, would say a prayer for the State of Israel, and in one place the president of the community quoted Theodore Herzl, "If you wish, it will come true."

When Shimon Peres, leader of the Labor Party in Israel, visited Bucharest, the Choral Temple was filled to capacity. The rabbi invited Peres and me to open the Holy Ark and blessed the State of Israel in Hebrew, after he had blessed the Romanian state both in Hebrew and Romanian. The choir sang "We brought you peace," "Hava Naguila," and "Jerusalem the Golden."

The reception for Peres at the community restaurant was attended also by some of the Romanian hosts. After they heard the speeches and saw the enthusiastic crowd, one of them said to me, "You are very privileged, as an ambassador, to have such a community!"

All that was made possible thanks to Ceausescu's positive attitude towards the Jews and Israel. Of course, in addition, the Romanians had concrete economic interests in the development of relations with Israel. We had signed a commercial agreement, but the trade balance was always in Romania's favor. There was also an agreement between the two countries for agricultural cooperation, and the Romanians gained on matters like repairing the soil, the improvement of plant types, betterment of livestock, and organizing research and training in agriculture. They were especially interested in learning the modern scientific systems being used in Israeli agriculture. On our part, this agreement helped to stimulate exports in agriculture, the sale of fertilizers and irrigation tools, etc.

When the Arabs demanded that the Romanians join the Arab boycott against Israel, the Romanians replied that this was interference in their internal affairs, and rejected the demand. Romania also had a significant income from Israeli tourists. The tourist movement between the two countries was mainly one-way, from Israel to Romania, because of the limitations that existed for the travel of Romanian citizens abroad, except to the Soviet Union. During one of my conversations at the Romanian Foreign Ministry, one of its top officials stressed the need for developing bilateral relations in all fields, especially economics, and noted, "Sentiments can be transient, but when they are based on concrete economic interests, they become much more firm."

Among the concrete interests of Romania was the emigration of Jews to Israel. This was linked to Romania's status as Most Favored Nation (MFN), granted by the United States. This status had to be renewed every year by the U.S. Senate and, before renewal, a Senate sub-committee discussed it with the administration and examined the problem of emigration from Romania to Israel, as well as to Germany and the United States.

While I was discussing the emigration to Israel with the president of the Romanian parliament, he told me a joke about an emissary of the Communist Party who visited a collective farm to encourage its members to increase production. The emissary explained how much the national income would rise in dollars if every member of the farm would increase the production of corn. One of the members of the farm rose to his feet and asked, "What is the situation with corn production in the United States?" The party propagandist rebuked him, "We are not discussing the situation in the United States, but in Romania." He went on to talk about tomato production, explaining the importance of increasing it. He was again asked, "What is the tomato production in Switzerland?"

He censured this one, too, and went on to explain the importance of increasing potato production. Then somebody asked, "Is it true that Israel is paying dollars to Romania for the exit of each Jew from Romania to Israel?" The emissary asked what the relation was between the question and what he was talking about, and the person explained, "Instead of corn, tomatoes, and potatoes, maybe it would be more convenient to grow Jews?"

Later, after Ceausescu had been overthrown and executed, a story appeared in the *Wall Street Journal* about Ceausescu having received $800 million from Israel deposited to his personal account in Switzerland for having permitted the Jews of Romania to immigrate to Israel.

Nothing had been paid to Ceausescu's personal account. Payments had been made from government to government, and the amounts paid by Israel were not very significant. During my years of service there, the average was about $1,000-1,500 per capita, and during the twenty-five years of Ceausescu's rule, only 40,000 Jews left Romania, so how could it be $800 million? Between the day of the creation of Israel in 1948, and my arrival there in 1978, 270,000 Jews had left Romania for Israel. During my five years there, about 5,300 Jews left. In those five years, more than 50,000 Romanians left for Germany, and more than 10,000 for the United States.

Germany, too, paid per capita, and a very much higher price, while the United States made a global payment of hundreds of thousands of dollars a year through renewal of the Most Favored Nation status. The Senate sub-committee renewed that status every year ignoring, rightfully, the payment issue.

Had the Russians agreed to Jewish emigration then, we would willingly have paid them, too, and Ceausescu had tried to help us to get Jewish immigrants from the Soviet Union. He agreed to let the Soviet Jews go to Israel via Bucharest and thus prevent the dropping out of most of them in Vienna. Moscow refused.

The author (left) presents his credentials as Israeli Ambassador to Romanian President, Nicolae Ceausescu

President Ceausescu invited the Heads of Diplomatic Missions to a traditional New Years' reception (1982). Aba Gefen is standing (on her left) next to Helena Ceausescu, wife of the President

XXXIII.

FIGHTING A NEW WAVE OF TERRORISM

Ceausescu was involved in all the stages of the war in Lebanon, which was the result of Soviet permanent support to the PLO as a terrorist force. Its aim to destroy Israel was openly set forth in the PLO proclamation, following the Yom Kippur War, "The Palestinian people have determined to recover their homeland through armed struggle and a long-term popular war....The restoration to the Palestinian people of their lawful rights in their homeland means the liberation of the whole of Palestine territory."

Unfortunately, the Yom Kippur War and the peace with Egypt had not changed the Arab position and they initiated new waves of terrorism, which the Soviets, in the absence of relations with Israel, supported directly. They were hoping to advance their hold in the Middle East within the framework of their global confrontation with the United States.

In its new wave of terrorism, the PLO killed the Israeli diplomat Yaacov Bar-Simantov in Paris in early April 1982 after the failure of its attack in November 1979 against our ambassador in Lisbon (one guard was killed and three wounded). It attacked our ambassador in London, Shlomo Argov. Argov was wounded in the head on June 3, 1982, when he left a diplomatic dinner at a hotel.

The next day at noon, our planes attacked Lebanon in a reaction to the criminal deed against our ambassador. Five PLO arms depots were hit at the soccer stadium in Beirut. A school for military training was also hit, and an ammunition dump exploded. There were many victims and thousands fled Beirut.

PLO terrorists increased their firing on Israeli settlements in northern Galilee. An Israeli helicopter was shot down and the two pilots were missing; a "Skyhawk" plane crashed; its pilot was seriously wounded and taken prisoner by the PLO. Israel decided to launch Operation "Peace for Galilee" in order to free the settlements of Galilee from the terrorist acts and to destroy the organization that had as its goal the annihilation of the State of Israel.

On June 6, 1982, Israel's Defense Forces (IDF) crossed the Lebanese border and advanced along the coastal road to Tyre, reaching Nabatiya in Central Lebanon, then to "Fatahland" in the east. The Israeli navy landed tanks and infantry north of Sidon, and IDF units reached the Beirut-Damascus road. Continuing the advance, the IDF clashed with the Syrian army. Forty-one Syrian planes were downed by the Israeli Air Force and nineteen Syrian ground-to-air missile batteries were destroyed. The IDF reached the vicinity of Beirut's international airport.

Israel accepted President Ronald Reagan's call for a cease-fire and proposed an arrangement to station a multinational force in southern Lebanon. But the PLO violated the cease-fire a few hours after it went into effect. The IDF besieged West Beirut, cutting off power and water, and occupied Beirut's international airport.

Ambassador Philip Habib, special emissary of President Reagan, continued his efforts to effect the PLO withdrawal from Lebanon. Syria, Jordan, and Saudi Arabia agreed in principle to absorb thousands of terrorists from Lebanon, and about seven thousand PLO people left. On August 23, 1982, Bashir Gemayel, the leader of the Phalange forces, was elected president of Lebanon, and on September 1, Prime Minister Begin held talks with Bashir Gemayel in Nahariyah. Two weeks later, Bashir Gemayel was murdered. IDF units seized West Beirut and surrounded the Palestinian refugee camps Sabra, Shatila, and Fakahani without entering them.

During the days of September 16-18, the Christian Phalange forces of Bashir Gemayel carried out massacres in the Sabra and Shatila camps, killing hundreds of civilians.

On May 17, 1983, an Israel-Lebanon agreement was signed, proclaiming the termination of war between Israel and Lebanon, and establishing the formation of a security zone. Both countries committed themselves to sign a peace treaty that would ensure lasting security for both. The Israeli and Lebanese parliaments ratified the agreement.

Israeli casualties were 657 killed in the "Peace for Galilee" operation. Under massive Syrian pressure and threats, on March 5, 1984, Lebanon unilaterally abrogated the Israeli-Lebanese agreement. A capitulation to Syrian dictates, it meant a death sentence for Lebanese independence and sovereignty.

Israel carried out a redeployment of its forces in the north, and peace is being ensured there by the IDF with the help of the South Lebanese Army, whose first commander was Major Haddad. After his death, General Antoine Lahad was appointed and given the mandate for maintaining the security and safety of the residents of the area. The actions of the South Lebanese Army reflect the refusal of the people of southern Lebanon, Christians and Moslems, to capitulate to PLO terror, and their decision to protect their families and homes.

Asked by journalists about the tasks of the South Lebanese Army, General Lahad responded, "I came to South Lebanon not to secure Israel's border, I came here on a mission...to bring peace and security to the region, so that Southern Lebanon and the State of Israel can live together in a neighborly fashion."

In June 1984, Israel and Syria exchanged prisoners: Israel returned 291 soldiers and 72 coffins, Syria returned three soldiers, three civilians and five coffins. Earlier, Israel and the PLO exchanged prisoners: Israel received six IDF soldiers in return for 4,600 terrorists. Ceausescu had tried to bring about the exchange of prisoners with Syria and the PLO two years earlier. I met with him on July 15, 1982, and delivered an urgent personal request from Begin. Begin asked Ceausescu to address President Assad of Syria to propose to him the exchange of prisoners. Israel would transfer to Syria all the Syrian prisoners in her hands, soldiers and officers, and the thousands of terrorists who were taken prisoners by the

IDF. In exchange, Assad would return all the Israelis who were in the hands of Syria and the PLO. Ceausescu promised to transmit our proposals immediately to President Assad. On various occasions, I inquired about Assad's reaction, and was told that Ceausescu never received an answer from the Syrian president.

Through the good offices of Ceausescu, Arafat and Begin exchanged messages on the Beirut crisis and, a couple of times during the war, Ceausescu sent his special political adviser, Vasile Pungan, with messages to Prime Minister Begin. Pungan's visits to Israel and his meetings with Begin contributed to the prestige of Romania in the West and in the East, as a country promoting an independent foreign policy, and trying to bridge the gap between the positions of the parties to the conflict.

This was especially important for Romania since the Soviet Union, having broken off relations with Israel, had excluded herself from the negotiations. On one occasion, Pungan left Begin's office in Jerusalem and Philip Habib entered it. Thus, the United States and Romania were active factors dealing with the crisis of the Lebanese war.

On November 13, 1982, I went to see Ceausescu for my farewell meeting. Most of the ambassadors met with Ceausescu only twice during their term of service, to present their credentials and to say goodbye. As a result of the exchange of messages between him and Begin, I had held ten meetings with Ceausescu. He thanked me and expressed his appreciation for my activity during my five years of service in Bucharest which, he said, contributed much to the development of good relations between our two countries. He asked me that, in my new position in Israel where I was to be appointed adviser to Foreign Minister Shamir, I should try to influence the government to take a more moderate stand on the PLO.

It was his opinion that most of the Palestinians were now in favor of a peaceful agreement with Israel. He said, "As long as the Palestinian problem remains unsolved, permanent danger will threaten Israel's existence, and if Israel counts on the arms she has, the Arabs, with all their money, will be able to buy any arms that they wish."

The president argued that Sadat, too, had said years ago publicly, like Arafat now, that his goal was the destruction of Israel, but in 1977 he changed his mind and peace was signed between Egypt and Israel. Ceausescu said he was convinced that a similar development could occur in the positions of Assad and the PLO. He asked me to transmit to Begin and to Shimon Peres, the leader of the Labor Party, his feeling that Jerusalem did not give enough consideration to his evaluations, did not respond to his proposals, clung to wishful thinking and to fixed patterns of thought, and thus missed opportunities for a peaceful solution of the Arab-Israeli conflict.

On my return to Jerusalem, I transmitted Ceausescu's message to Begin, Peres, and Shamir. After I had retired, Shamir visited Romania, in 1987 and 1988, as foreign minister and prime minister respectively. Before departing for Bucharest in August 1987, Shamir said at a press conference that he knew Ceausescu had recently met with various Arab leaders, among them Arafat, and he expected to hear from Ceausescu about those meetings.

On his return from Bucharest, Shamir said he had talked with Ceausescu regarding his meetings with Arafat. That meant a certain change in the attitude of Israel.

I recalled Ceausescu's request in August 1979, to send his special adviser, Vasile Pungan, to report to Begin about his talks with President Assad and Arafat, as I listened to Shamir describe Ceausescu's talks with Arafat. Begin responded that he would like very much to hear about the talks with Assad, but talks with Yasser Arafat, the head of a murderers' organization, could not be a subject for conversation with Israel's prime minister.

XXXIV.

MOSCOW'S EXCUSES

Ceausescu did not limit himself to friendly political dialogues with Israel and contribute to the peace process in the area. When the Chinese leader, Huah-Kuo-Fen, visited Bucharest, Ceausescu received me on Begin's request, and promised he would use his good offices for the normalization of relations between Israel and China. Ceausescu raised the question with Huah Kuo-Fen, first in Bucharest and later during his visit in Peking, but the Chinese were not yet ready.

On various occasions, I discussed with Ceausescu and with his foreign minister our relations with Moscow, and they told me they were constantly trying to convince the Russians to re-establish relations with us. In October 1978, when I asked to see Ceausescu to deliver Begin's message, he was busy with the Soviet foreign minister, Andrey Gromyko, who had arrived in Bucharest. But Ceausescu received me the same day, before his meeting with Gromyko. Ceausescu promised he would discuss the renewal of our relations with Gromyko.

I left his office, and Gromyko came in.

When Gromyko insisted that the Camp David Accord should be rejected, Ceausescu explained to him the importance of those agreements for the Arabs. "Sadat already got back part of the territories and will get all the rest," Ceausescu argued, and asked Gromyko, "Is it your idea that Sadat should abolish the agreements and return the territories to Israel?" Gromyko remained silent.

In those days, I maintained a friendly dialogue with the Soviet ambassador in Bucharest, as well as with most of the other ambassadors from the communist countries. The Soviet ambassador, Drozdenko, was the dean of the diplomatic corps in Bucharest, and I asked to see him in this capacity. He invited me to meet with him on February 20. It was the first time since the breaking of relations between our two countries in 1967 that an Israeli ambassador was going to officially visit the Soviet embassy, and it was at a time when relations between Jerusalem and Moscow were tense. The Soviets were extending every possible help to the Arabs, in the political and military fields, and a great amount of hate literature against Israel had been created in Russia. They even revived the "Protocols of the Elders of Zion" of czarist ill-fame. Jews were dismissed from key Government posts and institutions of higher learning barred Jewish students. It was not the best of times for meeting the Soviet ambassador, but I went.

I arrived at the Soviet embassy in my official car and the Soviet ambassador received me very cordially. We spoke Russian and English (through an interpreter) and at a certain point he remarked, "I have already seen you at the hunt, where you received your share." "You, too, Mr. Ambassador," I said.

The ambassador spoke extensively about the Soviet Union's role in destroying Fascism in the Second World War, about the 20 million Soviet citizens, among them many Jews, killed, and mentioned that every year on May 9 ceremonies were held in Bucharest to mark the end of the war and the victory over Nazism. Wreaths of flowers were placed in memory of the Unknown Soldier at four places, including the statue for the Unknown Soldier of the Red Army. He expressed his hope that I would attend these ceremonies, including the one at their monument.

I responded positively and explained to him that in addition to doing it in the capacity of Israel's ambassador, I had a good personal reason for doing it: I was liberated from the Nazi oppression by the Red Army. I then mentioned to the ambassador the Soviet Union's role in the creation of Israel, and quoted the speech at the United Nations of Soviet Foreign Minister Andrey Gromyko in favor of the Jewish state. I told him that his country had thus contributed to the change in my personal life.

On November 29, 1947, I was a refugee, and now I am the ambassador of the independent Jewish state. I added that with the help of the Soviet Union, we, the survivors of the Holocaust, have lived to see the miracle of the restoration of the Jewish Commonwealth, a privilege tragically denied to the lost millions of our brothers and sisters, mothers and fathers, murdered by the Nazis.

The ambassador reacted: "We both belong to the same generation, and certain events are part of ourselves, too deep in our hearts to be forgotten."

He said he would be happy to continue to converse with me, and he hoped that we would have many opportunities to meet.

When the Egyptian, Israeli, and American delegations convened at Camp David, I met the Soviet military attaché, General Kociumov, at a reception at the Portuguese embassy, and he asked me my opinion of the chances of Camp David. I replied that I was very optimistic, and added, "The Soviet Union could make my optimism come true."

"How?" asked the general, and I said to him, "As long as the Soviet Union plays an anti-Israel role in our area, she cannot be a partner in the negotiations to solve the Arab-Israeli conflict. But if the Soviet Union renews its diplomatic relations with us, she will become a partner to the discussions and could make a constructive contribution. This would be to the benefit of all the peoples of the Middle East as well as to the benefit of the Soviet Union herself."

He responded, "The policy of the Soviet Union has always been that Israel has the right to exist as an independent and sovereign state, but you must understand that the Soviet Union has interests in Syria, Algiers, Iraq, and other Arab countries, and therefore, the problem is not simple. I will, however, report about our conversation to the high command."

Who was his high command? Who were his superiors? The Soviet minister of defense? Or the head of the KGB? It was the general view that the military attachés at the Soviet embassies were KGB people and were responsible for all KGB activities. A week later we met again. He said he hoped that after Camp David some progress could be made in regard to the relations between Moscow and Jerusalem.

Nothing advanced, however, after Camp David, and the Soviets continued to publicly reject the agreements and condemn them. But they continued to keep the door open to us through their people in Bucharest. On March 26, 1979, at a cocktail party at the Greek embassy on the occasion of their National Day, I was toasting with the Egyptian ambassador the signing of the Egyptian-Israeli Peace Treaty to take place that very evening in Washington. General Kociumov came up and shook hands with us. I asked him, "Aren't you congratulating us on the signing of our peace treaty?"

"There are still nine hours," he replied, and added that Moscow will not change its position as long as the Arab countries had not changed theirs.

Two months later, I met the Soviet ambassador at the embassy of Liberia, who said, "I don't understand you Israelis. You may lose your opportunity to achieve rest and quietness. If you were generous on the question of the territories and agreed to an international conference, you could get guarantees from all: the United States, the Soviet Union, the United Nations, and others. The Arab forces will continue to increase and will become more than Israel's, who will not be able to stand up to them."

I explained our position to him in detail, and we continued our conversation in February 1979 at the traditional diplomatic hunt. While sitting at the table for drinks, the Soviet ambassador asked me to toast with him. I raised a glass of water and extended it toward him. He refused and said, "I know that it is forbidden for a Jew to travel on Saturday. I never heard that it is forbidden for a Jew to drink wine on Sunday."

I changed the glass.

On July 14, 1980, at the French embassy, I met for the first time the new Soviet military attaché, Commodore Terentiev, who had replaced Kociumov. He was very cordial and said that Kociumov had told him about our talks and had said that I was sincere and frank, and that I had good personal feelings towards the Soviet Union, being a Holocaust survivor who had been liberated by the Red Army. Terentiev expressed his hope that friendly relations would also prevail between him and me, and he immediately passed on to business. He said he was not a political person, but a military one, and therefore, whatever he would say to me would be his personal view. He thought that Moscow's breaking off of relations with Israel was a mistake. In his view, these relations should be renewed and he was convinced that they would be renewed. Only by maintaining relations with us will the Soviet Union be able to negotiate with us. "It is not in the interest of the Soviet Union to remain outside the peace process," he added.

I replied that the Soviet Union had broken relations with Israel and, therefore, the initiative for their renewal would have to come from her. Terentiev then asked whether he could consider our conversation as the first contact towards negotiations on the renewal of diplomatic relations between us. I replied affirmatively and at that point, the American military attaché, Colonel Womak, approached us.

Terentiev said to him, "I am talking with the Israeli ambassador about renewing diplomatic relations."

"If that happens, it will be wonderful," Womak replied.

My cable on my conversation with Terentiev reached Prime Minister Menachem Begin when he was on his sick bed. Begin replied to my cable from the hospital and asked that, when I see the Russian commodore again, I emphasize Israel's permanent interest in the maintenance of normal relations with the Soviet Union and the other Soviet bloc countries, as he, Begin, had noted publicly on June 20, 1977, and repeated in a public speech on July 7, 1980.

The prime minister also proposed that I remind the Soviet Military Attaché that Lenin had recognized Jewish nationality and the Soviet Union had recognized the Jewish state when it was established. It therefore makes sense that the Soviet Union should permit children of Jewish nationality to emigrate to Israel.

I transmitted Begin's reply to Terentiev on August 19. Terentiev said he would report to his superiors that Israel was ready to renew diplomatic relations. I agreed.

However, on January 22, 1981, the East German ambassador told me that no East European country would renew diplomatic relations with Israel as long as it knew that Moscow was against it and, to the best of his knowledge, Moscow was still against it.

On November 30, 1981, a Memorandum of Understanding for Strategic Co-operation was signed between Israel and the United States, and Radio Moscow broadcast an attack against Israel. The same day I met the East German ambassador again, and he said to me that the Israel-American Memorandum of Understanding had complicated the situation. This step will increase Israel's dependence on the United States, and will make it more difficult to advance toward the normalization of Soviet-Israel relations.

I told him that unfortunately all our efforts to get closer to the Soviet Union had failed. The Soviet Union has remained hostile to Israel and is acting in a way that endangers Israel's security, having transformed Syria and Libya into dangerous arsenals.

"Moscow is ready," I said, "to supply arms to anyone who proclaims a holy war against us, and I consider that behavior as an expression of anti-Semitism."

He replied, "How can you say such a thing in view of your contacts and conversations with me and with my colleagues from the other Socialist countries?" I answered that the Holocaust has taught us something, and we separated with a warm handshake.

A week later, on December 7, 1981, I received an invitation from the Bulgarian ambassador, Pitar Danailov, to a reception he was to host on December 10, for the diplomatic corps and the Romanian authorities, on the occasion of his departure from Bucharest. It was the custom that invitations to such events were sent a fortnight in advance. The invitation to me, at the last moment, must have been sent as a result of a consideration which did not exist when the other invitations had been sent out.

Despite the fact that on the invitation was explicitly written "Aba Gefen and wife," and on the envelope, "Aba Gefen, Ambassador Extraordinary and Plenipotentiary of Israel," I could not exclude the possibility of a mistake at the Bulgarian embassy.

It had not happened since 1967 that an Israeli ambassador was officially invited to an embassy of a communist country that had broken relations with us. I sent a cable to Jerusalem asking for permission to accept the invitation, and received permission.

During the two days before the reception, we were full of excitement. To go to the Bulgarian embassy in the official car, with the Israeli flag flying, was not a small thing. What will my colleagues say? What will the Arabs say? From my personal point of view, our visit to the Bulgarian embassy would be the climax of my contacts with diplomats from the Soviet bloc countries.

I did not believe that the invitation was a personal gesture toward me on the part of the Bulgarian ambassador. I had maintained much more friendly and closer relations with the Ambassadors of Poland, Vietnam, Czechoslovakia, and Yugoslavia, and they had not invited me to their farewell parties. The very fact that the decision to invite me was taken at the last moment was proof that it wasn't casual or personal.

Maybe, I said to myself, my words to the East German ambassador about the hostile attitude of the Soviet Union, and my insinuation about anti-Semitism, had helped to bring it about.

On December 10, I arrived with my wife at the Bulgarian embassy. When we entered the big hall, the Bulgarian ambassador and his wife welcomed us with a smile, shook our hands, and expressed their pleasure at our having come. Close to the Bulgarian hosts, the Soviet ambassador was standing, not surprised at all to see us. We shook hands warmly, and for an hour and a half we were the focus of the reception, the sensation of the evening. Ambassadors from the West and from the East approached us, some of them to greet us, others to express their opinion about our very presence there.

The Romanian Deputy foreign minister, Constantin Oancha, took me aside and said he was very happy to see me at the reception. He will report on it to the foreign minister, who will surely inform President Ceausescu, who acted constantly for the normalization of our relations with Moscow. I asked him whether my invitation could be a personal gesture towards me?

He replied, "It could have been a personal gesture if the Soviet ambassador were not present. Since he is here, it means that your presence here is neither casual nor personal. You may consider your presence here tonight as proof that Moscow is beginning finally to understand what we have understood all the time and were telling them. Your presence here is a significant step toward the renewal of your relations with Moscow."

Moscow, however, did not renew relations. The Russians turned this way and that with all kinds of excuses: the Camp David agreements, the peace treaty with Egypt, the Jerusalem Law, the Golan Heights Law, the International Conference, the destruction of the Iraqi atomic reactor by our air force, the Memorandum of Understanding, our increased world campaign for the right of Soviet Jews to emigrate to Israel, with increased Arab pressure on them not to permit emigration.

Although they always found a reason to say that it was not the right moment for renewing diplomatic relations, they never interrupted their contacts and relations with me.

Foreign Minister Yitzhak Shamir greets his newly-appointed Adviser, Aba Gefen, at a reception following Gefen's return from his mission to Romania (November 1982)

XXXV.

MASSIVE RETURN TO ANCESTRAL HOMELAND

When, with the establishment of the State of Israel, the gates of the country became wide open to receive every Jew who wanted to come, the three million Jews of the Soviet Union were not permitted to leave. The Arabs, whose opposition to the immigration of Jews to their ancestral homeland began many years ago, applauded the Soviets.

Shortly after Hitler took power in Germany, the Soviet Union started a cultural genocide against the Jews, and any attempt by a Jew to leave the Soviet Union was considered illegal and severely punishable. It was after the death of Stalin, and the Twentieth Congress of the Communist Party in 1956, that the truth of the persecution of Soviet Jewry became widely known. Only then did awareness of the Jewish problem in the U.S.S.R. spread throughout the West, and the global cry "Let my people go!" began.

Prolonged and tenacious efforts by Israel's envoys on every continent, at the U.N. and in other international forums, as well as the intervention of Jewish organizations, intellectual leaders in many lands, parliaments, and governments, drove the Soviet Union into a defensive moral quandary. In spite of strong Arab opposition, Moscow began to respond.

Israel's victory in the Six-Day War emboldened Soviet Jews. Prisoner-of-Zion Natan Sharansky arrived in Israel after having spent nine years in Soviet prisons and labor camps for his activities in the Aliyah movement of Jews who were struggling to emigrate to Israel.

He writes in his memoirs, "The Six-Day War made an indelible impression on me as it did on most Soviet Jews for, in addition to fighting for her life, Israel was defending our dignity. On the eve of the war, when Israel's destruction seemed almost inevitable, Soviet anti-Semites were jubilant. But a few days later, even anti-Jewish jokes started to change, and throughout the country, in spite of pro-Arab propaganda, you could now see a grudging respect for Israel and for Jews."

Younger Jews in particular, literally risking their lives, began to courageously demand the right to depart for Israel, whether under the family reunion concept or as repatriation to the historical homeland of the Jewish people. It is often said that the creation of Israel added ten meters of stature to every Jew everywhere. It is true. But it is no less true that our posture had been made even more upright by the courage and example shown by those young Jews in the Soviet Union.

While I was "repatriated" from Russia on false papers and under a false name forty-six years ago, by the 1970s large numbers of Jews could leave Russia legally. I had not dared to envision that in my wildest dreams. The Arabs declared war on that Aliyah and, at the end of September 1973, Arab gunmen broke into one of the trains carrying Jews from the Soviet Union to Vienna, kidnapped seven Russian Jews (including a seventy-one-year-old man, an ailing woman and a three-year-old child) and brazenly informed the Austrians that unless they instantly put an end to the assistance given the Soviet Jewish immigrants and closed down the Jewish Agency transit camp at Schonau Castle, not only would the hostages be killed but there would be violent retaliation against Austria.

Unfortunately, the Austrian Government gave in at once, with loud rejoicing both from the gunmen (who were immediately whisked away to Libya) and from the entire Arab press, which could hardly contain its glee at what it called "the successful commando blow to the movement of Russian Jews emigrating to Israel."

When the blessed massive Aliyah from the Soviet Union began, the Arabs' intensive opposition to it took on the rigid patterns of the past. They launched a propaganda and political campaign, sending letters, exerting pressure, and making threats directed not only against the Aliyah and Israel, but against the Soviet Union for opening its gates and against the United States for demanding that opening.

On April 10, 1990, at a meeting of PLO officials, Yasser Arafat said, "First, I want to say clearly: Open fire on the new Jewish immigrants, be they Soviet, Falasha, or anything else. I want you to shoot, on the ground or in the air, at every immigrant who thinks our land is a playground and that immigration to it is a vacation or picnic. From today on, the ball is in your court. I don't want to hear anyone say that political decision-makers prevent us from taking military action against the immigrants. It makes no difference if they live in Jaffa or in Jericho. I give you explicit instructions to open fire. Do everything to stop the flow of immigration."

The same day, a spokesman of the Islamic fundamentalist Hamas, addressing a rally in Amman, said that killing the immigrants was permissible and that Hamas would treat them as direct targets. On May 22, 1990, the General Command of the "Popular Front for the Liberation of Palestine" broadcast the following "welcome" message to the new immigrants, "On your feet you are coming to your deaths, on your feet you are coming to hell. New immigrants, you are coming to Palestine to see your deaths with your own eyes. Welcome!"

On July 9, 1990, Islamic Jihad issued a call: "We call on all our heroic agitators to continue to stab the Soviet Jewish immigrants with knives so as to perturb the enemy and sow fear in his ranks."

These Arab threats, however, have not affected the flow of the Aliyah. During 1990 and 1991, about 300,000 Soviet Jews arrived in Israel and hundreds of thousands more Soviet Jews are expected to come in the future. Thanks to Aliyah, the Jewish independent State has been re-established. As a result of Aliyah, the state has grown and developed. A constant Aliyah will secure its very existence, strong politically, militarily, economically, and demographically, and the Jewish people will have the chance to develop its capacity and creativity to the maximum.

In what was the Soviet Union, another million Jews are waiting to emigrate to Israel. They have postponed their departure because of the discouraging reports from relatives and friends about the absorption difficulties in Israel: thousands of new immigrants are unemployed; other thousands do not work in their professions; and there are problems of housing.

There is great hope in Israel that the $10 billion loan guarantee from the United States will help overcome the problems. But, large loan guarantees could be a dangerous burden on the economy of the country unless they are used for purposes of infrastructure development, the attraction of capital investment to export industries, and the creation of work sites for the successful absorption of newcomers. Only real structural reform will speed the arrival of those who hesitate. This is today the main challenge facing Israel.

By historic coincidence, the opening of the gates of the Soviet Union was followed with the end of the tragedy of Ethiopian Jewry. After years of alienation, Ethiopia resumed full diplomatic relations with Israel and permitted its remaining Jews to move to Israel. Thanks to the intervention of the American president, George Bush, with the authorities in Addis Ababa, 14,000 Ethiopian Jews were flown to Israel within thirty-six hours.

While the Aliyah of Soviet Jews presented Israel with the need to provide them with new homes and employment, the problems of the Ethiopian Aliyah went far beyond housing and work. It is literally a question of rebuilding their lives in every sense of the word. The absorption of all those new immigrants requires much imagination, vision, and dedication.

While only two thousand Jews remained in Ethiopia, more than two million Jews still live in the Soviet Union, where *Glasnost* and *Perestroika*, which made mass emigration of Jews to Israel possible, also opened all the anti-Semitic faucets, whose main operator is *Pamyat*. This organization bases its ideology on Russian nationalist sentiments and exploits latent anti-Semitic feelings. So, while governmental anti-Semitism is no longer Soviet policy, there is a considerable increase in anti-Semitic displays at the grass-roots level, causing grave concern and even panic among Soviet Jews.

Glasnost and *Perestroika* produced another result: the independence of the Baltic countries—a development justified in itself, but worrisome when seen through Jewish eyes. The Baltic countries, Lithuania, Latvia, and Estonia, lost their independence when they were occupied by the Soviet army as a result of the Hitler-Stalin pact of August 23, 1939. There is no doubt that these countries' demand to separate from the Soviet Union and renew their independent status was justified. But many Holocaust survivors, myself included, did not join in the enthusiasm most of the world displayed for the national aspirations of the Baltics.

Nor is our lack of enthusiasm caused only by the past of these three countries whose nationals, with the Ukrainians, were among the most vicious collaborators of the Nazis, but by their conduct at present. After having achieved independence, the Baltic countries are attempting to eradicate the history of their nationals' anti-Jewish atrocities during the German occupation, and to rehabilitate the murderers of Jews. I have a photograph of a monument erected near my native village, Simna, honoring Lithuanians who participated in the massacre of my brother Jews.

Fort IX in Kovno, which, like Babi Yar in the Ukraine and Ponary Forest in Vilna, was used exclusively for murdering Jews, is to be converted into a museum commemorating Stalin's atrocities. What a perversion of history! A similar distortion occurred at Ponary, where a monument was erected for the 70,000 Jews murdered there. The Lithuanians opposed the placing of an inscription on the monument that would say "the Jews were murdered by the Nazis and their local collaborators." They refused to include the word "local," which, they explained, would explicitly refer to the Lithuanians. They insisted on using only the word "collaborators."

This distorted inscription was permitted only in Hebrew and Yiddish, not in Lithuanian and Russian. Future Lithuanian generations will not know about the thousands of Lithuanian Nazi collaborators who committed sadistic murder. An additional desecration was made at Ponary by the setting up, at the very site of the monument for the murdered Jews, of tombstones for fourteen Lithuanians slain in struggle against the Soviets.

From a Jewish point of view, the Lithuanians, Latvians, and Estonians will deserve their recently obtained independence if they demonstrate their sincere repentance for the horrors their people perpetrated in the Holocaust, ask the Jewish people for forgiveness, prosecute the murderers of the Jews, properly mark the mass graves and all other sites where Jews were annihilated, and desist from the attempt to eradicate the memory of Lithuanian, Latvian, and Estonian atrocities.

Aba Gefen (far right) assists Rabbi David Moses Rosen during the Kol Nidrei on the eve of Yom Kippur (Bucharest, Romania)

XXXVI.

FACING ANOTHER HITLER

Arab opposition to Aliyah is motivated by a fundamental rejection of Israel's right to exist. This is why Israel considered Arafat's statement in Geneva, on December 14, 1988, purporting to renounce terrorism and recognize Israel's right to exist, as couched in fraudulent and misleading terms. Unfortunately, this statement made the United States forget the attack on the *Achille Lauro* cruise ship and the murder of Leon Klinghoffer, as well as the other Arab barbarities and atrocities. The very next day, Washington began a dialogue with the PLO, a dialogue that unfortunately made the Americans appease the Arabs at the U.N. at Israel's expense. This appeasement showed itself even during the discussions about the disturbances on the Temple Mount, after Washington broke off its dialogue with the PLO, having realized that Arafat's statement had been duplicitous.

The disturbances on the Temple Mount were caused by Arab terrorists who threw deadly rocks upon the heads of thousands of Jewish worshippers during the Jewish holiday of Sukkot. However, not a word against the homicidal terrorists, while all hurried to condemn the Israelis for defending themselves. Would the U.N. condemn the Russians, French, or British for defending themselves against terrorist attacks in Moscow, Paris, or London? Such is the double standard at the United Nations: one for Israel and another for the rest of the world. If there is any difference between Israel and the others, it is that Moscow, Paris, and London were unborn when Jerusalem was already the metropolis of a Jewish state.

The dialogue with the Americans and the appeasement at the U.N. have had no positive effect on PLO behavior. Infiltration attempts have continued, and PLO leaders have continued to call for "armed struggle" against Israel. On March 6, 1989, Arafat contradicted his December 1988 statement "renouncing" terrorism, when he declared: "The PLO has not given up the rifle and will not stop the armed struggle....It is fighting...for a political objective, namely, the liberation of the Palestinian soil and the establishment of a Palestinian state over every part of it from which Israel will be removed."

This policy of belligerence has been pursued by the Arabs since Israel's birth. The PLO refuses to repeal, revise, or amend its guiding document, the "Palestinian Covenant," which calls for the elimination of Israel; is not ready to disband terror units, and continues to carry out acts of terrorism.

Hence the PLO's increased efforts to fan the flames of the intifada, which broke out in December 1987 in Judea, Samaria, and Gaza. It sees the *intifada* as another facet of its campaign against Israel. Since its outbreak, murderous assaults have been unleashed not only against Israelis. The PLO has perpetrated savage assassinations of local Palestinians, men and women alike. In most cases, these Palestinian victims are accused of supporting a non-violent peace process or are suspected of opposition to the brutal strong-arm PLO tactics.

The violent riots of the intifada, largely instigated by agents of various PLO terrorist factions together with fanatic Moslem groups, have constituted yet another manifestation of the long-standing obsession of extreme Arab forces bent upon Israel's ultimate liquidation.

While the intifada had come to represent a sad sequel to past destructive excesses unleashed by Arab extremists, it is clear that the new methods have become more wily, insidious, and sophisticated. To achieve public relations gains and in order to provide avid representatives of foreign media with juicy and sensational scenes, terrorist ringleaders hide behind a human wall of children and old women, unashamedly pushing them into the front line. This cynical and shocking practice must be regarded as a supreme incarnation of heartless and inhuman cowardice. The ultimate aim is, however, unchanged: to undermine Israel's morale and hasten its demise.

It has long been obvious that PLO leaders are determined to impose their dictates upon the local Palestinians. Hence the PLO's entrenched rejection of the very concept and practice of free elections in the territories; elections that might produce an alternative legitimate leadership, capable of removing the PLO's monopoly of power. PLO death squads seek out and kill Palestinians as a means of enforcing political compliance. The murders are often committed in the most savage manner and represent another form of PLO terrorism. Since Arafat's press conference in Geneva, hundreds of Palestinians have been murdered by the PLO squads.

Arafat himself has publicly justified and taken responsibility for ordering such killings and, when Iraq's dictator, Saddam Hussein, invaded Kuwait and threatened Israel with annihilation, Arafat rushed to Baghdad to embrace Saddam Hussein whom President George Bush called another Hitler. The comparison of Saddam to Hitler was not a journalistic metaphor or propagandistic hyperbole. It was based on their characters and deeds. Both exemplified permanent aggression, both had territorial demands, and to both the Jews were not the only enemy.

Saddam used civilians to shield military targets by placing military installations, tanks, planes, and command-and-control centers in residential areas and villages and at archeological sites. Saddam used anti-colonialist, pan-Arabic and Moslem motives, and it is plain heresy for Moslems to complain of fathers, husbands or sons lost in battle against the infidel. That would imply disbelief in the happy afterlife promised by Islam to all its martyrs. Only infidel casualties count as losses, while Moslem deaths are gains.

Finally, their common Jewish point. For both Hitler and Saddam, the hatred of the Jews served as the ideal instrument to achieve their goals. In his book *My Struggle (Mein Kampf)*, Hitler "prophesied" that a new world war would lead to the extermination of the Jewish race in Europe. Saddam, in his book *Our Struggle (Unser Kampf*—the German edition, published in 1977), asserted that there must be a war in the Middle East to drive the Jews from Israel. Hitler used chemical means to liquidate the Jewish people, and Saddam threatened to liquidate the Jewish state with chemicals produced with the help of German technicians.

When, some time before invading Kuwait, Saddam declared: "In the name of Allah, we shall cause fire to devour half of Israel," world reaction was the same indifference it had shown to Hitler as long as the Jews were the only ones affected. As long as the Iraqi Hitler threatened Israel, everybody scoffed that Israel was exaggerating. There were even those who unashamedly insinuated that its warnings were designed to push away "the main issue, the solution of the Palestinian problem," in their words.

Despite Israel's warnings over a decade of the danger of selling sophisticated weapon systems and instruments of mass destruction to a monstrous dictator, East and West persisted in doing so, building up Saddam's arsenal of deadly weapons.

Companies, in Germany, France, Britain, Austria, Italy, Switzerland, Belgium, Spain, and the United States, supplied Iraq with conventional as well as non-conventional military equipment, and helped her to produce chemical, biological, and nuclear weapons. The Soviets supplied Iraq with armaments, ranging from battle tanks and supersonic fighters to Scud missiles. Western know-how enabled Iraq to improve the Soviet-made missiles. In 1988, the International Technological Fair took place in Iraq, and among the foreign participants were many American companies. They came to the fair on the warm recommendation of the American administration, including the president himself, since official advisers held Saddam to be a reasonable, Western-oriented Arab leader. On August 2, 1990, Saddam occupied Kuwait, using American technology to fight the Americans!

The entire world showed revulsion, outrage, and dismay at the Iraqi aggression. The U.N. condemned the invasion of Kuwait, and an anti-Iraqi coalition of 28 countries was formed. But Yasser Arafat stated: "We declare our support for Iraq...to achieve liberation from Baghdad to Jerusalem."

The Palestinians, for whom reality and fantasy intertwine, supported Saddam, and the world witnessed the Saddam-PLO alliance against the U.N. and against the U.S.-led coalition. As in the past, European cowardice came to the surface. Their leaders again degraded themselves with their readiness to sacrifice all principles of moral and national dignity, and to give in to another Hitler. Despite the fact that the invasion of Kuwait had nothing to do with the Israeli-Palestinian conflict, delegations rushed to Baghdad to save the Iraqi tyrant, proposing linkage between the Kuwaiti crisis and the Palestinian problem at Israel's expense.

Those efforts failed because there could be no linkage between Iraq's invasion of Kuwait, a clear act of aggression and classic example of a post-Nuremberg "crime against the peace," and Israel's conquests in the 1967 Six-Day War which resulted from self-defense against enemies sworn to drive it and its people into the sea, to wipe them off the map and out of history.

Iraq was a party to that concerted Arab aggression. To equate an Iraqi act of aggression in 1990 with an Israeli act of self-defense in 1967, or to link Iraqi withdrawal from Kuwait with Israeli withdrawal from the West Bank and Gaza, would not only license Iraq's act of aggression against Kuwait, but would retroactively reward the Arab aggression against Israel in 1967.

When war broke out in January 1991, the West faced the tough task of cracking British-designed "super bunkers" protecting Iraqi warplanes. Those bunkers, made of reinforced steel and concrete and partly buried in sand, had been built in Iraq with Western engineering skills to NATO specifications, to absorb any blast and to withstand a possible nuclear attack.

In spite of Israel not being part of the war coalition, Saddam launched the first salvo of eight deadly missiles against Israel before dawn on January 18. Sirens sounding throughout the country sent residents scurrying to hermetically sealed rooms in case of a chemical attack, as prophesied by *Isaiah* (26,20): "Come, my people, enter thou into thy chambers, and shut thy doors about thee: hide thyself as it were for a little moment, until the indignation be overpast."

Israelis across the nation clung to their gas masks day and night, and rows of water hoses were outside hospitals to wash down victims. Survivors of the German gas chambers watched with tears in their eyes as their Israel-born grandchildren donned masks in fear of German-made poison gas. For Holocaust survivors, every air-raid siren, each exploding missile, and every mention of the word "gas," brought back their private nightmare, and they were forced to re-live their past struggles for survival. Innocent civilians were killed and wounded, and enormous damage was inflicted to property.

We prayed for all our enemies to perish and found hope in the very Parashat Hashavuah (the Pentateuch's Sabbath weekly portion) following the missile attack: "Fear thou not, O Jacob my servant, saith the Lord: for I am with thee." (*Jeremiah*, 46,28).

As during the wars of 1967 and 1973, so it was in 1991, that the Talmudic saying that "All Jews are responsible for one another," proved true. Jews the world over stood behind the State of Israel as one. At a time when Israel was the victim of Iraqi aggression, they gave the Israelis encouragement and comfort and hope to overcome the traumatic Scuds, the danger of poison gas, and any political pressures.

On the other hand, the reaction of the world to the criminal attacks against Israel, was again the same as fifty years ago. When millions of Jews were tortured, maimed, and murdered by the Nazis in gas chambers, the Jewish communities that were not under the Nazi jackboot were entreated not to raise their voice too high, "lest supreme interests be damaged."

Now, the Jewish state was entreated not to react, "lest supreme interests of the coalition be damaged!" Even the Vatican, which did not condemn the missile attacks on Israel, called on Israel not to react. But the Jews are not the Jews of fifty years ago. Jewish statehood and sovereignty were the catalyst and Israel decided to retaliate.

However, the United States, too, asked her to refrain, committing publicly to consider the destruction of the Scud missiles as the highest priority of its war effort. With the knowledge that the elimination of Iraq's mobile Scud launchers was crucial to preserve Israeli restraint, American efforts in the search-and-destroy mission against the Soviet-made missiles were significantly increased. Throughout the world, people now realized how deadly dangerous the situation of the entire world would have been had Israel not destroyed Saddam's nuclear threat. Voices of repentance were heard all over the world for having condemned Israel's destruction of the Iraqi atomic reactor ten years earlier.

A U.S. aircraft carrier stood off the coast of Israel to help secure the safety of the Jewish state, and an emergency shipment of American Patriot anti-missile batteries was airlifted to Israel. American crews were brought in from U.S. military installations in Europe to man the Patriots.

All that took me back to 1944. When the Jews were being exterminated in crematoria and gas chambers, a young Polish Jew, Samuel Zigelbaum, met in London an American Jewish officer, Arthur Goldberg, who later became a justice of the United States Supreme Court and then U.S. ambassador to the United Nations. Zigelbaum begged Goldberg to transmit to the leaders of the Allies, to President Roosevelt and Prime Minister Churchill, the supplication of the Jews: "Stop the killing by bombing the extermination sites in Auschwitz and the railroads leading to them."

Goldberg transmitted the request immediately and the reply was not slow in coming: the Allied forces were busy with their war activities and were not in a position to bomb Auschwitz. While the synthetic rubber works four miles from the extermination sites were bombed, as well as the hospital and S.S. barracks some fifteen yards away, no action was ever taken against the unguarded camp installations easily recognized by the fires of the crematoria.

Samuel Zigelbaum committed suicide in front of the British Parliament to protest the apathy and indifference of the free and civilized world to the mass spilling of Jewish blood. How different the lot of European Jewry would have been fifty years ago had the Jewish state already been in existence then!

Since the existence of Israel is the overriding guarantee that extermination camps and gas chambers shall be no more than a dark memory of the past, never to happen again, one can easily imagine how lucky we were to have withstood all pressures for the establishment of an independent Palestinian state, even if in Gaza only. For rejecting the idea of a Palestinian state, the Israelis were accused of being stubborn, inflexible. If insistence on survival is being stubborn and inflexible, we plead guilty to those accusations. It saved us from a horrible disaster that would have been our lot if the Palestinian state were in existence when Saddam decided to launch deadly missiles on Israel.

Instead of launching the Scuds from a distance of four hundred miles and killing a limited number of Israelis, Saddam would have done it without any risks, from across the border, endangering our very existence.

President Bush called the war against Saddam a war to uphold basic principles of justice and sent 500,000 Americans to fight against unmitigated evil. The agents of that evil, PLO followers, stood on the roofs of their houses in Israel and applauded the plunging of Scud missiles on Tel Aviv and Haifa.

The real trauma of the Israelis, however, was the thought of what might have happened had Saddam not invaded Kuwait but decided to act against Israel as he had threatened. Jordan's King Hussein's unconditional support of Saddam showed the situation in which Israel could have suddenly found itself—facing, along the Jordan River, the Iraqi military monster with all its chemical, biological, and nuclear weaponry, hundreds of missiles and thousands of tanks.

The Hamas terrorist movement stated: "All of Palestine is ours and we want to liberate it from the river to the sea at one go. The PLO feels that a phased plan must be pursued. Both sides agree on the final objective. The difference between them is the way there."

George Habash, leader of the "Popular Front for the Liberation of Palestine," added, "I come from Lydda. My fight and struggle will not stop unless I return to Lydda....We seek to establish a state which we can use in order to liberate the other parts of Palestine...."

They mean what they say: they don't want peace with Israel. They want Israel piece by piece. In the words of the Psalmist: "I am all peace, but when I speak, they are for war."

We continue to hope that the Arabs will finally realize that the State of Israel is here to stay and is not, as so many of them imagine, a temporary phenomenon. They will understand that Israel has not come into being only as a result of Nazi persecution, that Jews have not just found a refuge here, but have come home, clinging to their historical roots and gathering the strength which assures the permanence of this state. They will have to recognize the reality of Israel: it is the only state in the world that speaks the same language, upholds the same faith and inhabits the same land as it did three thousand years ago. And if Israel will be strong, they will make peace with it. No one will make peace with a weak Israel.

Israel will always remember one of the wisest admonitions of this century: "Radical forces don't respect weakness. They prey on it. History certainly teaches us that much." So said George Bush on July 30, 1986.

It is our great fortune that Arab hostility, designed to restrain the growth of Israel, in fact spurred its energies, strengthened its resolve, forged its solidarity and national coherence, and thus contributed to its becoming a strong, vibrant, dynamic nation. It is a tragic paradox that the Jews, authors of mankind's oldest tradition of peace, must be most deeply concerned with keeping Israel's defense forces ready to deter any Arab country from initiating a war against Israel and, should the deterrent fail, to defeat the enemy quickly.

Israel's most important front is Syria with whom it shares a border. Since 1975, the Syrians have been deploying surface-to-surface Scud missiles, to enable them to hit the Israeli home front without needing to cross the border and jeopardize pilots and planes. Since 1980, Syria has been systematically deploying missiles with a shorter range (fifty miles) but which are far more accurate and capable of hitting Israel's army bases and airstrips. Over the years, the Syrians have improved their missile deployments, adding chemical warheads with missile attack capabilities several times more dangerous than those of Iraq. Our powers of deterrence have until now prevented Syrian President Assad from initiating a war against us, and he will not dare to attack us as long as Israel retains the ability to roll back the war into Syria's territory and retaliate devastatingly.

XXXVII.

CHANCES OR RISKS?

Following Saddam's attacks on Israel, we witnessed encouraging developments. Resolutions in the U.S. Congress extolled the Jewish state. American military aid to Israel was increased and the strategic cooperation between the two countries grew much closer. A significant *rapprochement* took place between Israel and the European Community, and the Germans, conscious of the damage done by their sale of poison gas and other deadly weapons to Iraq, offered Israel military and financial assistance. Relations with the Soviet Union also improved, and there were expressions of sympathy and support for Israel throughout the world.

All this increased the hope that, after it was clear that the Arab-Israeli conflict was not the main issue of the Middle East as so many wrongly insisted, the civilized world would change its policies, with good chances for a solution of the conflict acceptable to Israel. But we would not be too surprised if this should not happen, if Israel should face new risks. There was a similar situation following the Six-Day War. There must be something curiously attractive about threatened Jews.

Witnessing Saddam's launches of deadly missiles against Israel; seeing Neo-Nazis in Germany and elsewhere trying to raise their ugly heads again, and hearing the same calls for genocide that went unheard and unheeded fifty years ago, the world looked warmly on Israel.

There had been an outpouring of warmth also when Israel's existence was threatened in 1967. But the attitudes changed soon after the victory. It was a change that prompted the Israeli satirist Ephraim Kishon to write a piece entitled: "Sorry, we won!" We did not exclude that such a change might occur again and Israel would be vilified again. We even saw the possibility of being confronted with an American-Soviet initiative to resolve the Arab-Israeli conflict that would not be in our best interests. The first sign of such an initiative was the joint *communiqué* issued by James Baker and Alexander Bessmertnykh, the U.S. and U.S.S.R. foreign ministers, stating that Washington and Moscow would act together after the Gulf War to deal with solving the Arab-Israeli conflict.

"The old policy was wrong, and we changed it," James Baker said in his congressional testimony: the Soviets were promised a role in Middle East peacemaking. Washington almost bestowed a status of equality upon Moscow, which, after having hinted in August 1990 that its troops would join the multinational force, decided to stay out of the war and refused to send even a non-combatant, token representation. The Soviet Union was allowed to remain on the side and pose as a friend of the Arabs and the only "non-imperialist" great power.

Thus, the Soviets would be able to say to the Arabs and the Third World that, even after the fighting had begun, they had tried to bring peace. And while the U.S.-led coalition would be held responsible for all the harm done to Iraq, the Soviets will have gained favor in the Moslem world for trying to save an Arab country from ruin. The Soviets also tried to preserve one of their most lucrative markets in the arms trade. Before the war, every third dollar of their foreign income came from Iraq. By reestablishing patronage over Iraq and friendship with Iran, the Soviets hoped to hold cards that would serve them well in postwar "new order" arrangements.

Moscow's behavior recalled Soviet policies of the bad old days, that brought the Soviet empire to its sorry condition. One might have hoped that, after having revealed to the world and to themselves the enormity of the crimes committed by their own brutal regime, the Soviets would shun the likes of Saddam with greater determination than anyone else. It recalled for us the panic trip to Cairo by Soviet Premier Alexei Kosygin in the midst of the 1973 Yom Kippur War.

In both instances, the Soviets tried to save a client of their armaments from collapse on the battle-field. Kosygin showed then Egyptian President Sadat satellite photos that clarified the desperately grave situation of the Egyptian army and revealed to him that the Israel defense forces had crossed the Suez Canal and breached the Egyptian lines.

This time, President Gorbachev sent Saddam satellite photos of the heavy Iraqi losses that his commanders had been hiding from him. At the same time, Soviet spokesmen declared that "the Soviet Union could not remain indifferent to large-scale action close to its southern border." In previous Middle East conflicts, the Americans had taken such a Soviet statement into account and, given the long-standing relationship between Saddam and the U.S.S.R., the Gulf Crisis would have been far more dangerous to the world had the Soviets still possessed their former capabilities.

But the Soviet empire was now in decline, its status as a superpower had expired, with the Soviet economy in disarray and its military riven by ethnic strife and demoralization. President Bush could now expose the Soviets' impotence, and he ignored Gorbachev's peace proposals to force an Iraqi withdrawal from Kuwait only after a cease-fire.

The results of the ensuing war are well known and the world saw an unchastened dictator continue to manage and control his regime despite his defeat. With the liberation of Kuwait, the world understood the long nightmare of its occupation by Saddam. Over and again, liberated Kuwaitis spoke of murder, rape, and pillage by the occupiers. Britain's prime minister, John Major, declared that Iraq should be treated as an international pariah as long as Saddam remains in power.

The evidence from the emirate about the tortures to which innocent Kuwaitis had been subjected by the Iraqis and their Palestinian collaborators, was hair-raising. No Arab country had supported the PLO more generously than Kuwait. It gave Arafat billions of dollars over the years, and the Kuwaiti defense minister applauded the brutal PLO murder of eleven Israeli athletes in Munich in September 1972.

With the end of hostilities, the true face of King Hussein of Jordan was shown to the world: he had flagrantly violated the U.N. sanctions by sending arms to Baghdad during the war. It was also revealed that the Swedes, who have stringent laws against supplying war material to countries in war zones, supplied Iraq not only with military bunkers, but with land mines and Saab trucks for mobile Scud launchers against Israel.

For Israel, it was symbolic that Saddam, who promised the "mother of all battles," collapsed in the "mother of all defeats" on the 14th of Adar, the day on which the Jewish people celebrate Purim, the Feast of Lots. Purim commemorates the occasion when the Jews of the Persian empire were saved from destruction planned by their enemy, King Ahasuerus' senior minister, Haman, through the influence of Queen Esther and her uncle Mordecai. Thus, Saddam, called a new Hitler, acquired a new title, a modern Haman.

However, only one of Israel's sworn enemies was subdued in the Gulf War. It was certain that no coalition would be formed to protect Israel from its enemies, as would have never been done had Saddam invaded Israel instead of Kuwait. Unfortunately, there were signs that Israel must still be alert in the face of the Bush administration's postwar vision: to attain a "new world order."

One of those signs seemed to be the diplomatic incident of February 15, the very day Saddam tried his shrewd survivalist step. Washington published a condemnation of Israeli Ambassador Zalman Shoval's criticism of the U.S. administration's aid policy to Israel. Whether Ambassador Shoval had adhered to protocol in complaining to the press about delay in the American delivery on its commitments to Israel is only marginally relevant. The fact was that the administration was dragging its feet on numerous obligations, circumventing legislated commitments, and reneging on presumably air-tight promises to Israel.

Many of the projects, particularly those on strategic and scientific cooperation, should be as beneficial to America as to Israel. But holding up the aid to Israel could be exploited for purposes of political pressure. The ambassador charged that the Bush administration was giving Israel the "run-around" on promised loan guarantees of $400 million for housing Soviet Jewish immigrants. The administration held up the guarantees for over a year, guarantees that were a humanitarian gesture of an amount that was a drop in the bucket, in view of Israel's needs for the absorption of recent massive immigration. (One week after Shoval's criticism, the Americans signed the guarantees.)

Shoval also complained that, unlike its neighbors, including Saddam Hussein's ally Jordan, Israel was not to expect compensation for war costs. He said, "Not being part of the coalition, Israel has not received one cent of aid despite the fact that we have had immense direct military costs, not to mention the indirect economic costs."

The contrast between the U.S.'s indulgent reaction to King Hussein's speeches, which in effect charged the American army with genocide, and its scathing rude response to a mild criticism couched amid praise and appreciation by the Israeli ambassador, was evident. The fear was that while praising Israel's restraint for risking its deterrence credibility by failing to respond to attacks by Iraqi

Scud missiles, there was no change in Washington's solution of the Arab-Israeli conflict: "To trade land for peace."

Israel's prime minister, Yitzhak Shamir, warned that the end of the Gulf War would be followed by an attempt to establish a new pattern of Middle East arrangements likely to be at Israel's expense. Washington might still want Israel to return to more-or-less the 1967 lines, allowing a Palestinian entity to be established in Judea, Samaria, and Gaza for the very people who had been standing on their roofs cheering the Scuds aimed at Israel. It also considers the Golan Heights open to negotiations, and we asked ourselves: Is it possible that the Americans will learn nothing from their glaring misreading of the Middle East before August 2, 1990? Is it conceivable that Washington will ignore what was proven in the Gulf War, that a Palestinian entity would grant the PLO-Hamas terrorists access to the heart of Jerusalem and the outskirts of Tel Aviv? Does the U.S. realize that giving up the Golan Heights would increase enormously the menace of Syria's arsenal of non-conventional weapons to Israel? Will Washington disregard the dangers of its eventual postwar policy to Israel's very existence?

The world witnessed, before the Gulf War, an ardent, courting of Saddam by the U.S. and other Western powers. This included flattery by visiting senators, generous loan guarantees, support for Iraq's military buildup, tacit approval of its acquisition of non-conventional weapons from Western companies, and a consistently favorable press. Barely three days before Saddam swallowed Kuwait, the Bush administration vehemently opposed the mild sanctions against Iraq sought by Congress, and the U.S. ambassador in Baghdad, April Glaspie, assured Saddam on orders from Washington that the Bush administration would not interfere in such internal Arab affairs as his dispute with Kuwait. Saddam had good reason to see Glaspie's assurances as a go-ahead for his invasion.

With this handling of Saddam by the U.S. administration and the increasingly fractious U.S.-Israel relationship prior to the war, it is clear that the expectations of the United States and Israel from the postwar "Pax Americana" were contrasting, if not opposing. It was obvious that Washington would like to see tranquility and peace in the Middle East without great concern for the ways and means to that end.

For Israel, every step toward that objective is fraught with risk, and one blunder can be fatal. Israel insists, therefore, on peace with security. The history of this century has taught us that peace without security is no peace at all.

President Bush, however, was convinced that Saddam's collapse shook some conventions and created new opportunities. A short while after the end of the Gulf War, Secretary of State Baker began his efforts to convene an Arab-Israeli peace conference on the basis of the Israeli peace initiative of May 1989, which in turn followed the Camp David blueprint.

President Bush's eagerness to convene the conference made him oppose, in September 1991, the approval by Congress of the Israeli request for $10 billion in loan guarantees for the absorption of new immigrants, which will ultimately cost the American taxpayer nothing. Israel wanted to make the request in March, after the Gulf War, but the Americans asked for six months delay. Israel acceded to the delay and submitted its official application in September. However, Bush, with a vague plea "to give peace a chance," insisted upon a further delay of four months. In a direct appeal to the American people at a hastily called news conference, Bush vowed he would veto a Congressional decision in favor of the guarantees. Hitting the podium with his fist in a defiant gesture, he said he would put the cause of a peace conference ahead of politics, even if it damaged his 1992 re-election campaign. The president's outburst caused shock in Israel. It was difficult to understand how providing housing for new immigrants, whom President Bush himself helped to bring from the U.S.S.R. and Ethiopia, could adversely affect the peace process. Congress had no choice but to give in to the president's threat.

Shortly after his anti-Israel outburst, Bush demanded that the U.N. General Assembly repeal the 1975 U.N. resolution equating Zionism with racism. The president declared: "This world body will never be viewed as a peace-seeking organization until the resolution is eliminated. By repealing this resolution unconditionally, the U.N. will enhance its credibility and serve the cause of peace." Spokesmen of many nations supported Mr. Bush's demand to repeal the resolution, among them, the representatives of the countries of Eastern Europe, where dramatic developments brought the resumption of their full diplomatic relations with Israel. Thus, an era of bitter enmity between Moscow and Jerusalem came to an end.

The Soviet Union restored full diplomatic relations with Israel twenty-four years after severing them. The signing ceremony in Jerusalem for the renewal of the ties, on October 18, 1991, came just an hour before the Soviet Foreign Minister Boris Pankin joined American Secretary of State Baker in formally issuing invitations, on behalf of the presidents of the United States and the Soviet Union, to the Middle East conference.

Pankin spoke of a more evenhanded Soviet approach to the Middle East at a joint press conference with Baker. He said: "In the past, the Soviet Union tended to sort of side with the Palestinians and the Arab states, while the U.S. sided with Israel, and this did not bring any tangible fruit. The new approach now is not to have any *protégés* and support their positions no matter what they say and no matter how legitimate they may be."

Israel's agreement to participate at a regional peace conference was based on the following understandings with the Unites States:

1. The objective of the negotiations is the conclusion of peace treaties. This should be made clear to all participants in the bilateral talks.
2. States that participate in the bilateral talks should participate equally in the multilateral negotiations. This will be a major test of intentions regarding peace and coexistence with Israel.
3. The PLO will not be a party to the process, directly or indirectly. This relates to the Jordanian-Palestinian delegation and in particular the Palestinian element in that delegation, its composition, and conduct.
4. The bilateral negotiations must take place in the region, for many reasons and practical considerations that were explained in the preparatory talks.

The historic peace conference, with more than 7,000 journalists crowding the city, convened in Madrid on October 30, 1991, under the cochairmanship of Presidents Bush and Gorbachev. The Jews came to Spain, from where they were expelled five hundred years ago, to negotiate peaceful coexistence with the Arabs. But violence clouded the arrival of Israel's delegation, headed by Prime Minister Shamir.

In attacks in south Lebanon, Arab terrorists killed three Israeli soldiers and wounded six. In another attack Arab gunmen killed two civilians and wounded six others, five of them children. One of the dead was a mother of seven, and the other a father of four.

"Some might have expected that in the face of this terror Israel would not attend the conference." Shamir said, "but, despite this violence, our quest for peace is unrelenting."

Bush and Gorbachev made efforts to appear as honest brokers and assured the parties: Israel, Lebanon, Syria, Jordan, and the Palestinians, that the co-sponsors intended to act as catalysts, since any attempt by the United States or the Soviet Union to impose a solution, or in any way to interfere in the process, they said, could only guarantee failure. President Bush said: "The objective must not simply be to end the state of war in the Middle East and replace it with a state of non-belligerency. This is not enough; this would not last. Rather, we seek peace, real peace. And by real peace, I mean treaties. Security. Diplomatic relations. Economic relations. Trade investment. Cultural exchange. Even tourism."

Prime Minister Shamir's opening address invited the Arab delegations to break taboos and barriers, declare an end to war and to belligerency; and to conduct the direct bilateral and multilateral talks for the purpose of reaching a peace based on the mutual interests of Arabs and Israelis that would stand the test of time. After three days of formal speeches and responses, the moment Israel had been waiting for since the birth of the State, had arrived. For the first time, all the country's neighbors, including its most implacable enemy, Syria, had agreed to conduct direct, bilateral, independent negotiations without preconditions. It was a landmark achievement and it was historic, not only because direct negotiations are the only way to peace, but because they imply Arab recognition of Israel's sovereignty and legitimacy. It is the absence of such recognition that has been the root cause of the Arab-Israel conflict.

We cannot expect quick results from the Madrid gathering. President Bush said: "We come to Madrid as realists. We do not expect peace to be negotiated in a day or week or month or even a year. It will take time; time for parties to talk to one another, to listen to one another. Time to heal old wounds and build trust. In this quest, time need not be the enemy of progress."

Before leaving Madrid on November 3, Baker, whose efforts, patience, and tenacity had made the conference possible, said he was pleasantly surprised. Explaining why he was optimistic: "The direct face-to-face negotiations have begun. The parties are sitting at the table, bilaterally, and beginning to talk." Asked whether progress in the talks could guarantee peace, Baker smiled and said: "There can't be any guarantees. This is the Middle East."

XXXVIII.

A RELATIONSHIP BUILT TO ENDURE

During initial negotiations in Madrid no agreement was reached on the site or the date of the next meeting. The feeling was that there was a long way to go. The United States, however, was determined to push ahead with the first face-to-face bilateral peace talks between Israel and her Arab neighbors and, after a series of talks between U.S. Secretary of State James Baker and the various governments, the delegations agreed to meet in Washington on December 10, 1991.

The bilateral talks recessed on December 18, and resumed on March 2, 1992, again without tangible results. It became clear that serious progress could not be achieved before the parliamentary elections in Israel on June 23, 1992. On January 28, 1992, multilateral talks opened in Moscow. Five committees were established and convened for their first sessions in May 1992: in Vienna on water; in Ottawa on refugees; near Tokyo on the environment; in Brussels on economic development; and in Washington on security and arms control.

Syria refused to participate in the multilateral talks unless progress was forthcoming in the bilateral negotiations. Israel refused to participate in the discussions of the Committee on refugees because it objected to the participation of Palestinians living outside the administered territories.

President Bush continued to delay action on loan guarantees to Israel for the absorption of new immigrants. Tension grew. Bush refused to budge on Israel's request. He now made the guarantees conditional on Israeli acquiescence in a settlement freeze. But he admitted that his words about the "powerful Jewish lobby" might have been ill-chosen.

Following his attack on the Jews, representing them as a "powerful global evil," an uncomfortable White House was flooded with supportive messages from believers in the anti-Semitic Protocols of the Elders of Zion! Counteracting his unfortunate remarks, Bush assisted the world-wide campaign to repeal the U.N. resolution equating Zionism with racism. It was overwhelmingly reversed on December 17, 1991, by the General Assembly. Of the 165 member-states, 111 voted for repeal, 25 voted against, 13 abstained and 16 were absent.

Thus ended sixteen years of what Israelis had termed "delegitimization" by the world body. It was also the end of Israel's diplomatic isolation; even China and India established diplomatic relations with Israel. According to New York Cardinal John O'Connor, the Vatican, too, is considering a "historic shift" in its traditional attitude, including its opposition to Israeli sovereignty over Jerusalem. The Cardinal visited Israel in January 1992 and met officially for the first time with Prime

Minister Yitzhak Shamir and President Chaim Hertzog. After his visit, a joint Vatican-Israeli commission was formed to discuss matters of common interest, and reports suggest this could be a prelude to the establishment of formal relations.

It is doubtful whether these developments would have taken place without the demise of the Soviet empire. The Soviet Union ceased formally to exist on January 1, 1992, and was replaced by a "Commonwealth of Independent States." The red Soviet flag was lowered from above the Kremlin on New Year's Eve. Chairman Mikhail Gorbachev was replaced by Boris Yeltsin, the president of Russia.

Gorbachev's personal attitude and policy toward the Jews in the U.S.S.R. will always be remembered by us. As a result of his understanding and actions, Jews were given freedom to return to their ancient homeland where they are able to resume their national life. Israel will also remember his role in easing the process of normalization of Soviet relations with Israel.

Parliamentary elections in Israel also produced a political upheaval. Unexpectedly, the Likud was defeated and Labor Party leader, Yitzhak Rabin, became the new prime minister. In most countries, when the standard of living is on the rise, a large majority of the population is economically comfortable, and the country's standing in the world is dramatically improved, the incumbent government is reelected.

Indeed, only one short year before the elections, the Likud enjoyed unprecedented popularity, commanding the loyalty of almost half the population. Although its achievements have been remarkable in many areas, however, the majority of voters perceived the government as a failure. A media blitz in Israel and abroad over the government's exaggerated spending in the administered territories, its failure in absorbing new immigrants, and a serious rise in unemployment all contributed to the Likud's demise.

President Bush (who was ironically ousted in a similar manner) contributed significantly to the Likud's defeat by his hostility toward Shamir. Israelis are all too fearful of losing American good will to back a government which seems on a collision course with the United States. But what diminished the Likud's image more than anything else was a general impression of disarray, contentiousness, and political corruption.

Outside Israel, approbation for the new Rabin government was universal and not unexpectedly. Much of the world community sides with the Arabs, believing no doubt that stabilization and calm in the Middle East can be purchased by placating the Arabs with Israeli-held land. The world's leaders expect a Rabin administration, unencumbered by hawkish partners, to do what they would like Israel to do: withdraw to the 1967 lines, allow the establishment of a Palestinian state in the administered territories (with half of Jerusalem as its capital), and relinquish the Golan. They are aware that in Rabin's government there is a majority which favors this *dénouement* (except that it is opposed to the division of Jerusalem), and they clearly hope that, with Rabin in power, a "land for peace" solution to the Arab-Israeli conflict will become a reality. The world has made no secret of its desire to see an Israeli withdrawal from all "occupied territories" and it has pointedly applied this term not only to Judea, Samaria, Gaza, and the Golan, but to those parts of Jerusalem taken by Israel in 1967.

If Rabin's campaign rhetoric and his Knesset speech are any indication, the chasm between his position and those of the United States is not easily spanned. Though pledging a faster pace in the peace talks, Rabin has said that he does not consider a peace agreement to be a guarantee of security. Nor does he believe that building and expansion should stop in what he calls the "security settlements," the towns and villages in the Jordan valley and the Golan, nor does he consider construction activity in Jerusalem negotiable.

Although the Labor platform does advocate "territorial compromise," the prime minister opposes returning to the 1967 lines and the creation of a Palestinian state. Indeed, it is because he holds these positions that he led Labor to victory. Voters who have consistently supported the Likud felt the party needed a "rest." After fifteen years it was time for a change. While they would not have risked changing the Likud for a government headed by an outright dove, Rabin's background and his quasi-hawkish image, greatly enhanced by his years as defense minister under a Likud prime minister, made them feel safe in their choice.

The Israelis want peace, but not peace at any price. Most of them are ready today to consider territorial compromise, but only a minuscule number of voters are ready to consider rolling back to the 1967 borders. The argument is whether the state needs only the Golan, the Jordan valley, and the area around Jerusalem to survive, or whether it must have all of Judea, Samaria, and Gaza.

It is a legitimate argument which separates doves from hawks in Israel. As election results have shown, there has been no shift from the hawks' side of the fence to the doves'. Only the split in the ranks of the hawks made forming the government by Rabin possible. Following his victory Rabin received Bush's invitation to come to the Washington, and it was clear that Bush wanted to meet with him before the Republican National Convention.

Bush and Baker could not be expected to approve continued building in the "security settlements," nor could they give official recognition to Israeli sovereignty in Jerusalem. But Rabin believed that the Bush administration was ready to approve the loan guarantees with the understanding that no new settlements will be established, and that only construction already begun in the territories will be completed. Although the Labor victory made such a move easier and more natural, there is no doubt that Bush would have made a pronounced pro-Israel gesture even if Shamir had been reelected. Not only was the lack of personal "chemistry" between Bush and Shamir eliminated; the accession of a dovish, more flexible Israeli government was rewarded and encouraged.

It was also evident that Bush could no longer ignore American Jewry, who found themselves once again in the political spotlight. A year before the elections, when Bush seemed invincible and his reelection little more than a formality, he had no interest in wooing them. But with the November elections approaching, the administration was eager to mend its fences with the American Jewish community. Both parties wanted the Jewish vote which, concentrated in large, electoral-vote-rich states, is now potentially more formidable than ever before. Even a slight shift in its voting patterns may have made a difference in the national elections.

The United States has gone from a superpower to continued confrontations with international situations about which it can do little. President Bush, who in February and March of 1991 commanded the approval of nine out of ten Americans, suddenly seemed incapable of keeping his own party in line, and the race for the White House became wide open. Since then, he has been defeated for reelection, the economy has been slow to recover, and Bush's much-touted "new world order" is a mixed bag of embryonic democracies plagued with xenophobic, belligerent chauvinism.

Bush's adamant opposition to the settlements seemed reason enough to punish Shamir and Israel by withholding the loan guarantees, but at his later meetings with Rabin, Bush made scant reference to the settlement problem, and he seemed aware that he could not maintain his tough posture toward the guarantees forever.

Rabin, for his part, has not allowed the euphoria created by the loan guarantees and the heady improvement in U.S.-Israel relations to obscure the harsh facts of life. No expressions of friendship, and no easy-term loans, can divert Israel from the reality of its position, and Rabin reminded a Washington audience of that reality when he opposed the U.S. sale of seventy-two F-15E jet fighters to Saudi Arabia:

> I don't believe any responsible politician in Israel can but oppose the sale of arms to an Arab country that continues to state that they are in a state of war with Israel. To treat commitments and assurances of dictatorial regimes as anything other than cunning stratagems and hollow promises is to cling to illusions. We are told that Saudi Arabia is an American ally. But four months before the invasion of Kuwait we heard the same thing about Saddam Hussein.

He further stressed that the sales would not take place if the U.S. is truly committed to maintaining Israel's qualitative edge. Recalling the sale of tanks to the Jordanians in 1965, he added:

> They were tanks President Lyndon Johnson promised would never cross the Jordan river. In 1967 they crossed it. We have proof. We destroyed them all.

Rabin also mentioned the vast quantities of arms shipped to Syria from Russia, the Ukraine, China, and North Korea, adding that the Syrians now possess a Scud-C missile which can hit any target in Israel with double the accuracy of the older Scud-Bs.

In his view, the weakening of the Iraqi military in the Gulf War and the work of the U.N. inspection teams have postponed the threat to Israel from Iraq. But he predicts that within seven to ten years the Islamic world will make a concerted effort to develop nuclear and other weapons of mass destruction, and Israel may be in greater danger than ever before.

Rabin understands that Israel has become more threatened. This is not the rosy picture of the post-Gulf war Middle East that the Bush administration had painted. Nor is it a scenario in which Israel can take many risks for peace. Nevertheless, Israel is ready to make far-reaching proposals to withdraw from all of southern Lebanon with whom the bilateral talks are quite friendly. But Syria must agree to do the same from other Lebanese territory.

The Syrians have rejected Israel's proposals to discuss the definition of the peace process' objectives, or the issue of recognition of Israel, or even their readiness to negotiate without threats and terror. They have tried to dictate their views to the other participants in the talks. Will they change their attitude and enter serious discussions on an interim settlement toward a full peace treaty?

With the Jordanians, the talks have been quite cordial and a certain progress has been made. It was agreed that Resolutions 242 and 338 of the Security Council will be the basis for the negotiations and that the issues to be discussed should be: the achievement of peace, the refugees, the borders, and collaboration on water, energy, environment, tourism, and security. As for the Palestinians, they have refused to stop killing Israelis while negotiating peace, and consider the talks as a propagandistic opportunity by presenting lists of claims for an independent Palestinian state. Their proposals on the interim agreement have all the characteristics of a state, while Israel proposed to discuss interim arrangements in the framework of commissions on the various issues: administration, judiciary, agriculture, education, culture, welfare, religious affairs.

On the eve of the renewal of bilateral Arab-Israeli talks in Washington, on August 24, 1992, the Israeli government applied a series of confidence building measures: six hundred political prisoners were ordered released; the expulsion order handed down in January to eleven Palestinians was rescinded, and orders were given to permit free access to Israel of all Palestinians more than fifty years of age.

Israel, however, rejected the Palestinian proposal for a legislative council, which could set the stage for the creation of an independent Palestinian state. Israel's delegation to the Washington talks has outlined a timetable for the election of an administrative council for self-rule which would give the Palestinians the responsibility for day-to-day life on the West Bank and Gaza.

During this transitional period the Palestinians will govern their daily lives while Israel will continue to take responsibility for defense and security, for the Jewish settlements in the territories, and for foreign affairs.

The 1992 election platforms of both parties in the United States, mentioned full support for the interim arrangements proposed by Israel.

While Bush and Baker never expressed much "emotional" support for Israel, the relationship established by the Bush administration, beginning with the talks in Madrid, has been beneficial to Israel. Bush, at his meeting with Rabin, confirmed that:

The relationship between U.S. and Israel is a relationship that goes back more than four decades to Israel's birth in 1948. And this is a relationship that's been tested in times of peace and war, one capable not only of weathering differences, but of accomplishing good things and this is a relationship based on a shared commitment to democracy and to common values, as well as a solid commitment to Israel's security, including its qualitative military edge, and this is a special relationship, one that is built to endure.

...Literally hundreds of thousands of Jews from Ethiopia, from the former Soviet Union now make their homes in Israel, and this, more than anything else, is what the Jewish state is all about. In this regard, I am extremely pleased to announce that we were able to reach agreement on the basic principles to govern our granting of up to $10 billion in loan guarantees. I have long been committed to supporting Israel and the historic task of absorbing immigrants and I am delighted that the prime minister and I have agreed to an approach which will assist these new Israelis without frustrating the search for peace.

In a statement made in an earlier meeting with Rabin, the new Democratic president, Bill Clinton, pledged that he, too, was fully committed to maintaining the important relationship between the United States and Israel:

The central thing that came out of our meeting was our accord that we ought to continue the pillars, the bedrock, of America's relationship with Israel in terms of our commitment to the security interests of Israel, in terms of my support for the loan guarantees, and in terms of our complete commitment to the continuity of the peace process. I made it clear to the prime minister that I was committed to progress in that process, and that there would be complete continuity in that process after the election if I win in November.

I believe Bill Clinton will make good on his campaign promises and that there will be continuity in the special relationship between Israel and the United States.

The aid of the American government to Israel and its people, vouchsafed since the creation of the Jewish state, is a source of strength and inspiration now, as were American gallantry, magnanimity, and succor to the Holocaust survivors then. In those days, the help of the American officers and men enabled us to surmount all obstacles, circumvent all obstructions, and reach our destinations. So today, the amity and help of the American people and government are a source of infinite hopefulness and strength in our struggle for a lasting peace, that the prophecy of *Jeremiah* (23, 6) may be realized: "And Israel shall dwell safely."

INDEX

Defying the Holocaust

245